Navigating Liberty

Conflicting Worlds
New Dimensions of the American Civil War

T. Michael Parrish, Series Editor

School teachers from the American Missionary Association of New York pose with African American children (*far left*) in Beaufort, South Carolina, 1862. Courtesy Library of Congress.

Navigating Liberty

Black Refugees and Antislavery Reformers in the Civil War South

JOHN CIMPRICH

Louisiana State University Press
Baton Rouge

Published by Louisiana State University Press
lsupress.org

Designer: Andrew Shurtz
Typefaces: Benton Modern, Monotype Grotesque, Century Expanded

Maps created by Mary Lee Eggart.

Cover illustration: Freed slave children with their teachers,
Beaufort, South Carolina (1862). Prints and Photographs
Division, Library of Congress.

Library of Congress Cataloging-in-Publication Data
Names: Cimprich, John, 1949– author.
Title: Navigating liberty : Black refugees and antislavery
    reformers in the Civil War South / John Cimprich.
Other titles: Black refugees and antislavery reformers in the Civil
    War South | Conflicting worlds.
Description: Baton Rouge : Louisiana State University Press,
    [2023] | Series: Conflicting worlds: new dimensions of the
    American Civil War | Preface. | Includes bibliographical
    references and index.
Identifiers: LCCN 2022011975 (print) | LCCN 2022011976 (ebook) |
    ISBN 978-0-8071-7799-0 (cloth) | ISBN 978-0-8071-7878-2 (pdf) |
    ISBN 978-0-8071-7877-5 (epub)
Subjects: LCSH: Antislavery movements—United States—
    History—19th century. | Freed persons—United States—
    History—19th century. | Social change—United States—
    History—19th century. | United States—History—Civil War,
    1861–1865—Social aspects.
Classification: LCC E453 .C493 2022 (print) | LCC E453 (ebook) |
    DDC 973.7/114—dc23/eng/20220323
LC record available at https://lccn.loc.gov/2022011975
LC ebook record available at https://lccn.loc.gov/2022011976

Contents

Preface

As thousands of African Americans freed themselves from slavery during the American Civil War, they launched the major social change of emancipation. Hundreds of northern antislavery reformers responded by traveling to the federally occupied South to work with them. The Black refugees, seeking new privileges, generally could bring little or no property to help them build a free life but could contribute labor and skills. The relief workers, especially when organized by aid associations and serving under military superintendents, could draw upon more resources, as well as exert some influence on programs.

The two groups brought views and practices from their backgrounds, which could either help or trouble the transition from slavery. Enslaved African Americans had learned to act with independent-mindedness and wariness when dealing with whites. White reformers, excepting a small number of egalitarians, had absorbed racial stereotypes and assumed the superiority of their views. When northerners attempted to control freedom seekers or to coerce changes, it caused tensions. The disgruntled Blacks evaded, criticized, or opposed some programs created for them. Conflicts occasionally resulted in program modifications but also moved some Blacks to seek more autonomy.

Yet both groups wanted liberty for the enslaved, and some in each broadened their outlooks. Many Black refugees came to appreciate the reformers' ideals and charity. A minority of whites came to see Blacks as more equal humans. Individuals with very critical views of the other group maintained a degree of distance. The' most successful Black refugees and reformers evolved into a better understanding of the others. Working together resulted in some accomplishments.

A century later the Civil Rights Movement prompted more study of the role of the enslaved in emancipation. Historians now see them as self-assertive in initiating and struggling for their new status. Because many publications have touched on different aspects of the interaction between Black refugees and northern reformers,[1] this book partly synthesizes and partly adds to existing knowledge. It is the first comprehensive study of the subject, an important aspect of slavery's end in the United States. As such, the work examines factors that affected wartime interaction between the two groups, how those factors developed over time, and their consequences during the war. The book identifies and explains overall patterns, but also gives attention to local variations.[2]

Because this study focuses on interaction between Black refugees and reformers, each group's relations with slaveholders, secessionists, and federal officials appear when relevant but are not fully treated here.[3] In addition, the work only contains context essential to understanding the interaction of Black refugees and northern reformers.[4]

Geographically, the book's focus is on the federally occupied areas with slavery, plus a few peripheral locations. Chronologically, except for limited discussion of background and aftermath, the work covers from the war's beginning through the end of May 1865. After that time, interaction entered a new phase belonging to postwar reconstruction.

The chapters in Part One present a topical discussion of initial encounters between Black refugees and reformers. While they mostly cover 1861–62, they include similar data arising from the same developments starting in new places during the later war years. The chapters in Part Two focus on patterns that show further developments during 1863–65 in the relationship between the two groups.

Available source materials raise two issues of balance. First, African Americans left far fewer relevant accounts than the reformers did. Northerners' versions of the words and deeds of Black people can reveal much if read judiciously and carefully. Since prudence could lead to guarded speech from the Black refugees, their actions are especially telling. Second, one aid organization, the American Missionary Association (AMA), had more workers and preserved far more evidence than any of the others, although some documents remain from some other aid organizations, several of the freedmen's departments created by most federal territorial commands, and the American

Freedmen's Inquiry Commission (an investigative body). Granting a few recognizable differences, the evidence in these collections is very similar. Thus, the greater quantity of AMA data should not appreciably distort the analysis. The evidence tells an important story: unusual circumstances opening new possibilities, social movement for change, challenges within and without the movement, and limited results.

I am grateful to Thomas More University for several research grants that financed the beginning of this project, and for extended access to the college's computer system after my retirement. T. Michael Parrish provided a number of very useful bibliographic leads. An anonymous reader beneficially urged me to think more deeply about the subject. My wife Vickie Hucker Cimprich—as well as good friends Stanley Harrold, David Lee, Jack McKivigan, Carol Rainey, Sister Evelyn Reinke, and Steve Ash—helpfully critiqued portions of the manuscript. Steve, a longtime friend, passed away before this book's publication and shall be greatly missed.

The project benefited from the assistance of staffs at the National Archives, Library of Congress, Abraham Lincoln Presidential Library, American Antiquarian Association, Indiana Historical Society, Massachusetts Historical Society, Ohio Historical Connection, Southern Historical Collection, State Historical Society of Wisconsin, Western Reserve Historical Society, Boston Public Library, Cincinnati and Hamilton County Public Library, Kenton County Public Library, Duke University Library, Earlham College Library, Haverford College Library, Howard University Library, Indiana University Library, Oberlin College Library, Ohio State University Library, Southern Baptist Theological Seminary Library, Swarthmore College Library, University of Cincinnati Library, University of Michigan Library, University of North Carolina Library, Wilmington College Library, and Thomas More University Library (especially Jim McKellogg and Joyce Vorderbrueggen).

I would like to dedicate this book to my late friend and mentor, Merton L. Dillon. He was an unfailing source of encouragement, guidance, and inspiration.

I.
Initial Interactions

1

First Encounters

Fort (or Fortress) Monroe sat on a sand spit on the northern side of the mouth of the James River, where it emptied into Virginia's part of the Chesapeake Bay. As the largest and strongest of the defensive works along the Atlantic coast of the United States, the fort remained in federal hands after Virginia joined the seceded Confederate States of America. The state had more enslaved persons than any other (see Table 1, p. 3), and a few of them, probably having heard secessionists claim that northerners wanted to free them, sought liberty at the fort during the Civil War's first weeks in 1861. The garrison refused to admit them; some Union forces elsewhere actually returned Black people to their enslavers. After all, President Abraham Lincoln had defined the war's purpose as preserving the Union rather than interfering with slavery, a stand soon reaffirmed by Congress.[1] Still, the most daring of the enslaved continued to think that civil war would open an opportunity for them to escape bondage and to gain liberty. They did not expect that their eventual acceptance by Federals would draw antislavery volunteers from the North to assist and support their cause.

The Fort Monroe Incident

A significant shift started after a month of war, when Shepard Mallory, Frank Baker, and James Townsend on May 23 asked to speak to the fort's new commander, Gen. Benjamin F. Butler. The three Black men reported that their owner, a Confederate colonel, planned to send them to build fortifications in North Carolina. Wanting neither to go far from families nor to help the proslavery Confederacy, they offered their services to the Federal forces instead.[2]

General Butler involved himself during most of the war with the issue of slaves who became refugees. He was no stranger to controversy and bold opinions. A Democratic Party politician from Massachusetts, he had opposed slavery's expansion in 1848 but later supported his party's proslavery wing in the 1860 national election. Since the latter stand affiliated him with many subsequent leaders of southern secession, it devastated his political career, which he then sought to revive through prominent military service for the Union. Butler, needing more laborers in 1861, chose to take the three African American refugees on their word. In a bold move he became the first federal commander to publicly appropriate and designate slaves who escaped as "contraband," enemy property potentially confiscatable because of its use for military purposes. When a Confederate officer representing the owner of those three refugees came to the fort to request their return, Butler responded that secessionists could not expect enforcement of rights under the United States Constitution without first restoring their allegiance. He would only send a receipt for the slaves.[3]

Word of Butler's action spread quickly. Hundreds of the enslaved refused to leave with slaveholders who hastily evacuated the nearby town of Hampton. These Blacks became refugees from slavery simply by staying put when owners fled. Some from the surrounding area departed owners for the fort. The men gained entry by stating that they worked on local Confederate batteries. Butler allowed their families, who did not fit his original criteria for admission, to come in on humanitarian grounds. The general had rations issued to all. The men, if not hired as officers' servants, lived in tents inside the fort and received assignment to various work crews. The dependents received housing in buildings outside the moat, and a limited number of the women may have found work too. Butler ordered the recording of military laborers' work hours and upkeep expenses for a future financial settlement.[4]

Anxious to have his actions approved, Butler not only wrote his superior on May 24 and 27 but additionally sent his brother to Washington to explain matters. From the Republican Party's beginning, most members, including Lincoln, had criticized slavery on various grounds yet had only advocated stopping its further spread in the hope that it would die out in the future. While many Republicans wished that secession would somehow undermine the institution, none seemed to have anticipated that the enslaved would flee to the Union army. Certainly, no one had planned for such a contingency. Now, an executive

Table 1. Major Slave Populations in the United States, 1860

Location	Number	Percentage of State Population
Virginia	490,865	31
West Virginia counties	17,715	5
Other counties	473,150	38
Georgia	462,198	43
Mississippi	435,631	55
Alabama	435,080	45
South Carolina	402,406	57
Louisiana	331,726	47
North Carolina	331,059	33
Tennessee	275,719	25
Kentucky	225,483	20
Texas	182,566	30
Missouri	114,931	10
Arkansas	111,115	26
Maryland	87,189	13
Florida	61,745	44
Indian Territory	7,369	14
District of Columbia	3,185	4
Delaware	1,798	2

Sources: US Department of the Interior, Census Office, *Population,* vol. 3 of *Eighth Census:* iv, xvi, 598; Theda Perdue, "Indians," in *Dictionary of Afro-American Slavery,* eds. Miller and Smith, 356.

cabinet discussion resulted in Secretary of War Simon Cameron approving Butler's actions with the provision that "The question of their final disposition will be reserved for future determination."[5] The administration continued to let commanders exert discretion in their responses to Black seekers of sanctuary.

Butler's pragmatic policy won him the national attention he craved. Through the rest of the war both the northern masses and even the Black refugees themselves commonly used the term "contraband" to mean a person who sought liberty by leaving slavery. Only the abolitionist minority, who for decades had advocated freedom and equal rights for the enslaved, objected to the term as dehumanizing. At the fort, the Black population had, by summer, risen so high that Butler had to resettle most of them at Camp Hamilton near Hampton. A new garrison at Newport News also attracted Black refugees. Although those admitted during 1861–62 remained legally unfree property subject to army supervision, they generally experienced some degree of freedom

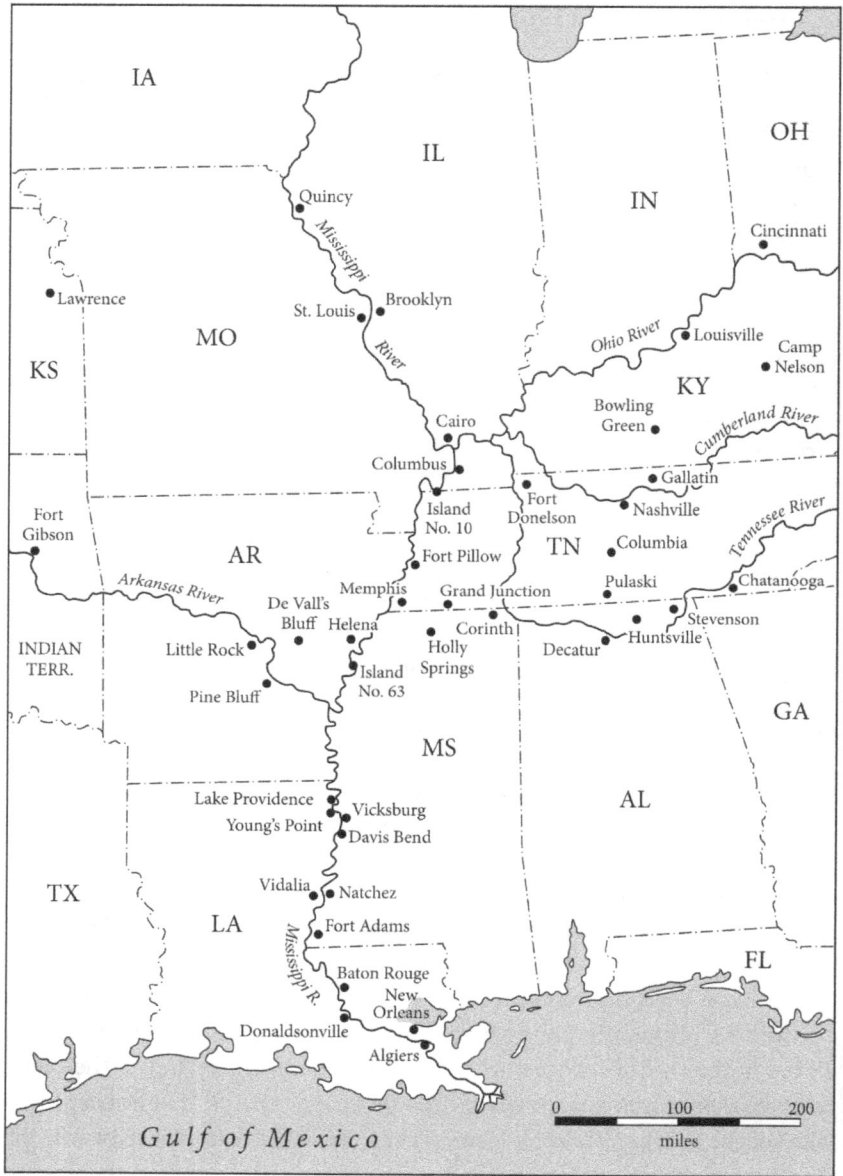

Major Western Sites for Freedpeople

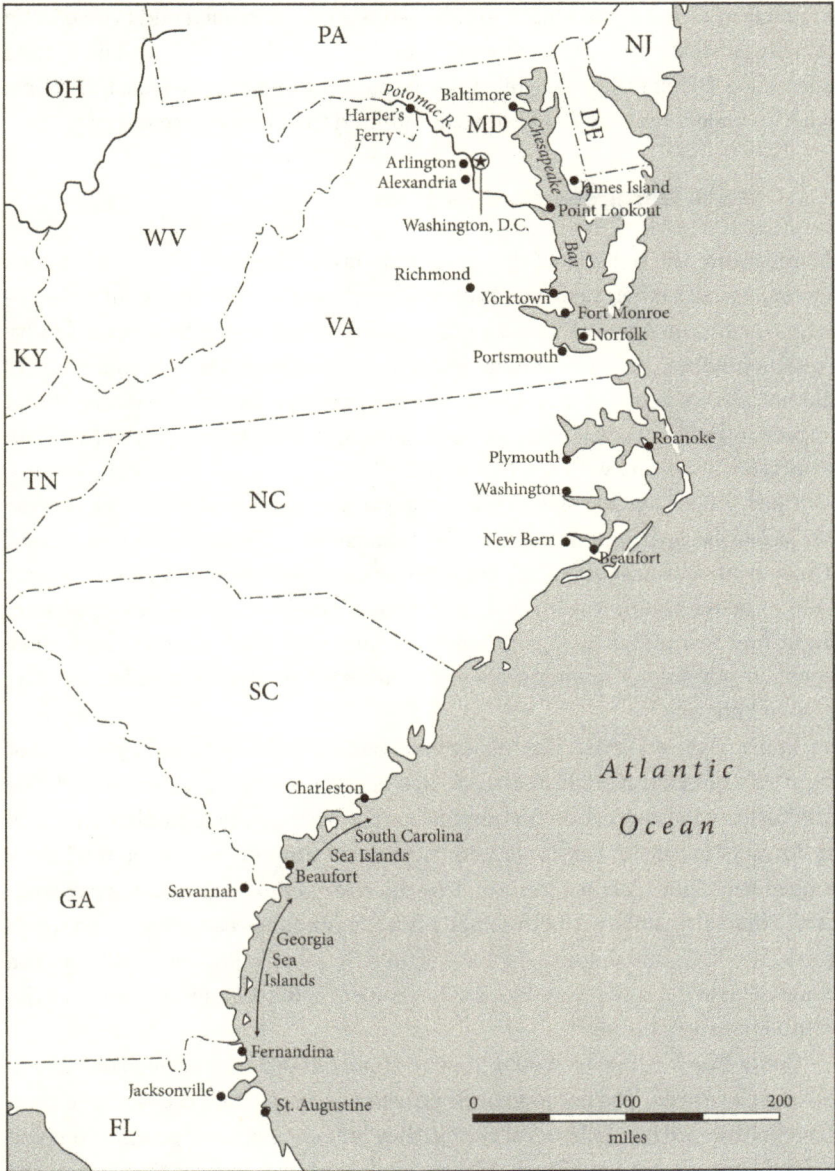

Major Eastern Sites for Freedpeople

in practice. Contraband status simultaneously had beneficial and problematic meanings. Butler returned a few to Unionist slaveholders who took an oath of allegiance. Black refugees, while feeling that they ought to be free, had to live with an uncertain future, a reality that limited the number escaping.[6]

Black Refugees: Perspectives

At first only the boldest of discontented slaves attempted to reach Union forces, usually when nearby. Many others viewed northerners with skepticism or caution. A few of the remaining ones felt genuine and personal loyalty to slaveholders. Yet even having what the enslaved called a "good master" did not always keep them at home, due to yearnings for equal treatment and opportunity. As one Missouri slave observed, "I likes to own myself and my work; that's the way with the rest of folks."[7]

Most Blacks leaving slaveholders early in the war, like those in the prewar period, were young men travelling by themselves or with one to two others. Those confronting substantial distances or obstacles tended to go with a light load in order to minimize noise and delays. However, those facing a short flight and few difficulties preferred to travel with their families and more goods, if possible. A small number of southern free Blacks blended into the flow to Federals.[8]

Many of the enslaved, like Moses Washington, believed that they were "not rightfully held a slave and the whole system was a plan of wicked men." The institution's most dreaded features probably were physical punishment and splitting of families.[9] Venus wanted "nobody to whip me nor dribe me." Suzy judged that "dey treat we too bad. Dey tuk ebery one of my chilen away from me." Some also suffered from sexual abuse, inhumane restrictions, too much work, too little subsistence, or having, like Scipio, "feelins hurt all[,] all the time." Slavery made many Blacks desirous of a better life and wary of the white majority's power.[10]

Some Black refugees would appear almost every time that Federals entered a slave area. The immediate circumstances separating the enslaved from slaveholders varied. In general terms, they launched an escape upon sensing a good opportunity. One Black refugee explained to a Federal that "we heard your guns, massa, and dey seemed to call us dis way."[11] Some Blacks, such as those at Hampton, refused to evacuate with fleeing enslavers. When Federals came near, some slaveholders, exasperated with discontented slaves or suffering financially, would evict the more troublesome and least useful of the enslaved. By 1862 some Federals, motivated by anger against either slavery or secessionists, occasionally removed slaves by force, whether or not the slaves themselves were ready to leave. When taken by soldiers, the elderly Polly Graham grieved for her comfortable home, although she "likes to be free." Others *"would rather be free* even if they were in rags and out of doors."[12]

Black refugees held various outlooks upon the future. Some believed with great hope in a predestined divine deliverance. Baylor Pollard declared that "the Lord was going to rescue his brethren from bondage as he did with the Israelites." Another believer in providential deliverance told soldiers: "Dun' yer t'ink *yer* did it all. De Lord d'unt it all. He jus' use *yer,* dat's all." The reformer Julia Wilbur later observed that the idealistic ones, most likely believers in deliverance, optimistically expected big changes: "They seem to feel that the world is all before them, and if they only work for it, they can have a share of all the good things the world contains."[13]

Other Black refugees did not hold this religious perspective but thought that the disruptive forces of civil warfare would likely open doors to freedom. The refugee Aleck advised slaves to flee a harsh owner, but warned that "if they have good homes that they had better stay where they are [because,] . . . if they run off[,] they have no homes and perhaps can't get work." The pragmatists were uncertain, if not skeptical, about the extent of likely benefits beyond freedom, as most of the enslaved had experienced whites as hostile.[14] Regardless of one's view on the future, all Black refugees shared a hope for freedom.

The liberty seekers at first encountered few Federal commanders who copied Butler's policy. When they did, it often did not last, because a superior or a successor insisted on demonstrating that the Federals meant no harm to the institution. While some officers restored Blacks to owners, most chose excluding them from Federal lines, considering it as a middle road that neither helped nor hurt these refugees.[15] The Fort Monroe incident helped to move the United States Congress to pass the First Confiscation Act on July 6, 1861, confiscating all slaves who worked for the Confederate military. This law had limited impact, as commanders mostly applied it in the relatively few provable cases, such as the construction crews captured at Fort Donelson, Tennessee, and Fort Pulaski, Georgia. A month after the law's passage, the Lincoln administration encouraged its commanders to adopt Butler's contraband policy in the Confederate states. It directed that Federals neither remove nor entice slaves from owners and should allow their voluntary return. The navy adopted the contraband policy, while many army officers with legal qualms did not. The President still let commanders choose their policy, as he tried to stay above the controversial issue. Of course, both exclusion and return disappointed and discouraged Black refugees.[16]

Northern Reformers: Perspectives

At Hampton during July 1861, many refugeeing males encountered Pvt. Edward Pierce, the first northern reformer to work with them. Granting that reform movements of the time focused on many different causes, "reformer" in this book will serve as a shorthand label for those, mostly northerners, who worked behind Federal lines to improve the lives of Black refugees. General Butler assigned Pierce to organize and direct a Black crew in constructing a major set of earthworks. This Massachusetts abolitionist tried to convince the abandoned African American males living on their own in Hampton to participate. Realizing that this activity would anger secessionists, they wanted to know if they would be freed. Pierce could only reply that he believed that they deserved it. As a minority, African Americans knew that they could only try to influence the dominating whites. Given the potential benefit in public support of the Union, the men decided to take the risk. Before Pierce's short-term enlistment ended, he concluded that his workers "will accomplish more when treated at least like human beings." Army officials could seem like new masters to the escapees, who probably viewed Pierce as the beneficent type, but many of his successors as tyrants. The Black refugees quickly learned that many northerners held racial prejudices and did not want to end slavery.[17]

The abolitionist leaders of the American Missionary Association (AMA), a large evangelical Protestant organization, wrote Butler for permission to take Black refugees north for jobs. As this would raise legal, political, and social issues, the general countered with a request that the group instead send down winter clothes for the Blacks. The AMA became the first organization to enter aid work with Black refugees, and providing necessities became the original task drawing civilian reformers to the South. In September 1861, the AMA sent the Reverend Lewis C. Lockwood to inventory the needs of the Fort Monroe–area Blacks, and soon shipped donated clothes. After distributing them and urging the refugees to rely on self-help as much as possible, Lockwood stayed for over a year to gather more input and to offer various services. By autumn the fort area had fewer than a thousand Black refugees, and Pierce had returned home after his military term ended.[18]

Developments in the South Carolina Sea Islands would move matters to a larger scale. The islands between Charleston and Savannah are lowlands cut off from the mainland by streams and bays. They comprised an isolated and unique region, where Blacks retained more African cultural elements than elsewhere and grew high quality long-staple cotton, rather than the far more common short-staple type. On November 7, 1861, a fierce attack by the

Federal navy on forts outside the port of Beaufort led to the withdrawal of Confederate defenders and the flight of nearly all white people. Most of the islands' enslaved, like those at Hampton, refused to leave with owners. The thousands of Sea Islanders left behind composed a group far larger than that abandoned in any other locality.[19]

Slaves left behind at their old residences retained their possessions, while often having the materials to raise food and cash crops, advantages over refugees who left. Still, some adventurous young male hands departed and, along with refugees from the mainland, took jobs with either the military or the Treasury Department agents who confiscated the cotton crop, despite the plantation dwellers considering it their property. Gen. Thomas W. Sherman, worried about footloose Blacks becoming hungry and disorderly, set up the first supervised contraband camps at Beaufort and Hilton Head for these two groups.[20]

The Treasury Department appropriated the abandoned plantations because—unlike those at Hampton—these lands sustained a very valuable crop. Since the Republicans favored an active government involved in the economy, Secretary of the Treasury Salmon Chase, an abolitionist, asked Edward Pierce, a personal friend, to examine the situation of Sea Island Blacks and to design a plan for them. The former supervisor of African American laborers at Fort Monroe had returned to civilian life and so could visit the Sea Islands in January 1862. He promised the Blacks that they would get pay, the elimination of corporal punishment, family unification, and education. "If they were to be free," he demanded that they prove themselves to be hardworking and obedient. Since racists among the soldiers and cotton agents had already provoked a degree of distrust, he opposed the possible leasing of plantations to white businessmen in fear of more abuse. Instead, he advised Secretary Chase that the Treasury Department quickly install antislavery supervisors practicing "paternal discipline" to restore cotton cultivation for northern markets.[21]

Chase approved the plan as an experiment in economic and social change. Pierce agreed to get it started. By working for Federal authorities in occupation zones, he and other reformers would gain a share of the supervisory power and access to governmental resources. Pierce travelled to Boston, New York, and Philadelphia to spark the creation of charitable organizations to support the project. The Educational Commission of Boston, the National Freedmen's Relief Association in New York, and the Philadelphia Port Royal Relief Committee resulted.[22]

Smaller groups, like the Kansas Emancipation League and Cincinnati's Contraband Relief Commission, formed around the same time. Free Blacks with better incomes—who had run southern African American organizations in the past—most likely led the formation of their own aid societies, such as the Contraband Relief Association in Washington. Contending that Black refugees benefited the Union war effort with their labor, the new associations proceeded to raise donations and train volunteers.[23] While the names of these groups sound secular, they generally espoused a nonsectarian Christianity and sometimes sponsored missionaries. Some existing religious organizations—the American Baptist Home Mission Society, American Tract Society, American Bible Society, and several Quaker groups—also joined in work on behalf of Black refugees.[24]

Most volunteers who headed south needed the low salaries provided by the sponsoring entities. Very few went on their own resources, and Laura Towne may have been the only one to have done so throughout the war. The great majority did have the independence of single status, but a minority went as married couples. When a pair had young children, the wife usually focused just on their care. Other married reformers left their spouses and families in the North (women did so only if children had reached adulthood) but returned periodically to visit.[25]

The reformers held some type of antislavery views, although only a minority took the controversial stand of abolitionism upholding racial equality, since northern culture cultivated widespread racial biases. Relief workers sought to maintain separation of the escaped from their enslavers. Yet during 1861–62, most felt awkward about discussing emancipation with Black refugees, since the government had not committed to it. Nearly all believed that Blacks needed help to rise above some degree of damage from slavery in "preparation for freedom," as Thomas Howard wrote. Many white reformers, even some abolitionists, espoused the supposedly scientific belief, called romantic racialism by historians. It held that, despite a very basic human equality, the races had different innate characteristics, some positive and some negative. So, while some reformers anticipated a relatively quick elevation, others expected it to take many years, if some weaknesses could ever be overcome. Most considered subordination appropriate for Blacks during the process. The middle-class background of most relief workers also caused them to expect Black refugees to adopt their lifestyle and values. Blinded by a superior self-image, they often misunderstood their charges.[26] Some were very open in stating their stereotyped beliefs; others only occasionally expressed such views to other whites. Many of these individuals would not sound reformist today.

Relief workers—white as well as Black—felt motivated fundamentally by the ideals of American liberty and Christianity. Elizabeth Botume wrote in the context of the national crisis: "I now belonged entirely to my country, to labor for that country's good." Julia Wilbur added that "I have always felt that, if opportunity was ever offered me, I w[oul]d do something for the negro. And it seems all the while as if the Lord would guide my steps & bless my efforts." As with the enslaved, personal factors could affect an individual's decision to take action. Volunteering helped Wilbur get past a deep sorrow. When her sister had died, the husband left the couple's baby girl with Julia, then living with relatives in western New York, but in less than two years her brother-in-law took the toddler back and cut off all contact without explanation. This likely heightened Wilbur's sensitivity to injustice.[27]

Women who felt wrongly restricted by social norms for their gender gained more freedom and authority by going south for reform work, although the aid societies paid them less than the men and rarely rewarded their efforts with management positions. Some of the unmarried women, especially Wilbur, Harriet Jacobs, Laura Towne, Ellen Murray, Harriet Buss, Cornelia Hancock, Emily Howland, Lucy Chase, and Sarah Chase, believed in a life of selfless Christian service, sometimes called "blessed singleness." They considered improving society as a more important and fulfilling female calling than performing domestic work for relatives. The new tasks made Harriet Buss very happy, more than ever before in some ways. The opportunity to benefit Black refugees primed them for a great burst of personal development made possible by newly found economic independence and self-determination.[28] They likely realized the affinity between their goals and those of the African Americans.

Reformers were divided over three basic strategies for their task. First, paternalists thought that escaped Blacks could make the tough transition to freedom only with much parent-like care, guidance, and control, although their expectations about the length of the process varied. These reformers differed over how possible equality was, but they all considered the Black refugees as in an inferior condition, at least initially. Frederick A. Eustis, a white southerner who had moved to the North and turned against slavery, wrote: "We are dealing with a people almost dehumanized by slavery, and it will be a long process to elevate them. . . . they should not be abandoned to their own ignorance. I never before have been so impressed with the necessity of exercising an absolute control over them."[29] Paternalists ranged from those like Eustis, who emphasized tight management of Blacks, to those like Edward Pierce, who stressed care. Paternalistic reformers predominated during the war, probably because of widespread destitution among Black refugees, the military's need for order behind the lines, and the prevalence of racial stereotypes.

A second group, the laissez-faire advocates, believed in the promotion of self-help and free choices along with minimal intervention in the lives of Black refugees. Reuben D. Mussey, a reformer enlisting Black troops later in the war, proclaimed: "No man is a swimmer until Cork Jackets are off him—as well as manacles. Do let him exercise his selfhood and Manhood, working out his own destiny." This minority granted that some charity would be necessary during the climb out of the impoverished state of slavery. The laissez-faire proponents all thought that individuals should ultimately succeed or fail depending on their abilities and effort, but, like the paternalists, they ranged widely about how much natural capability they thought Blacks possessed.[30]

The third division, the egalitarians like the Reverend Lockwood, believed in equal rights, and listened to the concerns of Black refugees. Not surprisingly, northern Black reformers fit here, but few white reformers shared this viewpoint early in the war. Austa French did, because "surely there are principles of right necessarily eternal, since God is." The abolitionist Julia Wilbur added that Blacks "are *very much like white folks.*" The key to taking this position was developing and acting with respect for the Black refugees. Austa and her husband Mansfield French went so far as to advocate redistribution of Confederate land to Black refugees.[31]

The perspective of most individuals fit primarily into one of the three groups, but some of the more independent-minded reformers mixed in views from the other two. Edward Philbrick practiced laissez-faire in his dealings with Blacks, but also favored some paternalistic guidance by employers. Laura Towne provided paternalistic direction to African Americans and made a few demeaning comments about them to other whites, but treated her students as having equal mental abilities. Behavior and ideas occasionally became inconsistent or changed.[32]

These differences over strategy among antislavery reformers led to some very sharp contention. Laissez-faire advocates believed that the generous help of egalitarians and paternalists would undermine Black initiative and build dependency. The other two groups responded that the laissez-faire position ignored the extent of need. Paternalists held that Black refugees were ready for neither the laissez-faire group's full freedom nor the egalitarian group's equal rights, and they alleged that rushing toward either goal without extensive preparation would guarantee failure. The paternalistic Maria Mann contended that "for one generation, if not for two, under the best arrangements, *that race* would not, could not, but by miracle, become independent of superior, directing minds." The laissez-faire and egalitarian viewpoints agreed in seeing paternalists as harming the freedom to which Blacks aspired. Egalitarians insisted on listening to refugees about their needs; they judged the other two groups as disrespectful if not prejudiced. The paternalistic and laissez-faire reformers assumed that they could design aid programs best and were more realistic.[33]

The Rise of Contraband Camps

During 1862 Federal policies continued to evolve. In March the United States Congress enacted a new article of war that prohibited the military from returning Black refugees to owners. This generally spurred commanders either to protect all Black refugees or to establish strict standards for responding to civil enforcement of the Fugitive Slave Act. Moved by racial hostility or bribery, some Federals tried to circumvent the new rule in various ways. Some treated Unionist slaveholders as legal exceptions, although neither the article of war nor the First Confiscation Act did so.[34]

Commanders opposed to interference with slavery—like Generals Henry Halleck, Don Carlos Buell, George McClellan, and John Dix—persisted in excluding Black refugees from the lines in their territorial departments. But rank-and-file troops—moved by antislavery convictions, shocked by seeing the realities of slavery, or angered by the hostility of most white southerners—turned against exclusion starting in 1862. These soldiers hid or defended Black refugees in the face of orders to the contrary.[35] Some even attempted to smuggle them north, much like the prewar Underground Railroad.[36]

Even commanders upholding exclusion came to exempt those who brought in helpful military information, but the main hole in the policy arose from the desire for numerous laborers, as in General Butler's case. Soldiers could perform a great deal of the work, but replacing them with African American refugees freed more troops for combat. At first commanders did this as a temporary measure, often for quick fortification of a position. Ongoing crews evolved, as forces moved with the workers to new sites needing defense and as more tasks were assigned to the African Americans.[37]

While expediency expanded use of the contraband policy as a means of advancing the war effort, the Black refugees themselves often became a lower priority. Many labor supervisors partly or even completely left crew members on their own to find necessities beyond rations. That approach resulted in deteriorating health and morale for workers, as well as disorder from theft of food for family members and recapture attempts by slave hunters. The better foremen tried to oversee adequate food, shelter, medical care, and security but otherwise left laborers alone.[38]

The more pragmatic commanders came to see a need to start contraband camps (see Appendix A) under a superintendent responsible for military-style order and discipline, as well as the residents' welfare. Gen. Thomas Sherman quickly perceived this after invading the Sea Islands, but elsewhere supervised camps started during Spring 1862 or later. Major contraband camps lay near Federal garrisons, which always sat along transportation routes such as the seacoast, rivers, or railroads to facilitate communication and resupplying. Superintendents included officers (especially chaplains), enlisted men, and civilian employees. Commanders mostly appointed antislavery superintendents, perhaps believing that sympathetic men would do the best job. Yet some assigned racists to the position. For assistance, superintendents could get detached soldiers and volunteer civilians funded by aid societies. Some charities sent out scouts, such as Lockwood, to examine possible sites for relief work, determine needs, and verify military tolerance for aid workers. Camp staff members sometimes had useful experience managing military supplies, businesses, charities, schools, or missions, but none had ever worked in what today is called a refugee camp. During the prewar period the army had rarely dealt with refugees and did not accumulate relevant knowledge.[39] Camp residents had to endure much, as staffs independently figured out logistics and developed practices.

In July Congress enacted a Second Confiscation Act by which the government took possession of and freed slaves belonging to those supporting the Confederacy. A few commanders would try to implement it by issuing free papers to those whom they judged eligible. By this time under mounting pressures from the continuing stream of Black refugees, Federal difficulties in the increasingly bloody war, and Republicans wanting tougher war policies, Lincoln had decided to issue a war order on the matter but delayed doing so until Federals won a victory of sorts at Antietam. On September 22, 1862, he released the preliminary Emancipation Proclamation, which threatened to end slavery in all areas that did not restore allegiance to the United States by the new year. The series of war measures in 1861–62 showed the President and Congress moving very cautiously against Confederate slavery.[40]

As Federal policies changed, contraband camps slowly appeared behind most war fronts in 1862. In March, Pierce returned to the Sea Islands, soon incorporated with other Federal toeholds on the Georgia and Florida coasts as the army's Department of the South. He briefly served as the first superintendent of contrabands there. Similar officials (see Appendix B) would gradually appear under a variety of titles to manage the army's programs for Black refugees in most territorial departments, each of which operated in its own way.

During most of 1862, relief workers in the Sea Islands probably outnumbered all those elsewhere. Across the islands Pierce scattered teachers, doctors, and charity distributors funded by the three associations initially supporting the experiment. He quickly took over the army's two contraband camps and ended the independence of abandoned slaves by imposing supervisors on plantations. In an unusual case, Frederick A. Eustis became supervisor on his father's plantation. Eustis's background and refusal to pay the house servants made the laborers there fearful of reenslavement. Several of the other supervisors evoked similar worries through strict management, especially the retention of the old slave code rule that prohibited leaving a plantation without a written pass. Essentially, a plantation abandoned by secessionists and focused on large scale agriculture became a type of contraband camp, which this book will refer to as a plantation camp. When Pierce left in June, control over Black refugees passed from the Treasury to the military, the usual location of that authority. Gen. Rufus Saxton, a career soldier and very compassionate abolitionist from Massachusetts, took charge as the department's contraband superintendent for the rest of the war. Late in the year he had Black workmen construct the new village camp of Mitchelville.[41]

At Fort Monroe, the Reverend Lockwood secured permission from Gen. John Wool, the new commander of the Department of Virginia, for the Black refugee William Davis to leave temporarily on a speaking tour in the North to raise funds for the needs of his community. Davis's speeches included an appeal for an end to slavery. This and Davis's extension of his tour prompted proslavery officers to accuse Lockwood of slave-stealing. After some waffling, Wool exonerated the minister.[42]

The general soon appointed a departmental contraband superintendent, the wealthy businessman and abolitionist Charles B. Wilder. The army commissioned him and some later superintendents on the southeast coast as quartermaster captains, probably in the hope of facilitating supplies for contraband camps. If so, the appointments did not always inspire the cooperation of other quartermasters. Expanding occupation in eastern Virginia led to new camps under Wilder at Norfolk, Portsmouth, and nearby Craney Island.[43]

During the war, several officials selected vacant islands at a distance from shore or in a major river for camps because of the security they offered from the soldiers of both sides and southern whites. It eventually became clear that islands were vulnerable to flooding, they largely depended on outside sources of supplies, and they offered restricted opportunities for earning money. John Oliver, a northern Black reformer, described the Craney Island camp as "what Elba was to Napoleon a place of confinement and hard bread . . . cut off from every facility of aiding themselves only to depend on the Commissary." During its short existence Craney Island did earn attention for its organization and sanitation.[44]

Along the southeastern coast, starting in late 1861, the navy created self-managed and mostly small camps for Black refugees whom its patrols picked up from a variety of vessels. It settled them on several islands along the coasts of Maryland, South Carolina, Georgia, and Florida. An enclave on South Carolina's Edisto Island grew large enough to become a contraband camp under Pierce's supervision. Residents of villages on the other islands had little interaction with reformers, except for some naval officers. After a reduction of nearby Federal forces, Confederate threats caused the closing of the settlements at Edisto and Georgia's St. Simons Island in 1862.[45]

When Federals took control over the northeastern coast of North Carolina, Gen. Ambrose Burnside, the commander, accepted Black refugees and prohibited them from departing on ships, because of their contraband status. He selected Vincent Colyer, a missionary, as departmental contraband superintendent with camps at Hatteras Island, New Bern, Beaufort, Roanoke, and Washington. When Edward Stanly, a southern Unionist and military governor appointed by Lincoln, allowed a fellow Unionist to recapture a Black refugee in New Bern, African Americans held a protest meeting, which a few northern whites attended in support. Some of the military laborers, expecting to be reenslaved, either returned to owners on their own or went into hiding. However, antislavery soldiers quickly freed the recaptured slave, and the military governor dropped the issue.[46]

In the spring of 1862, the reassigned Benjamin Butler led an invasion of southern Louisiana, where he encountered a situation very different from eastern Virginia. The captured area had too numerous an enslaved population for the army to provision many, as well as too many Unionist slaveholders to ignore. In an effort to establish order amid increasing labor unrest, he briefly experimented with several policies and then settled upon what he saw as a compromise semislave/semifree system that required the enslaved to labor for owners but without whipping and for pay. Butler forcibly imposed the new order: noncooperating Blacks received harsh confinement, and noncooperating owners lost their workforce. Expelled or escaped African Americans became unpaid military laborers or field hands on a plantation camp at Algiers. General John W. Phelps, a post commander and reformer, wanted to enlist Black men but resigned after Butler rejected the idea. No aid association sent workers to Louisiana until 1864. Because the enslaved considered themselves freed by Federal occupation, they had ongoing tensions with slaveholders and most Federals.[47]

As commanders in the western theater of war invaded Alabama, Arkansas, and Tennessee, they tried to maintain an exclusion policy. When Federals enforced this in Alabama, the barred Black refugees poignantly responded: "It is very hard, Massa." Constantly encountering Black refugees who offered their services in return for protection, Gen. Samuel Curtis abandoned exclusion, as he fought across Arkansas in 1862. He left large numbers of Black military laborers in Helena, where his campaign ended. The general issued freedom papers to those who said they had worked for the Confederate army.[48] Around the same time in western Tennessee, Gen. Ulysses S. Grant also came to judge exclusion as impractical. Like a few other commanders who sought to reduce the drain on army resources and help Black refugees find jobs, Grant tried shipping them northward, in his case to Cairo, Illinois. Because this action stirred up controversy during that state's election season, the new Secretary of War Edwin Stanton temporarily halted it. Consequently, Grant's forces, which had advanced further south, established contraband camps at Grand Junction, Tennessee, as well as at Corinth and Holly Springs, both in Mississippi. In December, the general appointed Chap. John Eaton as contraband superintendent for the Department of the Tennessee. Eaton, an antislavery Ohioan, would play a prominent role in the work with Black refugees.[49]

In the upper trans-Mississippi theater during 1861–62, Federal expeditions into western Missouri, northwest Arkansas, and the Indian Territory (today's Oklahoma) opened flows of Black refugees into Kansas. The Indian Territory's wartime situation was unique. The five main tribes there had undergone much assimilation that included the acquisition of slaves while living in southern states before the US government moved them westward. The Federals withdrew from the territory at the war's beginning, and all five tribes signed alliances with the Confederacy, which bordered most of their lands. New pro-Confederate leaders of the Seminoles reestablished slavery, which their predecessors had recently ended. Black refugees who reached Kansas from neighboring areas settled at a safe distance inside that free state's eastern, more populated end. Some received help from local aid societies, but most struggled to provide for themselves.[50]

In Delaware, Maryland, Kentucky, Missouri, and the District of Columbia, the slave areas loyal to the Union, civil authorities retained power to uphold the institution. A Federal in Kentucky overheard a slave say that "they would all run away if they could get a chance." As in the prewar days, small numbers did flee across borders into free states despite the Fugitive Slave Act, which provided a legal process for their return. Delaware, which had the fewest slaves among all southern states (see Table 1, p. 3), experienced the least change, because it lay well out of the war zone and proslavery Democrats firmly dominated the state. Wanting to keep the border states on the Union side, Lincoln treated slavery there very carefully. He offered to support funding for gradual emancipation in willing border states, but their officials sharply rejected the proposal. During 1861–62, only a trickle of Blacks sought freedom with Federal troops stationed within border states, because garrisons generally followed an exclusion policy.[51] A few army posts would use either a need for laborers or the new article of war to admit some Black refugees. Most attempts by Federals to sneak southern Blacks into the North required a hazardous passage through these states.

Throughout the war, some of the enslaved in Maryland escaped into Pennsylvania or the District of Columbia. Early in 1862 a post commander accepted Black refugees as hospital workers at Point Lookout, Maryland. However, his successor treated them like prisoners and promised to return them, once the owners took the oath of allegiance. Abuse, including whipping by Federals, upset Abby Gibbons, the head nurse, who lamented: "So much of my time is consumed in pleading [unsuccessfully] for the poor contrabands." She did obtain clothing they needed from an aid association.[52]

Kentucky, which held an especially intense commitment to slavery, had a slave population larger than the total in the other border states and the District of Columbia combined (see Table 1, p. 3). When Blacks, some carrying freedom papers, accompanied Federal regiments through the state, Kentucky officials used the state fugitive slave law to seize and auction off all those not claimed by owners. White Kentuckians also tried to prosecute or sue a few northern officers for assisting slave escapes.[53]

Starting in the early summer of 1861, some Black refugees from Kentucky and possibly Missouri managed to cross the Ohio or Mississippi river to Cairo, Illinois, where the post commander admitted them. As the town evolved into a major supply depot, military officials needed more laborers. The quartermaster at Columbus, Kentucky, also assembled a labor crew from male Black refugees in May 1862. Poor provision for the needs of workers and their families at both posts spurred commanders to create contraband camps with superintendents in late 1862.[54]

In Missouri, despite Halleck's exclusion order, a few regiments accepted Black refugees as laborers. Halleck himself decided to employ a group held in the St. Louis jail by claiming that they probably had worked for the Confederate army. One of his subordinates restricted the city's police to seizing Blacks specifically identified in court orders, but never if they were laboring for the Federals. When General Curtis replaced Halleck, he briefly applied the Second Confiscation Act to some of Missouri's enslaved.[55] Aid associations would not operate in the state until 1863. Other than some small exceptions, Federal commanders in the border states during 1861–62 sought to avoid interference with slavery.

The District of Columbia had a low number of slaves, but location in the national capital gave them symbolic prominence. Congress, which governed the district, enacted emancipation there with slaveholder compensation effective on April 16, 1862. Many of the freed left their former owners in search of new employers.[56]

During the war's early months, the commanders of the Department of Washington had tried with limited success to exclude Black refugees from Virginia and Maryland. Civil authorities and slave hunters often lodged captured individuals in Washington's jail. The army and navy hired some as laborers. Late in 1861, the army began to keep Black refugees claiming to be from Virginia in a section of the Old Capitol Prison. The prison superintendent hired out many and issued protection papers to them.[57] In March 1862 he moved the growing population to larger quarters at nearby Duff Green Row on Capitol Hill. The Reverend Danforth B. Nichols from Massachusetts became camp superintendent and relocated the residents in July to the still larger Camp Barker, a former military barracks to the north. As it grew overcrowded, he moved some residents to the new Camp Todd in nearby Virginia. Formerly the head of a reform school for delinquent boys, Nichols was prone to vehement outbursts and harsh discipline, along with behavior seeming to indicate alcoholism or mental health problems. Laura Towne, who knew him when he briefly taught in the Sea Islands in April 1862, judged him as having a "poor head . . . [with much] Conceit." His charges either endured the treatment or rushed into jobs that earned enough for independent living.[58]

During the summer of 1861, the Department of Washington also sheltered and fed Black refugees in a number of appropriated buildings at Alexandria, Virginia, a short distance down the Potomac River from the capital. Appalled by the camp's overcrowded condition, the reformer Julia Wilbur and the city's mayor separately but successfully urged the War Department to build a large barracks for Black refugees in the town.[59]

Early in the war, African American freedom seekers appealed to the sense of military expediency on the part of Federal commanders. The large number of the enslaved abandoned in the Sea Islands prompted the creation of new relief associations, which joined the American Missionary Association in funding antislavery volunteers to work with Black refugees. Where the army admitted African Americans in occupied areas, it primarily did so to take advantage of their labor. The refugees gained a degree of liberty under the insecure contraband status. Although some Blacks tried to live independently, reformers in supervised contraband camps provided for the destitute near most fronts.

In the loyal border states Black refugees found themselves in a precarious situation. All of these developments may not have looked like the initiation of social change, but it had begun. Rejecting slavery, the refugees and reformers would work toward change, but differences of opinion among the two groups would lead to difficulties.

2

Provision of Necessities

In old age Mary Barbour remembered escaping slavery with her parents and siblings in a wagon pulled by mules during the dead of night. Arrival at Federal lines in coastal North Carolina brought her family great relief and rejoicing. The pickets (military guards) admitted them but took away the mules and wagon. Federals generally confiscated all valuable property from Black refugees on the assumption that it belonged to secessionists and so went for army use or occasionally the picket's own profit. In either case, the victims and some reformers considered this to be robbery. The experience of those allowed through the lines could easily become more painful. Besides verbal abuse, rape, or other violence inflicted by racist Federals, many refugees suffered from an immediate need for life's necessities. Black refugees could either seek aid from northerners or seek maximum independence on their own. William Davis of Hampton "asked nobody to take care of him. He had been taking care of his mistress and himself too."[1] Others, like Barbour, entered a contraband camp, if they had one at hand and needed help badly enough.

Regardless of their choice, many Black refugees sooner or later would encounter a northern reformer, a development they had not anticipated. Appreciation for help could build some trust in those providing it. As one Black woman observed, "It was the first time in her life that a white person had shown any interest in her or her children." But if African Americans saw a reformer as part of the new power structure, it could put some cautious distance into dealings.[2]

Aid Workers

Before northerners became aid workers, few had interacted with Blacks in a meaningful way. The northern states' share of American Blacks in 1860 was only five percent, mostly those descended from slaves emancipated after the American Revolution. Joanna P. Moore admitted that "I had scarcely ever seen a colored person, and had never spoken to but one." Many northerners brought unexamined preconceptions, rather than knowledge, about their charges to relief work. The poverty and unfamiliar culture of Black refugees stunned reformers. Laura Towne, an abolitionist sent from Philadelphia to the Sea Islands, added that the whole situation in occupied areas "certainly takes great nerve . . . not [to] be disgusted or shocked or pained so much as to give it all up."[3]

Black reformers, like Charlotte Forten, a young woman from a wealthy family in Philadelphia, also had little experience with enslaved southerners. She had faced racial exclusion and segregation in the North; now enslavement in the South loomed if caught by Confederates. Obviously, northern African Americans treasured their liberty and fervently desired social change. Forten wished the Black refugees "all the blessings of freedom, and may you be in every possible way fitted to enjoy them." Some, agreeing with southern Blacks who believed in a providential liberation, saw themselves as carrying out the divine plan. The northern experiences of Harriet Jacobs and Sojourner Truth led to strong advocacy of personal and economic uplift. Black refugees from isolated rural areas found educated Black northerners amazing; a few felt resentment or distrust.[4]

Benevolent workers from both races, especially if not living with other reformers, found themselves associating most of the time with African Americans. Southern whites and prejudiced northern ones angrily rebuffed naïve requests to support the charitable work. Additionally, the refugees did not always welcome the reformers' guidance. Sojourner Truth, a famous African American missionary and speaker who had gained freedom long before the war, got thrown out of a Black refugees' gathering for calling them disgracefully dependent on charity. Such a strong statement about individual uplift offended the deeply destitute.[5]

Relief work itself could be hard, dirty, and understaffed. Julia Wilbur delivered rations by "trudging through the mud as no other white woman of my status would do." Superintendent Danforth B. Nichols complained: "Oh how tired we all get working from light to 10:00 P.M. all the time with 1, 2, 3, 4, 5, 6, or more questioners at our heels." Turnover among aid workers was high. Yet a writer using the initials "M.H.C." took a positive perspective on her tasks: "This is a most absorbing life—there is so much to be done, one never feels like stopping anywhere through the hours of the day . . . I have never worked with more earnest purpose." Being busy also tended to distract relief workers from loneliness and homesickness.[6]

Like modern refugee camps, the priority for the contraband camps was providing the destitute with necessities. Like many other reform movements of the era, the camps drew on both governmental and private resources. The number of destitute in a camp during 1861–62 ran from hundreds to around a thousand residents. While the camp staff had responsibility for meeting needs, some residents participated in the process.[7]

Food

Many new arrivals came hungry. Food in the early contraband camps, as in slave quarters, generally took the form of measured-out, weekly rations. Slaveholders most commonly had issued pork and cornmeal; Federals generally provided pork or beef alongside hardtack (a very hard, cracker-like bread). In both situations, Blacks might receive coffee and vegetables.[8] Many Black refugees disliked the hardtack and beef. Hardtack needed some form of softening to make it edible. Given the huge quantity of the army rations issued, some arrived spoiled. Food gone bad or unfamiliar might lead to digestive challenges, especially for children, the elderly, and those who were ill. Blacks could supplement rations, if it were feasible and permitted, by fishing, hunting, gardening, or the gathering of wild plants, just as was done in slavery. Some camp residents served as butchers, ration distributors, and mess hall cooks.[9]

Various circumstances could interfere with rations. Production or transportation issues occasionally caused shortages. Some Federals stole the food of Black refugees. Some officials either reduced rations or restricted them just to military laborers, not dependents. In those cases, much suffering resulted, unless the officials paid the workers and allowed purchasing of extra rations. Aid associations rarely attempted food shipments, because of the distances involved. Black refugees not living in camps or on farmland needed to earn enough to buy food.[10]

Because many camps opened with little or no equipment, the residents might have to cook meat, vegetables, or dampened flour by improvising the use of stick spits and either pieces of wood or bark as containers carefully nestled among hot coals. Otherwise, groups had to take turns using available equipment, which could lead to long waits and even fights. Much of the cooking took place outdoors. Fort Monroe and Camp Barker seemed alone during 1861–62 in organizing communal food preparation in mess halls.[11] As in slavery, most Black refugees ate with fingers, while on the ground or a floor, when they had the time. Reformers hoped to move them toward holding family meals around tables with utensils at set times.[12]

In or out of camps, the alternatives for the hungry were to starve, beg, or steal. One Black refugee insightfully explained the appropriation of food: "We learned it from childhood up. When we raised de corn and put it in de master's Crib, and he would not gib us enough, we didn't think it very wrong to go and take it. And when de corn in de master's crib was all gone, den we had to go to de neighbor's crib."[13] Those who stole food in desperation unfortunately reinforced the preconception of some reformers that Blacks were inherently larcenous.

During 1861–62, some reformers had to buy their own food, although some aid associations may have provided a food allowance. At this time, it seems that only commanders at Alexandria and the Sea Islands granted rations to aid workers. Harriet Tubman, a prewar escapee and Underground Railroad operative, at first received free rations when she worked as an army scout in the Sea Islands. Black refugees perceived her as a privileged northerner and kept their distance. She had to give up the rations and earn her food before she could work more closely with them. No other reformer did this, but a few raised private supplemental funds from supporters back home to help with expenses. When Black refugees with gardens or domestic animals appreciated a particular aid worker's service, they rewarded that person with eggs, produce, and other food treats. Reformers might later reciprocate with small gifts obtained when visiting the North. Because preparing meals consumed much time and some considered it below their dignity, better-off aid workers preferred to live in boarding houses or to hire servants. Reformers sharing quarters could make workable table cloths and napkins by cutting up a sheet, but in many cases they had to order kitchen wares from the North.[14]

Housing

Shelter for Black refugees, like cabins for slaves, varied widely in quality, such that camp quarters could be better or worse than previous residences. Many settled into vacant structures, not only houses, slave cabins, and empty barracks, but also animal sheds, factories, warehouses, and public buildings. Quarters badly deteriorated or not intended for human habitation often had either too little or too much ventilation. Some became uncomfortably hot during summer, while others could not retain much heat during winter or shed rain at any time. Black refugees accustomed to poor cabins could cope better with these buildings than those who had better homes in slavery. Structures lacking fireplaces led refugees during winter to light fires on an earthen floor or, in the case of a wooden floor, on a pile of dirt or stones. Either way, they had to endure the smoke. This might have led to carbon monoxide poisoning, except that many of these buildings were not airtight. Large, open-floored buildings with many residents could not help but be noisy and lacking in privacy. In all but the worst cases, repairs or renovations of defective structures by residents or quartermaster crews could help immensely.[15]

Other types of quick housing involved assembly in an open area, preferably with good drainage. Army tents, often worn or discarded, tended to provide the poorest cover, especially for those with vulnerable health. Brush arbor huts, made from large branches, provided minimal cover if retaining the leaves or coated with mud that hardened. Inhabitants sometimes dug the floors down several feet for a little more room.[16]

When the quality or quantity of housing was grossly inadequate, superintendents might seek a location for new construction. Blacks often did the work themselves. Wood was the standard building material as logs (if the crew had mostly axes), slabs (if it also had splitting tools), or lumber (if it had saws). A steam-powered sawmill, such as Gen. Rufus Saxton and Capt. Charles B. Wilder obtained for their departments, greatly sped up the process. The residents desired the privacy of family-sized cottages and often built them, if allowed. Some resembled the cabins that soldiers quickly constructed for winter quarters, usually smaller than slave cabins. Quartermasters, concerned about sheltering as many as possible, favored long military barracks with room divisions added. In 1862 some were completed at Fort Monroe and started at several other camps. The army tended to arrange new structures and tents in a grid, like troop housing.[17]

Some construction crews erected new quarters roughly, others skillfully. It was easiest and quickest to make new housing without windows, like many slave cabins, but that limited daytime lighting. Cutting shuttered openings into buildings allowed for more light and ventilation but would also reduce heat retention in winter. Residents could get a bright light for fine work, like sewing, by burning either a pine knot or a sliver of cloth in fat. Many kinds of shelter had dusty dirt floors, although these could be covered with planks or bricks, if available.[18] At a few locations during winter Federals forcibly took over the better-built cabins of Black refugees.[19]

The early shelters rarely had furnishings, the most desirable of which was bedding, especially in winter. Most residents had to sleep on the ground or floor at first. Some gathered rags to use as mats. Aid workers sought to get them blankets or quilts, if not also bed ticks (mat-like bags stuffed with straw, corn shucks, or dry moss). Camp Barker, followed by others later in the war, had wooden bedsteads arranged as bunk beds in order to house more under a roof. Besides bedding, furniture was scarce in the early camps.[20]

Good housing also benefited from certain facilities, like fireplaces. Poorly designed chimneys let smoke escape into a room. Mud-and-stick chimneys were easily built but ran the risk of catching on fire. Stone or pipe, if available, was better. The Cairo camp seems to have been the first one to get a heating stove. Rural sites often had woodlands, although the collection of firewood could involve a long, cold walk during winter for the under-clothed. Dependence on others to haul in wood or coal meant periodic shortfalls. The worst cases required rationed distribution and armed guards at the woodpiles.[21]

Housing required two types of detached facilities. The cleanest water generally came from wells, springs, or piped systems, but sometimes streams, lakes, or marshes were the only option. As with firewood, a close source made life easier. Officials suspected that the location of Camp Barker's well in an old graveyard caused illness (mosquito-breeding pools nearby were likely the main problem). Fort Monroe's dependence on hauled-in water soon limited the number of Black refugees housed there to essential military laborers. At least Camp Barker and the Corinth camp had bathtubs; some other camps used nearby water bodies for personal washing.[22] The second facility, the privy, did not exist in sufficient numbers at Camp Barker and many other overcrowded sites. This explains the frequent references to filthy and foul-smelling buildings or grounds in the camps.[23] Obviously, problems with these facilities constituted a threat to health.

Bad experiences with Federals, distrust of whites, and desire for independence caused many African Americans to live outside of contraband camps. Of course, urban settings offered more safety and jobs than rural areas, but any place could come with problems regarding water, sanitation, fuel, and crowding. New arrivals first filled up a town's abandoned and rental buildings, both of which included decrepit structures. Black refugees also built shanties out of scrap materials and generally close to one another. In the unusual case of Hampton after Confederates burnt it in 1861, Blacks constructed a shanty-town out of the rubble and incorporated the chimneys that were still standing. When Julia Wilbur visited those living on their own in Alexandria, she judged the shelters as "a lower depth of degradation than I had yet seen. What can I do? Nothing unless they can have shelters fit for human beings."[24]

Reformers had several choices for their own housing. At plantation camps, like in the Sea Islands, they always occupied the planter's house and expected Blacks to live in the slave cabins or to build additional ones. This caused conflict with any refugee who had moved into the big house. In these camps the northerners became a new and—in their eyes—better elite replacing the slaveholders. Paternalists took to the role as substitute masters and mistresses in a "princely" life. While revising the labor system, these reformers retained pieces of the old plantation glamour, such as poorly compensated house servants and a genteel living style. The egalitarians, however, likely paid servants better or did without them.[25]

Aid workers in towns sometimes received a housing allowance from their sponsoring organizations but competed with numerous federal officials for rentable spaces. Wilbur reacted negatively to her first room in Alexandria: "What a place I have found! How can I stay here? It is too uncomfortable to sit down & write." Reformers at times could only rent lodging from free Black homeowners, something egalitarians, like the Reverend Samuel G. Wright, more readily did, although critics "say that it is disreputable and that we make the cause unpopular." He thought living in a Black person's home was "making ourselves only equal with them." Relief workers in a contraband camp usually could have a free room there. Emily Howland's friends convinced her at first to take respite away from her workplace, but she, like many other reformers, eventually found that residing in camp was more convenient. Those rooming far from work sites would need extra funding for a horse or public transportation.[26]

Small groups of aid workers, especially in the Sea Islands, could obtain housing appropriated by the army. They usually found the furniture removed, and might substitute wooden shipping boxes for some pieces. The most prudent reformers brought at least bedding, if not beds. The rest had to sleep on the floor, until they could have it shipped to them. Elizabeth Botume remembered: "Our house was a cheerless place at first. It took time and patience to bring around us anything like homely comforts."[27]

Reformers mostly preferred shelter that matched the lifestyle of their social class in the North, although some had the ability to rough it better than others. Esther Hawks commented: "I often wonder if it is my *duty*, to live in this way—if I am doing just as *much* good as I might be in some other sphere." After a long workday, satisfactory quarters facilitated beneficial relaxation and recreation. In the cases of single females who had previously resided with relatives, gaining their own living space enhanced their new independence.[28]

Clothing

Black refugees had great need for clothing, as they often arrived at Federal lines "scantily clothed" in scraps of rags, blankets, carpets, or cotton bagging held together by patches, thorns, or sharpened sticks. Most had received few new clothes per year, and many slaveholders in war zones stopped issuing replacements due to wartime inflation, scarcity, or concern about the flight of the enslaved. Besides warmth, clothes were necessary for any public activity, like work, church, or school.[29] Reformers strongly advocated modest and clean clothing. Black refugees arriving with little or no clothing probably stayed indoors as much as possible until they could get enough. Only after they had a second set, would they do laundry outdoors with large boiling pots and washboards.[30]

The army could do little for this need. It could only distribute some blankets during 1861–62. In Norfolk desperate mothers made clothes for their children by cutting up and reworking the blankets. When novice soldiers tossed what they considered unnecessary apparel, Black refugees quickly picked it up. However, in Alexandria, officials who suspected African Americans of stealing military clothes and blankets stripped them of items not officially marked as discarded.[31] When dealing with small labor crews in 1861–62, a handful of officials with access to sufficient funds purchased an initial round of cheap clothes for their charges. They then expected reimbursement if the men ever received wages.[32]

Everywhere camp officials became dependent on aid associations for large amounts of durable clothing, especially as winter approached.[33] Not all of what the organizations shipped was helpful. Very worn, luxurious, or conspicuous attire was not practical. Henry Rountree complained that some donors thought that "anything is good enough for the niggers." So, relief workers wrote public letters, as charities still do, advising donors against sending such items. The contributed clothes did not always cover a sufficient range of sizes, although one reformer cut a hole in the shoes' uppers in a way that enabled them to fit more feet.[34] Aid workers and the seamstresses among the Black refugees modified or repaired some donated items. If sent bolts of fabric, they could also cut and sew made-to-fit clothes. A number of female reformers began classes to teach sewing to the women who had not learned the skill. On rare occasions a reformer would make a dress for a favored Black refugee.[35]

The early donations arrived slowly, and occasionally an intense desire to have more clothes than in slavery led a Black refugee to wear old rags to try soliciting a few more items by deception. Clothes distributors, whether instructed by their sponsors or not, reacted by evaluating need through home visits. Lovey Eberhart observed: "This plan took me to places of destitution, starvation and suffering, such as I hope never to see again . . . I had to harden my heart to get rid of them without giving them everything I had."[36]

Clothes formed the core of the stock in the handful of camp stores opened by superintendents and aid associations during 1862. A few organizations fixed prices for all items, whether donated or bought for stores. With prices ranging from cost to 25 percent (occasionally more) below retail, camp stores made it possible for African Americans earning an income to afford goods. Charities earning more than store costs spent the money on more stock. Some stores permitted free goods for the destitute, but in the Sea Islands the availability of jobs led stores to charge everyone. Paternalists who worried about fostering extravagance would charge high prices for donated luxury items. Employed Blacks sometimes could make credit purchases, since they often received pay irregularly.[37]

Stores not run by reformers often cheated Black refugees, many of whom had little, if any, experience with money or understanding of costs. Black refugees, like slaves who obtained a little cash, typically bought small quantities of clothes, sewing materials, and food. A limited and fast-moving stock sometimes caused purchasers to take what they could get, rather than what they would prefer. Still, reformers urged careful consumption and thrift on customers.[38]

Some camp store managers requested that their sponsors ship them clothes made from a heavy and coarse cloth in the manner of slave clothes, due to concerns about low cost, durability, and possibly class distinctions. However, the customers with a choice would not purchase anything with the appearance and discomfort of slave clothes. Stores could only give these outfits to those in desperate need. One refugee declared: "we don wan to war *dat* kind o' stuff no more[;] . . . we wans to dress like de white folks now." Investigating Quakers concluded: "Their taste is the same as ours." Attractive clothes, such as girls' straw bonnets in the latest style, sold well to employed parents. However, some refugees and reformers complained that all prices were too high. One Sea Island store was twice broken into and robbed.[39] From the beginning, camp stores gave rise to conflicts as well as new opportunities.

Because reformers hauled trunks of clothes with them, they initially eliminated worries about their wardrobes. Not surprisingly, they usually dressed better than their charges. Several Black refugees tried, as they had likely done with mistresses, to obtain some of a reformer's clothes as gifts, but only the most needy cases moved a few aid workers to do so. A few reformers did their own laundry, but most probably paid for the service, due to the time it required.[40]

Medical Care

Black refugees with a long or difficult flight often arrived at Federal lines wounded, injured, or ill. Once there, inadequate food, shelter, fuel, outhouses, and clothing, as well as overcrowding and impure water, threatened health. Many African Americans preferred home remedies or sought help from the group's herbalists and "granny doctors" (females given some training by southern white doctors). Black midwives commonly saw to the pregnancies and births of refugees.[41] Many aid workers administered home remedies. Esther Hawks, Laura Towne, and Rhoda Smith had some medical training that they put to use. Yet the challenge of meeting other needs of Black refugees generally took precedence over medical care during the early war years.[42]

In some contraband camps, relief workers endeavored to institute the public health measures of structural ventilation, regular removal of human waste, bathing, and prompt burials. Whitewashing gave buildings a smooth, easily cleaned surface. Spreading lime powder on the ground outside buildings was believed at that time to have a disinfecting effect. Most of the sanitation practices arose from the prevalent idea that foul air carried disease.[43]

Federal army posts had military doctors who obviously had to prioritize care for soldiers and so might not have time left to treat Black refugees. Some physicians refused to care for African Americans or treated them poorly, such as one at Helena who ordered several patients whipped. On the other hand, naval surgeon Samuel Pellman Boyer provided treatment whenever his ship stopped at an island settlement of Blacks.[44] The aid organizations associated with the Sea Islands experiment sent some doctors to ride circuits around plantations there, and other societies subsequently recruited physicians. They also sent medicines, although one Quaker association refused to provide medicinal liquor.[45]

In 1862 Fort Monroe obtained the first army doctor assigned to a contraband camp. By the year's end at least the camps at Washington, Alexandria, Hampton, and New Bern also had doctors. Like regimental surgeons, they set up small hospitals to simplify care and to control contagion. Most had separate male and female units. Camps without a doctor sometimes secured a ward for Black patients at the post's military hospital.[46]

Many African Americans who had lived under a slaveholder disliked and avoided care from white doctors, because much of the medical treatment in the era before the discovery of microorganisms was frightening, painful, or not very effective. Also, physicians may have incorrectly thought Blacks to be naturally immune to certain diseases and extremely vulnerable to others. Another common white misapprehension claimed that slavery or the African American character promoted disorderly lives that increased illness within the race. Black families, fearing the hospitals as places of death, tried to hide ill members from aid workers. Thus, officials forced the seriously ill into hospitals, an action that made the patient feel like a slave despite the medical reasons for it.[47] The quality of hospitals varied. Some began in dilapidated structures or tents. Many lacked an adequate staff. Some army doctors resented being assigned to contraband camps and gave poor care to the patients.[48]

Because Black refugees from rural, especially isolated, areas were very vulnerable to communicable diseases, the crowded camps and shantytowns facilitated epidemics. In early 1862 smallpox broke out in the Sea Islands and spread northward along the coast to Washington, where the dangerous disease killed several camp doctors. Another outbreak occurred in Kansas. In each area officials quarantined infected Blacks in special smallpox hospitals and vaccinated as many of the others as possible. The common practice of burning the patients' clothes to reduce this epidemic's spread led to new clothes for survivors, a significant drain on the supply of donated garments.[49]

Other illnesses and conditions raging at times among the Black refugees were whooping cough, chicken pox, measles, mumps, diarrhea, dysentery, and various fevers. Much of the South was known to have unhealthy months in the summer or fall, but no one then knew about the mosquito's role as a disease carrier. The most beneficial forms of care at the time were bed rest, regular washing, and special diets. The last two were not always provided to African American patients. One historian estimates that as many as 25 percent of those who lived for a substantial time in contraband camps died from disease.[50]

High death tolls posed a challenge for disposal of the bodies. Burial crews likely consisted of several soldiers or male camp members. As had long been done at epidemic sites, crews used carts to make daily rounds to collect the deceased, wrapped in a blanket at most, for quick deposit in a mass grave.[51]

Aid workers generally knew about the southern environment's seasonal dangers and seem to have had no difficulty getting medical care. Julia Wilbur noted that "a person needs good health and strong nerves to endure this work," although a few disregarded their frail conditions to volunteer. New or worsening illness caused a fair number to resign and to depart. Even so, just four aid workers—all in the swampy Sea Islands—died from disease during 1861–62.[52]

Security

An additional necessity, often taken for granted in times of peace, is security. In the occupied South, hostile civilians threatened Black refugees and reformers. As Wilbur understood, "It was Federal bayonets alone that made it safe for us or for the contrabands to stay," although prejudiced soldiers contributed to the problem at times. Black refugees living on their own generally lived close together to provide some safety in numbers. Military laborers usually had a guard of Federals that provided some protection from Confederates and slave hunters. Many contraband camps had soldiers posted either at or near the site.[53] In the absence of available or sympathetic troops, the camp superintendent recruited Black guards and secured arms for them. A leader of the African American settlement on St. Simon's Island, Georgia, organized a guard with muskets provided by the navy. Camp guard forces drove off small-scale Confederate raids at several locations. When more serious threats arose from Confederate advances, Federal commanders preferred to relocate Black refugees. That caused Grant to send women and children from Corinth to Cairo in late 1862.[54]

Reformers had adequate protection from Federals most of the time. The one exception was an aide to Superintendent John Eaton who was murdered during 1861–62. Black enlistment potentially could expand security, but few reformers advocated it until the Lincoln administration authorized it.[55]

In the militarily occupied South, the reformers' fundamental task of keeping Black refugees alive, Maria Mann observed, "needs an exhaustless fountain to supply these demands [for necessities]." Aid workers only occasionally faced some challenges in meeting their own needs. Many refugees, especially independent ones, had limited resources and had to utilize all their talents to manage. The military and the aid associations had resources to provide help, especially for camp residents. All the same, the quantity and quality of the necessities provided varied widely, as in slavery. Federal military needs always came first, and that periodically threatened the welfare of camp residents. The reformers' exertion of control over clothes and medical care sometimes caused tension in what was otherwise constructive interaction. Despite much physical suffering, the majority of Black refugees persevered. "We will endure this suffering in patience," said one, "for the sake of the prospect of freedom. We are patient through all, because we see a good time coming." Few came to doubt their new life's worth so much that they abandoned the Federals and reformers to return to owners.[56]

3

Seeking New Privileges

Amid thick smoke from firepits in a long stable that housed Black military laborers and their families at the Mississippi River port of Columbus, Kentucky, the reformer Samuel G. Wright overheard an African American preacher compare his audience's situation with the biblical story of the Israelites' escape from Egyptian slavery: "Brethren, we's come to de Red Sea. Dat is jes where we em. De Giptians is behind us. De river is afor us. God will speak by and by through Massa Linkum and say Go forward. Den wel march. We must have *patience*." Legal freedom would require governmental action, but even Black refugees living in Unionist slave states had some liberty in practice that they hoped to apply to work, religion, social life, and education.[1]

Northern reformers, relying on the antebellum philanthropic model borrowed from Europe, after some provision of immediate necessities, turned to modifying assumed character flaws of the needy. Paternalists hoped to guide them through a great transformation incorporating the northerners' values. They expected the instilling of these traits to require work supervision, evangelizing, home visits, and formal education.[2] Aid societies lined up volunteers not only as charity distributors and doctors, but also as farm supervisors, missionaries, counselors, and teachers. Individuals often performed multiple tasks. Some had relevant training or experience; others had little or none.[3]

While the enslaved had assimilated portions of the white majority's culture in the past, they had tenaciously developed their own subgroup culture. This pattern would continue, as Black refugees would adopt only new ideas and practices that they freely found meaningful.[4] Naturally, they clung to treasured customs and thinking, while trying to attain new opportunities. The reformers supported their own goals for African Americans through resources provided by aid associations and authority gained from participation in federal supervision. Sometimes clashes with their charges' preferences resulted.

Employment

Black refugees aimed to enter the free labor system, which to them meant at least no whipping, a less intense work regimen, and some sort of compensation. Many Blacks quickly sought to become servants for either soldiers or reformers, even though those who had never performed domestic service risked being replaced, if they lacked the skills needed to meet employers' expectations. During 1861–62, only a limited number obtained wages, ranging from meager to generous. Commissioned officers had access to funds for hiring servants, although some did not bother to apply or ran into technical issues. Many aid workers with low salaries tried to avoid spending their money on servants. Officials provided no oversight of these agreements, although Edward Pierce advised his subordinates in the Sea Islands to pay servants.[5] Many employers made verbal agreements to compensate labor with subsistence (often just army rations and/or aid society clothes). A number of African Americans, like one woman, initially accepted this: "I don't kere if dey don't pay, so dey give me freedom." Other Black refugees, like John Washington, sought only wages from the start, because "I felt for the first time in my life that I could now claim Every cent that I should Work for as My own. I began to feel that Life had a new joy awaiting me." To live an independent life outside a contraband or military camp, especially when supporting a family, obviously required pay.[6]

Some Black refugees earning just a subsistence soon grew dissatisfied and quit their jobs, especially if the employer behaved in an overbearing way, never issued promised compensation, or failed later to introduce a wage. The smaller numbers of reformers outside of the Sea Islands tended to be absorbed in the immediate need for providing necessities in contraband camps and initially involved themselves but little with the economic transition. One philanthropist in Kansas bought tools and materials for a group of craftsmen, who gradually reimbursed him after marketing their products. Others just hoped eventually to cultivate the wage labor system along with its values of hard work, thrift, and self-improvement in whatever job opportunities came along for Black refugees. A few thought that "the negroes are very tractable, and under a proper influence, would soon be capable of taking care of themselves."[7]

Some Black refugees could draw upon business experience during slavery. With their owner's permission a few had sold small goods and services to townspeople or fellow slaves. Others had owners who had offered little sums for good work, certain tasks, or produce raised. All of these individuals had learned some skills helpful for economic activity, such as bargaining, counting, or currency values (many local currencies with fluctuating values existed at the time).[8]

With or without these skills, a number of independent-minded persons started inexpensive enterprises, most often involving gardening, fishing, oystering, or cooking to sell food. Others engaged in services such as laundering, clothes mending, transportation, teaching, barbering, peddling (firewood, fodder, etc.), crafts, or various day labors. Some sold the cotton abandoned by their fleeing enslavers and then raised more of it. Harriet Tubman supported herself by making and selling root beer and pastries. She also set up a workshop that enabled women residents at the Beaufort camp in South Carolina, to earn money from baking, sewing, and clothes washing. While most Black refugees aimed for a reliable income, a few sought more economic mobility. Enterprising Black refugees who came into Federal lines with some savings, of course, had an advantage; they might even hire Black employees.[9] A few in Kansas had enough to rent farmland. Reformers either became customers or took a dim view of Black business.[10]

The flight of some white southern businesspersons and the arrival of numerous Federals increased marketing opportunities. Yet many African Americans could not make a living from small business, especially when too many tried it. Also, Black entrepreneurs periodically encountered malicious Federals paying in counterfeit or nearly worthless currencies, denying remuneration, and sometimes directly robbing them.[11]

The most available work, especially for males, was on military crews, which had lost most white laborers to enlistment or higher pay in the North. Many Federal soldiers, such as Sam Evans, wanted Blacks rather than themselves to fill this crucial gap: "My doctrine has been anything to weaken the enemy. The same negro has been the means of sustenance to the Rebels in the way of building fortifications [and] furnishing supplies." By making up the majority of the army's labor crews, Black refugees significantly aided the Federal war effort. Most of the work supervisors came to prefer Black hands, because they were accustomed to the southern climate and therefore could toil in it better. Also, the army paid Black workers less than whites, if it paid them anything.[12]

The contraband concept and prejudice commonly led Federal officials to exploit Black workers as appropriated slaves. One quartermaster later claimed: "These persons being idle, and thus supported by the government, it was deemed proper to make them work for their subsistence . . . without pay." Some commanders required Black refugees to perform any work needed by the army. The worst moved them to work sites away from their families, and sometimes allowed the use of physical punishment.[13] Many officials held that the Black refugees' legal status was too uncertain to qualify for payment, and a few actually paid supposedly Unionist owners for their slaves' work. Some did not even keep work records.[14] Obviously, all of these actions could make Black refugees suspicious of reenslavement.

Unskilled Black refugees performed many types of military work. Quartermasters and engineers needed numerous workers as axe men, earthmovers, construction workers, and teamsters. The commissary assigned laborers to transfer and haul supplies. Many Black women served as laundresses and hospital attendants. If paid at all, women earned less than men at that time. Harriet Tubman spent much of the war caring for hospitalized soldiers. She and Abraham Galloway, as two prewar escapees who took a big risk in returning to the South, served the army at times as spies and scouts. They may not have asked for pay, but presumably received funds to cover operational expenses. All these workers lived under military discipline and organization usually overseen by officers. Good work occasionally won them some respect. Sophronia Bucklin at first judged her crew of laundresses as lazy but soon realized that the workplace was inefficiently arranged. Reorganization resulted in much more work done in less time.[15]

Skilled Blacks—like wheelwrights, carpenters, blacksmiths, and ship pilots—were more likely to receive pay, and at a substantial rate, from various branches of the military. After Robert Smalls, his crew, and their families escaped from slavery in Charleston, South Carolina, on the Confederate supply ship *Planter,* the navy not only paid him a salary as its navigator but also prize money. When promoted to the *Planter*'s captain, he earned even more and probably became the best paid of the Black military employees.[16]

Congress passed the Militia Act of July 1862 to try to rectify matters for Black military workers by establishing freedom and a low, standardized compensation for them. Many officials questioned the law's validity and would not cooperate, even if a commander ordered pay. For a time at Fort Monroe, General Wool ordered token payments in cash and put most earnings into a freedmen's charity fund. Even when officials did honor the law, the cash usually came infrequently.[17] Black laborers with little or no compensation refused to work at some posts but found themselves forced back on the job by armed guards. Coerced roundups of Blacks for unpaid military labor launched the practice of impressment. The impressed men deserted whenever possible, and a few even returned to their slaveholders.[18] Reformer Julia Wilbur criticized the practice as just for the "benefit of Government, *not for the benefit of the Negroes.*" Reverend Lewis Lockwood called it "government slavery." He and Superintendent Charles Wilder strongly advocated wages for workers at Fort Monroe. They won a congressional investigation and secured an opportunity for the current crew members to take other jobs, but they could not gain regular payment for the laborers there.[19]

Reformist or pragmatic foremen, if permitted, did the paperwork to get their workers paid. All federal employees, military and agricultural, got pay in the Sea Islands. The Department of Washington since the summer of 1861 employed Black refugees, primarily for fortifying the capital, an important enough task to require good pay to attract and retain enough hands. Wartime inflation had also raised local wages and costs in the District of Columbia area. Officials in both Washington and the Sea Islands, though, additionally imposed a tax on employed Black refugees during 1862 to make them contribute to care of the destitute in contraband camps.[20]

Unlike the army, the navy practiced no racial discrimination in laborer compensation until late in the war. The navy hired a number of Black refugees for good-paying work at its construction and repair facilities. It began enlisting Black refugees in September 1861, but only at the lowest ranks. The navy reliably issued wages for Black sailors at $10 per month, part of which could be mailed to the enlistee's family and part of which was held back until discharge. Access to some promotions and a pension became available in late 1862. The Secretary of the Navy Gideon Welles, an antislavery Republican, implemented these policies.[21] Of course, harassment by prejudiced white personnel created difficulties on ships, as it did elsewhere.

In contraband camps the residents' lack of activities and the staff's need for help led superintendents to assign unpaid work to as many as possible. Residents collected and cut firewood, butchered meat, cooked or distributed rations, constructed housing, cleaned the camp, and buried the dead. No one on record objected to helping out. Only in a few camps during 1862 did ways of earning money for the group develop. A superintendent at Norfolk had his charges make baskets and pick oakum from old ropes to earn small sums for that camp's fund.[22]

Farming on abandoned plantations could put the largest number to work. Grand Junction Camp's residents picked cotton on such places nearby. Along the southeastern coast the navy directed its island contraband camps to feed themselves by farming, which worked well only at small camps. The residents at larger camps, probably viewing their placements as temporary and certainly alert to an entrepreneurial opportunity, sold the food they raised to passing ships, while they continued to draw naval rations.[23] Superintendent Wilder, probably intending to copy the Sea Islands experiment in wage labor, decided in the spring of 1862 to disperse his charges onto eastern Virginia's abandoned plantations. But since the sites had little or none of the necessities for farming, Wilder found more preparation necessary and postponed the plan until the next year.[24]

The large-scale Sea Islands experiment included an introduction to wage labor very early for workers. The Treasury turned the sales receipts from the confiscated 1861 cotton crop into a fund to finance the experiment. The fund covered purchases of implements, seeds, horses, and mules. Some plantations needed the work animals to replace those appropriated by the military. The fund additionally provided wages for Black workers and for the agricultural supervisors sent by aid associations to conduct training for hands in self-support. Actually before supervisors arrived in the islands, many of the Black foremen had started spring planting with their crews. Of course, the hands knew much more about their tasks than the new managers did. Most islanders had favored planting food crops to sustain themselves during wartime uncertainties and to avoid the work required by the long-staple type of cotton, much more intense than that needed for the short-staple variety raised on the mainland. Some laborers had even disassembled cotton gins and hid the parts. However, northern mills had suffered from the loss of access to the raw material, grown only in the Confederacy. The government wanted to reopen the flow of cotton and to maximize revenue from the experiment. This issue led to clashes. Further conflict arose when the monthly pay came late or food supplies fell short, matters beyond the reformers' control. Most plantation superintendents, though, meticulously kept up with doing the required paperwork for the hands' low pay.[25]

Discontented laborers soon started a work slowdown, stole needed food, and engaged in intimidation. Edward Philbrick, a plantation supervisor, felt bad about the workers' just grievances, and spent some of his own money on supplies for employees who returned to work. Like all supervisors, this businessman from Massachusetts needed to get the planting done on time. The supervisors threatened to report the strikers "to Massa Lincoln as too lazy to be free," to cut off all food, or even to abandon the Blacks to Confederates. Management ultimately triumphed only by calling upon military force. Even Philbrick used it once to arrest a hand who menaced him. A local commander, fearing that dissatisfied workers might seek more regular and better pay as military laborers, limited the number of passes for those jobs. Ironically, northerners instituted the new free labor (non-slave) system by forcing plantation residents into it.[26]

Farm supervisors, like slaveholders, monitored the quality of each day's work but only punished poor work with fines. Some realized that learning names and cultivating personal relationships encouraged better work. Most northern supervisors in the islands saw no sense in the local task work system, which required each laborer do a measured amount of toil in the plantations fields and then allowed him or her to tend to personal matters, such as vegetable gardens. These supervisors instituted gang labor in the cotton fields. Philbrick, who made the effort to learn about long-staple cotton production, came up with a compromise satisfying his workers by setting a workday task for each family.[27]

Most enslaved females had labored as field hands, and Superintendent Pierce continued the old practice. "Better a woman with the hoe than without it," he concluded, "when she is not yet fitted for the needle or the book." Many northerners considered it acceptable, though not ideal, for low-income women to do hard physical work. Only Austa French and Julia Wilbur recorded opposition to requiring women to do field work.[28]

The eventual arrival of pay relieved everyone, although it continued to come late. Philbrick once kept his hands working by advancing his own money to issue pay on time. Some of the Black hands, however, assumed that wage labor continued all of a slave laborer's privileges. They objected when weekly issues no longer included tobacco or the same types and amounts of food rations. One woman who failed to complete all her work was upset to find her pay docked. Those, who requested and received a little cash early, misunderstood it as a gift rather than a pay advance. Thus, the new regimen kept generating new causes of friction and distrust.[29]

William C. Gannett, a supervisor and laissez-faire reformer who advocated that the experiment "let all the natural laws of labor, wages, competition, etc., come into play," believed that the new fiscal experiences would prepare Black refugees for success in freedom. Reverend Mansfield French, a Methodist from New York and a prominent reformer in the Sea Islands, on the other hand, worried that the wage labor system substituted economic need for whipping as a compulsion for work. His wife, Austa French, took a hopeful outlook: "Imagine the trade set in motion the moment they get wages." The hands who adjusted quickly to the new system even hired replacements when they could not work.[30]

In late spring 1862, Gen. David Hunter, the Department of the South's commander who lost a part of his forces to a campaign in Virginia, tried recruiting

Blacks but soon switched to conscripting the able-bodied men. Wherever Federals forcibly rounded up and removed male refugees, it provoked anxiety about reenslavement. Many Blacks and whites decried the involuntary service, separation of families, and loss of wages. Pierce feared that the draft would destroy the farming program without producing much military benefit. Plantation supervisors struggled to get the remaining, mostly female, hands back to work. Some men, like Prince Rivers, wanted to enlist: "I was gettin' big wages in Beaufort, but I'd rather take less, and fight for de United States, for I believe de United States is now fightin' for me, and for my people." When Hunter could get no pay for his unauthorized Black regiment, he put most of the men on indefinite leave.[31] General Saxton subsequently issued weapons to every plantation for creating a militia. Fearing another conscription, some residents refused to practice drilling. In October Saxton received special permission to recruit a regiment of Blacks. The new unit quickly drew in Hunter's eager enlistees as well as refugees from the mainland hoping to rescue their relatives, but the former conscripts refused to join. Hunter's mass conscription also worked against the free labor experiment's financial success in 1862.[32]

A few contraband camps came to have a staff member who sought out local, private sector jobs (mostly as servants) for camp residents. Some of those hired, especially in the District of Columbia, then found themselves with an employer who refused to pay. This pointed to a need for official follow-up. Some Black refugees in Kansas independently obtained work as farm hands in warm weather but found winter work scarce.[33]

In response to a wartime labor shortage in the North, in September 1862 Secretary of War Edwin Stanton permitted a Midwestern hiring program at Cairo for the Black refugees, whose numbers had increased through shipments from several downriver commands. Given the limited private employment in most occupation zones, some reformers elsewhere urged Black refugees to accept jobs in the North.[34] But many Blacks preferred familiar landscapes, and expressed reluctance to relocate in a colder northern climate. Many wanted to stay put in the hope of locating relatives separated from them by slaveholders. They especially opposed sending their youngsters off for jobs with distant strangers for fear of losing them to the same kind of permanent separation as in slavery. The small number who readily agreed to migrate feared recapture by especially determined and resourceful owners. Some who did relocate got northern employers who mistreated them and paid little or nothing.[35]

Concluding that meaningful change in white attitudes was hopeless in the United States, some Black refugees became attracted to colonization abroad.

Such movements had long existed, and President Lincoln was now advocating it. In 1861–62, a number of Virginia's Black refugees participated in an emigration program, which lined up employers for them in the Caribbean nation of Haiti, ruled by Blacks. With funding from that nation's government, the white abolitionist James Redpath organized the operation. Bernard Kock, a white profiteer with a different Haitian colonization scheme, won the support of Superintendent Nichols at Camp Barker and then tried to recruit Blacks in Hampton. However, Reverend Lockwood, favoring instead the improvement of race relations in the United States, talked the interested Black refugees out of going, which helped to stall Kock's plan.[36]

Adjustment to economic activity came quicker to some; lack of financial experience hindered others. Henry Clay Bruce, who left Missouri for Kansas, "found myself almost as helpless as a child so far as . . . providing for personal welfare and the future." He found himself slowly learning how to judge the prices and quality of goods. Only by gradually overcoming slavery's training that "it was a crime for me to dispute a white man's word," did he start to bargain with storekeepers. Many Black refugees took some time to understand the ultimate costs of credit purchases. A large number of the employed could accumulate little or no savings, due to meager pay and wartime inflation.[37]

Only a limited number of Black refugees succeeded in gaining the important privilege of earning money during 1861–62. The more enterprising Black refugees tried to earn money on their own. Hampered by responding to the refugees' immediate needs and the legal status of contraband, the reformers did not attempt much transition into the wage labor system, except in the Sea Islands and the Washington area. The compensated work programs supported by reformers mostly consisted of employment as subordinate laborers. Jobs enabled some residents to depart from camps and cut government costs. Some found unpaid work reminiscent of slavery, as numerous white employers did not recognize them as free laborers and benefited. Reformer Austa French realized the difficulty for "a race to be elevated by the same people that had so long oppressed them." The Black worker Andrew, when asked by a reporter at Fort Monroe if he would get full freedom, responded that "Dar, now, dat's jist what troubles me all the time a thinkin' on it."[38]

Church

Many slaves placed Christianity at the center of their lives and their survival. A Portsmouth Black told Martha Kellogg that religion was "all I's got. If I hadn't known how to pray I should have been dead." Another explained to

Reverend Samuel Wright that "despite troubles . . . I know God's up there & his sperit is here in my heart and I'se well content all the time to let my Lord manage all these things."[39]

Most religious slaves participated in an evangelical Protestantism. Although some slaveholders had forbidden religious activity among those they enslaved, most just banned services that were without white supervision, which nearly all slave codes required. While many masters had their laborers attend a white church, a largely underground church—fundamentally independent of whites—developed a folk religion with its own preachers. The slaves' religion had its own style of services, sometimes at night and occasionally running until dawn. All evangelical Christianity had a strong emotional tone, and the slaves' type especially so, in order to energize the faithful and help them cope with suffering.[40] The most distinctive religious service, practiced at least in the coastal southern states from Virginia to Mississippi, was the shout, a circular dance of African origin with repetitive singing. The movement and singing grew more intense with each hymn. Most northerners, like Laura Towne, at first found the ritual "savage," but she and Charlotte Forten came to enjoy it. Col. Thomas Wentworth Higginson thought that "it is impossible for anyone who has an ear not to partake [in] the rhythmical excitement."[41]

A few of the first Black refugees requested permission to pray from Federal officials, but learned that the military only concerned itself with gatherings that disturbed public order. Most African Americans assumed that escape enabled them to hold services openly and to organize congregations. An elderly Sea Islander voiced a common view when he prayed "thanking God out of the depths of his soul that at last they can meet together for worship without fear or restraint." Blacks in some locations quickly set up their own chapels, ranging from open-air ones to wooden buildings. On Roanoke Island they built a simple timber frame thickly covered with leafy branches. Underneath sat long construction horses for benches and a stack of empty wooden boxes for a pulpit. Most unusual at Yorktown was an outdoor pulpit, which had an artistically carved lattice through which live ivy twined.[42]

Reformers sought involvement in the church formation process. They generally insured that contraband camps had a meeting hall for use as a church and school and that a reformer usually controlled it. Missionaries asked existing Black congregations for an opportunity to hold services or at least to preach. They also rushed to organize their own assemblies. Aid workers divided roughly by denomination in their reaction to the slaves' religion. Presbyterians, Congregationalists, Unitarians, and Quakers—all groups that emphasized reasoning in religion—generally held that the Black refugees' emotional services needed much taming. The Reverend William S. Bell complained that the Black refugees' religious practices, "like many human preferences[,] are not founded on wisdom." These nonevangelical missionaries sometimes found that Black preachers challenged them by holding competing services nearby.[43]

Evangelical reformers—such as Baptists, Methodists, and Disciples of Christ—had enough in common with Black refugees' religion generally to show a little more understanding. The Reverend James A. McCrea wrote that the Black refugees "manifest a true Christian & zealous spirit, & far exceeding my expectations. My own heart has been greatly cheered and refreshed in attending these meetings & I cannot but trust that they are & will be crowned with the divine blessing." Hedging a little, Mansfield French, a Methodist missionary, stressed the need to honor strengths of the slaves' religion, while offering a few carefully worded criticisms of weaknesses. Black refugees received Evangelical missionaries more favorably but generally preferred their own preachers, who after all had an advantage in familiarity with the black refugees' traditions.[44]

Denominational frictions appeared at times. The northern evangelicals' American Missionary Association generally tried to avoid it by holding nonsectarian services for all residents at contraband camps. To implement that policy, Reverend Lockwood wanted to give communion to anyone wishing it and the Reverend W. W. Wheeler allowed no one else to preach at his services. However, both offended some Baptists, who walked out to hold separate services under their Black preachers. Some existing Black Baptist churches barred missionaries of other denominations from giving guest sermons. Protestant aid workers unsuccessfully sought to convert or at least reeducate Black Catholics, mostly present in Maryland and Louisiana.[45]

Southern white churches granted official membership to no more than a large minority of slaves before the war. By 1862 a growing number of African American refugees exhibited interest in conversion, much to the satisfaction of both northern and formerly enslaved preachers. However, paternalist missionaries worried that either slavery had warped consciences or that Blacks had inherent moral weaknesses. Romantic racialism stereotyped Black refugees as having tendencies toward some combination of stealing, lying, intemperance, profanity, laziness, unchaste behavior, and social irresponsibility. Its believers insisted that Black refugees needed more preaching about morality. Northern evangelicals with higher standards also condemned recreational dancing and card playing. At Craney Island camp, the Reverend William O. King went so far as to warn those attending a service that God sent them much suffering there to push them toward more moral lives.[46] Needless to say, these northerners created more tensions than converts to their denominations. One Black refugee in Washington advised: "Do not come among us with your hastily-formed opinions, backed up by hearsay, but bring us light . . . and not so much faultfinding."[47]

Egalitarian reformers, such as Mary E. Green, looked more benignly on the character of refugees: "What some people mean by saying these people are neither affectionate nor grateful, is more than I can tell—they are eminently so here, industrious, persevering, patient, and many of them bright examples of what a Christian should be." When a Black refugee at New Bern asked Juliet B. Smith to help a needier person instead of her, the "poor helping the poor" deeply impressed Smith. G. H. Hyde, understanding that Blacks comprised a range of the good and the bad, criticized "some professed friends of contrabands . . . [who] did not think the people would steal or break the Sabbath and when they see them as much like white people, say 'well modified slavery is best for them.'" The Reverend Henry Clay Trumbull, despite his preconceptions, admitted that the Black refugees' religion consistently taught that each person's actions would be judged by divine standards.[48]

Evangelical missionaries with an egalitarian perspective tried to cooperate with Black refugees' religion. Lockwood and several others organized prayer meetings jointly with Black preachers. Disturbed by the practice at Fort Monroe's hospital chapel of seating Blacks in the back pews during services, Lockwood encouraged the refugees to raise funds to build their own combined church/school building. Several white chaplains of contraband camp chapels allowed times for Black preachers to hold their own services there. Near the end of 1862, John Oliver, a northern free Black, entered one of Norfolk's African American churches, over the objection of the southern white minister in charge, to announce the imminent likelihood of emancipation and access to bibles. Some missionaries visited homes in order to read the scriptures or to hold scripture study groups. As Laura Haviland made such a circuit in a contraband camp, several Black youths followed her, because "we have never heard white folks talk like you talks in our life. Da never talks for our own good."[49]

At several locations along the Atlantic coast in 1861–62, both white missionaries and some black congregations organized Sunday schools to encourage religious conversion and sometimes to teach basic reading. The weekly programs could include hymns, prayers, recitation of memorized verses, and scripture reading. If they lacked printed materials, Sunday schools relied on oral instruction. Aid workers, literate African Americans, and antislavery Federals helped to instruct the classes.[50]

Reformers commonly appreciated several aspects of the Black refugees' religion, such as prayers for Lincoln, the Federal army, and the volunteer teachers. They assumed that the religion cultivated an admirable commitment to patient endurance and forgiveness, but even African Americans who held those virtues had human limits. When a missionary tested a refugee named Obman by asking if he would feed a hungry rebel, the man replied affirmatively, but added, "I should want him to leave mighty quick after he'd got his victuals." The Reverend Vincent Colyer could get freedmen to volunteer to care for wounded Confederates only by much use of the Biblical directive to "Love thy enemies."[51]

Family and Social Issues

Counselors used home visits not only to evangelize but also to practice an early form of social work. "M. J. P." engaged in "reproof, consolation, and cheering." Reformers assumed a need to cultivate middle-class domestic values, especially self-control, orderliness, cleanliness, hard work, and punctuality. For example, Frederick A. Eustis (the man who became supervisor on his father's plantation) advocated the ideals of "a tidy house—a family dinner around the same table—undressing at night—washing and dressing in the morning—trivial in themselves, yet so essential," but the necessary furnishings were not easily obtained.[52] Even though the enslaved mostly kept cabins clean and could face punishment if they did not, many northerners saw what they expected to see. Shabby housing could not undergo effective cleaning, and few camps had a private place for personal bathing.[53] Criticism on these subjects probably came across to the refugees as irrelevant, annoying, or even offensive.

While the counselors could be aggravating, they could also be helpful. Relief workers aided Black refugees on a variety of matters. They offered constructive advice, arbitrated squabbles, and visited the ill. Those who won the refugees' trust were consulted on many issues brought to them. This included, according to Edwin L. Williams, that "discouraged men ask my intervention . . . with slack and often heartless officials." Refugees at times needed the intervention of a white person in order to obtain basic necessities, passes, burials, or restoration of property. Reverend Wright concluded from his experiences that simply the presence of an advocate could reduce abuses at a post.[54] Tacy Hadley believed that women, probably because of common belief in their mothering instincts and moral fiber, were more effective than men at guiding and helping. Julia Wilbur was deeply sensitive to injustices: "My soul is sick with every day's report of wrong and outrage."[55] She took on so many battles that she lost a fair number, but the successes strengthened her self-confidence to continue. Wilbur provided sympathetic support to many deserving individuals.

The reformers firmly believed in lifetime monogamous marriage cemented by a public wedding ritual, but all southern states had denied legal marriage to the enslaved. Unions usually required the owner's permission, and some slave-holders even chose the spouses. Many marriages began without ceremony and ended when enslavers broke up a significant number of slave couples through sales, relocations, or divorces. Separated mates commonly married someone else. Not surprisingly, Black refugees often refused to stay with undesirable spouses forced upon them in slavery. When reformers encountered refugees who had had a series of spouses, many jumped to blame either a flaw rooted in race or a weak marital commitment created by slavery.[56]

Horrible wartime situations added to the number of split-up families. Some slaveholders withheld children from departing parents, while expelling or abandoning troublesome adults. Some adults had to leave family members behind in order to escape successfully. Hurried movement of refugees by Federals sometimes fragmented families. Black refugees demonstrated a deep attachment to family by venturing far outside Federal lines to attempt the rescue of relatives, and by extensive searching for lost family members. They increased chances of finding or learning about kin by living in large communities of African Americans.[57]

Some Black refugees approached reformers to ask for formal marriage. One contended that "we'll be more like people if we's married." Lockwood first obtained military authorization for it and proceeded on a voluntary basis. General Saxton ordered Reverend French to conduct weddings for all Sea Island couples under a rule that couples who had a ceremony in slavery or had conceived children must marry. Despite the questionable legality of such weddings under state laws, officials soon issued marriage certificates and tried to enforce them in contraband camps. Charlotte Forten, though she judged one bride's headdress as "ridiculous," was "*truly* glad that the poor creatures are trying to live right and virtuous lives." By late 1862, a few reformers had just begun to realize that the innovation of a binding, formal marriage created special difficulties and differing reactions among the Black refugees.[58]

Aid workers also advised mothers about children. Julia Wilbur, when approached by a woman worried about having a child out of wedlock, counseled that it was only a small wrong. Probably influenced by her long-freed friend Harriet Jacobs who experienced sexual harassment during slavery, Wilbur showed much understanding: "I may not forget for a moment that these poor women have been more sinned against than sinning & that I may ever be patient with them & make all the allowances I ought to. . . . [White men] seem to think that a colored girl can't be virtuous." Dr. James Hawks encouraged the family bond by giving new mothers a card with their baby's name and birthday, the latter being information that few slaves knew about themselves. Both the nonviolent Laura Towne and the pacifist Lucy Chase objected to physical punishment of children, a common practice then. One mother retorted to Chase: "I will beat my boy just as much as I please." When neighbors of Towne believed such a punishment necessary, they simply conducted it out of her earshot in a distant woods.[59]

Many children lost their parents due to illness or wartime chaos. As had long occurred in slavery, other African American families quickly absorbed some orphans, but in wartime many children remained on their own or gathered in independent groups. Harriet Jacobs took one set of Washington orphans to a Black orphanage in Philadelphia in 1862. That year Rachel G. C. Patten, a white aid worker, established an orphanage at Camp Barker. She hired Black women to tend to the children's daily needs, a common practice in later camp orphanages. As soon as possible, caretakers typically would commence the bathing of orphans, followed by issuance of new clothes and bedding. The institution provided the children with a comfortable home, subsistence, religious activity, and education. Patten obtained a cooking stove and Christmas toys for her orphanage. When the District of Columbia's military governor wanted to cut costs by binding out orphans to employers, she joined Black residents in opposing it.[60]

In contraband camps the army tried to establish orderly communities through military discipline. Reformers rarely mentioned it in their writings, perhaps because of the well-known harsh regulation of men in arms. Camp superintendents probably focused on poor work, disobedience, absence without permission, insubordination, fighting, and theft, but had much discretion in such matters. Baxter K. Lee at the Hilton Head camp in the Sea Islands began with physical punishments: male violators spent time standing on a barrel, and female ones were locked in a dark room. As already noted, some work supervisors used whipping.[61] If a post provost marshal (the official in charge of police matters) had appropriated a jail, some offenders probably went to it.

Just as strong community bonds helped the enslaved endure slavery, Black refugees sought to live together. They especially benefited from living near longtime friends, but camps and shantytowns contained numerous strangers and a great deal of transience. Even if a slave community fled together, some members would eventually go their separate ways. New camp and neighborhood identities would slowly form, as refugees built new relationships and shared activities. In Washington several free-born leaders called a meeting of the city's African Americans in 1862. They passed resolutions urging the local establishment of a Black orphanage, a hospital, and a home for the destitute elderly, all of which became reality during the next year. Teachers, both Black and white, commonly initiated public celebrations in their schools, a common practice among whites. In a Hampton school decorated with evergreens and patriotic images of George Washington and Daniel Webster on Christmas 1861, the Black instructor Mary Peake held a choral concert followed by distribution of small presents to the children and refreshments for the audience. Such events might include speakers of either race, who typically presented their thoughts on the current situation of community members.[62] In coming years community meetings would broaden to cover more topics.

Relief workers drew upon their resources to support the drive of Black refugees for religious and marital privileges. They performed other constructive services as well. Black refugees, like Caroline Andrews, came to feel a deep gratitude to "those who, leaving home, kindred, and friends, came to labor for the advancement of the temporal and eternal welfare of my race."[63] African Americans independently raised funds and provided labor to establish their own churches as part of building their new neighborhoods. They upheld their religion and values as well as initiating orphan adoptions and official marriages. This sometimes occurred in the face of paternalist criticism about religious and domestic practices, arising from those reformers' preconceptions and leading to attempts at control.

Education

All southern states prohibited slave education, except Kentucky and Tennessee, and even there, white hostility and some local laws still hampered it. Black refugees desired education, especially for children. It would obviously aid personal independence and have practical use in financial matters, information gathering, Bible reading, and family records. One study counts, at the war's outbreak, about forty secret schools operated by southern free and enslaved Blacks who had gained a degree of literacy.[64] African Americans opened the first wartime schools for Black refugees in many occupied localities and in Kansas. They did so with minimal equipment and funding but much community support.[65] Even individuals with limited literacy might begin a class to get children started, if "none more competent present themselves," according to C. P. Letcher, one such teacher. After school sessions, eager students commonly assisted one another with the difficult material.[66]

Mary Peake, a Hampton free Black who had conducted a secret school in her house before the war, consulted with Reverend Lockwood about a reopening, after children asked for it. Lockwood encouraged the efforts of Peake and several other Black educators. He also convinced the American Missionary Association to pay Peake for a brief time before illness took her life. In other places during 1861–62, either Black refugees convinced friendly northerners to teach, or aid associations inaugurated schools (primarily in the Sea Islands). Cautious instructors at first conducted classes secretly or requested military protection in the presence of many white southerners. In the mostly secure Sea Islands, parents got some of the numerous northern educators to start morning classes just with the younger children and to teach the older ones later in the day after they completed field work. If large numbers enrolled under a few instructors, teachers divided pupils into short daily sessions of one to four hours. Believing that reading, writing, and thinking skills would make Black refugees unfit for reenslavement, the teachers saw schools as quietly but subversively working for emancipation.[67] Both reformers and Black refugees began this activity with enthusiasm, although African Americans who distrusted whites preferred Black instructors, when possible.

However, in New Bern, North Carolina, the wishes of Military Governor Edward Stanly caused Vincent Colyer to close his schools. After the students responded with "such sobbing and weeping I hope I may never see again," Superintendent Colyer took the matter to Lincoln, who gave permission for the schools' reinstatement. The highly publicized incident probably minimized subsequent obstacles from commanders. Still, the aid associations did not make efforts during 1861–62 in Louisiana, Tennessee, or the border states (except possibly at Columbus, Kentucky), probably due to not appearing safe enough. In the unique case of the District of Columbia, Congress repealed the restriction on the education of Black people after enacting emancipation there.[68]

Teachers of Blacks in the occupied South comprised a varied lot, but some generalizations can be made about them. Few belonged to abolitionist organizations, although they generally had antislavery views. Those with the most stereotyped views minimized teaching, much to their students' dissatisfaction. During the war, women probably made up the majority of instructors. The Reverend Asa Fiske illustrated common assumptions about gender by stating that women had a "peculiar adaptation to the work," by which he meant motherliness. Reverend Lockwood added that, if women worked alongside men, they would make much better assistants than males would, "because there will be less conflict in regard to superior authority." Many educators were young, and nearly all needed an income. Those unaffiliated with an aid association, mostly southern Blacks, made their living from tuition. Some teachers had substantial education and experience; some did not. Two young women, upon arrival in the Sea Islands, "visited different schools, and saw how *unfitted* we were for teachers" but still decided to try it in a small school at a minor post. Educators led busy lives, as aid societies expected instructors to handle day and evening sessions, participate in a Sunday school, and provide other services outside the classroom. Many teachers lasted for just a brief time doing this demanding work.[69]

Since the first schools in many places opened under immediately available shelters, the quality of the structures varied as widely as had initial housing in the contraband camps. Large shade trees, brush arbors, and tents were suitable only in the summer. Basements and former animal shelters (like barns) could be unpleasant settings. Rooms in empty houses accommodated small classes well, but often drew competition for such prime spaces. Southern Black instructors primarily used their homes and church halls, the latter of which also attracted northern educators.[70]

Unheated buildings and those without solid roofs might shut down on rainy or cold days. In the latter case, some very determined teachers tried to persevere in winter gear, although the children with the least clothing often stayed home. J. W. Coan noted that at times the attending pupils' "tears would roll down their cheeks, as they shivered." E. Frances Jenks admitted that without heat in winter, "There is nothing here but the love of learning to stimulate them." Writing lessons stopped, when cold fingers could not handle it. Parents could greatly aid a school by repairing structures or raising funds for that.[71]

At first most schools had primitive furnishings and little, if any, equipment. The teacher's table might be a crate. Improvised seating often was uncomfortable: barrels cut in half, empty boxes, logs (whole and split), split-logs fitted with legs, or rough-hewn planks over various types of support. Most of this kind of furniture could not be easily rearranged. Night classes required lighting, usually candles.[72] Teachers could use large roof slates or painted wood for a chalkboard; the alternative of charcoal on a plank did not work as well. Boards over barrels or barrels alone could substitute for writing desks. New schools especially needed blackboards, slates, alphabet cards, word cards (today known as flash cards), and textbooks. Lack of texts severely limited a school, but the donated ones might include too many types or be too advanced to use.[73]

A northern soldier remarked that "it seems quite like home when I see these children flocking to or from school with their books under their arms." This is not surprising, since most of the educational practices derived from existing white schools. Some are still in use today, and others have long since passed out of favor. Because schools drew mostly first-time student children, teachers quickly needed to establish classroom discipline and order. This was hard not only for instructors but also for children. Many juveniles began with rude, noisy, restless, profane, or combative behavior. They laughed at others' mistakes, wandered about, ate, drank, and pulled pranks. Angelina Ball observed that her students were "so full of fun and frolic that it is difficult for them to sit still long at a time." Tacy Hadley added that her students threw paper or mud wads "across the room as accurately and swiftly as white pupils."[74]

The most effective teachers obtained order through kindness, charisma, and rapport. Laura Towne and Ellen Murray only used praise and affection in their school, Mary Ames had to reinforce that with stomping and shouting.[75] Many instructors and some Black parents of the time firmly believed in corporal punishment, such as whipping, switching, or hand-rapping. Others preferred less painful physical consequences, such as prolonged standing on a seat or in front of the class, perhaps on one leg. The most common noncorporal punishments were sitting in a corner or on an isolated seat, losing recess, and staying after school.[76]

Some women, handicapped by inexperience and the gender roles of the time, could not control their students. In such cases, supervisors assigned a strong, classroom-hardened male teacher to the school. Charles P. Day handled all discipline at the Hampton school, because "*Our* children are *all children*. Sometimes they need punishing with the *rod* & that severely but always in love, & they realize it."[77]

Learning for the great majority of the students started with the alphabet. A large printed or written version was essential. As preparation for writing later, some teachers had pupils draw each letter with a finger in the air. Most schools aimed first for a basic literacy. A few northerners experimented with the new word method. The simplest form, called sight reading today, focused just on word recognition without alphabet training. A more elaborate approach introduced one new word every day. It started with the shortest words and worked toward longer ones. After explaining each word's letters, sounds, meaning, and use, the teacher drilled the class on this information and had each student read a passage using the words covered so far. Other instructors endorsed the more common phonics method that required the children to learn the sounds of letters and syllables for pronouncing, reading, and spelling new words.[78]

Many teachers, like Emily Howland, focused on "teaching to give them such knowledge as they would need immediately." So, beside basic reading, schools often focused on mental arithmetic (calculations that could be done in one's head). The few with usable surfaces added writing. Early in education, most teachers brought in music, at least hymns and songs familiar to the educator. The better schools usually added spelling, grammar, and geography. In the Sea Islands one instructor taught gymnastics.[79] Many teachers, desiring to remake the children with their own middle-class norms, assumed, like James M. Hawks, that "Their minds are blank and readily receive such impressions as you see fit to make." Most instructors worked basic Christian religion and other values into lessons. Many taught cleanliness; one included a display of the insects on a pupil's head. Several lectured on the war's meaning and on prominent figures in African American history, topics not generally featured in white schools.[80]

Many teachers held evening classes primarily for working adults. Mature students might have to struggle more to learn, but lacked the children's disciplinary issues. Teachers, like Caroline Johnson, generally found them "a great pleasure to teach, they are so persevering in their efforts." Many adult Blacks with a religious bent strongly preferred using the Bible as the reading text. A few teachers unfortunately used condescending books of advice for freedpeople in their classes. In 1862 Clement Robinson, a well-educated Black refugee in Alexandria, had the foresight to start the first course to train some as teachers.[81]

In that era, the traditional style of teaching focused on memorization, exercised in individual and small-group recitation of lessons. Physical punishment typically reinforced effort as well as order. A newer style of education replaced most physical discipline with privilege loss, while emphasizing incentives, enthusiastic involvement, and respect. This approach used more lecturing and visual aids to achieve understanding and skill development. Both approaches had advocates among the more talented teachers.[82]

As a means of handling large student loads inexpensively, some instructors adopted the Lancastrian or monitor system that originated in England. This method subdivided the pupils into small groups that, when not receiving instruction from a teacher, conducted exercises directed by assistant teachers (monitors) drawn from either the better students or literate adults. Monitors sometimes received advanced lessons. During the early war years, Black instructors rarely could hold any other post in the earliest schools run by northern whites.[83]

Instructors used many means to motivate students. M. E. Burdick favored group recitations on the grounds that "Children love to hear the sounds of their own voices—they learn by the ear as well as by the eye. Hard lessons are thus rendered easy and animation given to school exercises." Teachers offered the incentive of prizes gained by earning points or reaching a learning goal. A. L. Etheridge, however, thought he could fire up pupils by telling them that Confederates wanted Blacks to remain ignorant.[84]

From the start, education faced various challenges. Tardy pupils really aggravated some teachers, who had trouble understanding those outside a middle-class lifestyle. But a few realized that the Black refugees, lacking clocks, determined time roughly by the sun. Elizabeth Botume simply told her children to come to school right after getting up, and thereafter they all arrived at dawn. A more traditional solution required obtaining a bell to assemble a class.[85] Some teachers excluded pupils with too little or ragged clothing. This caused many impoverished parents to withhold their children, lest the youngsters feel ashamed. A parent who could stay secluded during a school session could loan a child his or her own outfit, if it was presentable enough and fit. The teacher Mary Ames thoughtfully issued needles, thread, and patches to families who could benefit. Most instructors required cleanliness for entry, on both practical and idealistic grounds. The more tactful ones either relied on persuasion or provided some water and soap. During her first spring on a Sea Island, Ames had advised a boy to wash in a creek. Later she learned with horror that he could not swim, got caught in the tide, and drowned. In a rare case, a group of dirty and poorly dressed boys who really wanted schooling moved Superintendent Orlando Brown to ask Sallie Daffin, a Black teacher, to admit them. She prudently first obtained agreement from her class to accept them without ridicule.[86]

Children of working parents sometimes needed to bring and to care for younger siblings. If allowed to stay, this occasionally caused disturbances, but if sent home, the caretakers fell behind in class. During 1861–62, no one seems to have come up with a solution. In the Sea Islands the local Blacks' creole dialect, Gullah, baffled instructors, just as the northerners' speech puzzled the pupils. Both groups gradually came to understand each other. The process reoccurred later in the war with the Cajun dialect in the lower Mississippi Valley.[87]

Education obviously benefited freedom. During a speaking tour in the North, William Davis from Hampton joked that the equalizing experience of schooling was "so much like the way master's children used to be treated, that they [Black children] believed they were getting white." Understanding the value of independent group self-help, African Americans who could develop or support their own schools often did so. Many reformers echoed the sentiments of a missionary who observed that "The intense desire of the Negroes to learn to read is beyond anything I have ever witnessed." Edward Pierce candidly noted: "At a time [in the Sea Islands] when the people were chafing the most under deprivations and the assurances made on the behalf of the government were most distrusted, it was fortunate that we could point to the teaching of their children as a proof of our interest in their welfare and of the new and better life which we were opening before them."[88]

Many of the initial patterns in the activities of Black refugees and reformers alike would recur in newly occupied areas throughout 1863–65. Part One has included evidence from those years, when the actions clearly did not arise from later developments. Throughout the war, slaves reaching the protection of Federal forces hoped to carve out a better life somehow amid the war. Although poor, they mobilized their energy and determination. They clearly wanted full freedom that came with respect and more rights. Northern reformers sought to damage slavery by preparing a vanguard. Yet during 1861 the relatively low number of relief workers, mostly concentrated in the Sea Islands, limited their efforts elsewhere.

From the start both groups experienced hostility from slaveholders, secessionists, and northern racists. The military and government, which wield the most clout in wartime, restricted them at times. While the US government gingerly moved toward some degree of emancipation, the future of the Black refugees remained unclear.

Refugees and reformers did not always align their efforts for change. The two groups brought somewhat different cultural backgrounds with them. The paternalistic and laissez-faire aid workers thought they knew what was best. When they tried to control the Black refugee transition, they often conveyed disrespectful beliefs in African American shortcomings. At times, their charges just had to endure the sometimes offensive, preachy, and demanding northerners in order to gain desired help. Blacks brought with them a wariness around whites, and soon had numerous reasons to be suspicious and assertive. They sought to manage some of the charitable, religious, and educational activity through collective, autonomous effort. Individuals created small businesses on their own. Real conflicts sometimes arose regarding religion, compulsion, and work compensation. Among the few thoughtful reformers who soon perceived that the Black refugees did not fit northern preconceptions, Mansfield French made a rare confession: "Many of us need much more wisdom and grace for the peculiar work around us." A Black preacher holding a service in Norfolk in 1862 simply prayed that President Lincoln would "maintain the rights of all."[89]

II.
Later Developments

4

Emancipation

The release of Lincoln's final Emancipation Proclamation came in midafternoon on New Year's Day 1863. By then Camp Barker's Black refugees had endured a long wait after holding a midnight watch service. White reformers had organized the activities but allowed for significant Black participation. The staff presumed that the document would free the Virginians who made up most of the residents. All had indulged in cakes and pies; children had received toys from the aid workers. Celebrants reassembled in the evening, after Superintendent Danforth B. Nichols finally obtained a copy of the document, which not only freed slaves in most of the Confederacy but also opened military enlistment to Blacks. As he read it, rejoicing broke out. He finished by urging the men to consider enlisting and all the adults to accept low-wage jobs at first. Then refugee preacher William Beverly prayed for the President, the freedpeople, those still enslaved, and the Union war effort. "Thank God our sufferins all dun away!" he exclaimed, "Han' cuffs, beatin's all dun away! Never part from children again!"[1]

Most areas occupied by Federals would receive Lincoln's decree only later in the month. Yet on New Year's Day, Blacks in Norfolk, Virginia, held their own celebration, one manifesting a different tone from the one in Washington. They derided secessionists by burning an effigy of Jefferson Davis, the Confederacy's president, and parading through the city with a wagon on which Black women ripped up and trampled Confederate flags. Those who later learned that the proclamation excluded Norfolk's county and five others on the Chesapeake

Bay informed a journalist that they would refuse to accept reenslavement. The issue arose from Lincoln's promise in the preliminary Emancipation Proclamation to exempt the parts of the Confederacy that in his judgment restored allegiance to the United States. Yet, outside of two counties on the state's isolated Eastern Shore (the peninsula between the Bay and the Atlantic) where little had changed, the spread of the contraband policy in the area allowed slaves to leave enslavers at will. Consequently, Black refugees around Norfolk, Hampton, and Yorktown ignored exception from the proclamation.[2]

Besides these counties and the ones that would soon form West Virginia, the President excluded southern Louisiana and all of Tennessee. In occupied Louisiana Gen. Nathaniel P. Banks, the Department of the Gulf's new commander and an antislavery Republican, maintained Butler's semislave/semifree system and, bowing to slaveholders' fears of insurrection, prohibited festivities on January 1. No evidence of Black refugees celebrating in Tennessee has surfaced. The proclamation also did not apply to Delaware, Maryland, Kentucky, and Missouri, the slave states loyal to the Union.[3]

In the Sea Islands reformers held a well-attended festivity in the late morning on January 1, 1863, at the Black regiment's camp near Beaufort. Except for the presentation of regimental flags, they may have modeled the event on northern abolitionists' commemorations of Britain's earlier liberation of enslaved Jamaicans. After the flags' reception, freedpeople spontaneously sang "My Country, 'Tis of Thee," which deeply touched the northerners. Then a series of speakers, mostly whites, praised emancipation, and the preliminary Emancipation Proclamation was read. The festivity concluded with a banquet for the attending African Americans provided by Superintendent Rufus Saxton. Days would pass before celebrants could confirm that Lincoln had definitely liberated them.[4]

The South Carolina and Georgia Sea Islands lay among the Federal toeholds that Lincoln did not exempt. Other localities, where Black refugees immediately gained freedom, included several spots on Florida's coast, northeastern North Carolina, three eastern Virginia counties (around Alexandria, Williamsburg, and Newport News), two sections of northern Mississippi (around Holly Springs and Corinth), and two parts of Arkansas (the northwestern corner and around Helena). These places had a substantial but uncountable number of Black refugees alongside the enslaved who still lived with slaveholders. The total freed certainly fell well below the hundreds of thousands living in the exempted counties (see Table 2).

The impact of the final Emancipation Proclamation lay in establishing emancipation as federal policy for mostly future application to the bulk of

Table 2. 1860 Slave Population in Areas Excluded from the
Final Emancipation Proclamation

Location	Number
Southern Louisiana (13 parishes)	93,152
Tennessee (all counties)	275,719
Western Virginia (50 counties)	17,715
Eastern Virginia (6 counties)	34,911
Total	421,497

Source: US Department of the Interior, Census Office, *Population,* vol. 3 of *Eighth Census:* 91, 93, 465, 509, 511, 513.

the Confederacy, and instituting Black enlistment as immanent policy behind Federal lines. This affected freedpeople more emotionally than materially (except enlistees, who generally were better fed and clothed in the military than in contraband camps). The federal government had made a commitment to most slaves and had tied their hopes for more opportunities to the Union's preservation. This changed the context, not the basic patterns of interaction between Black refugees and northern reformers. Even though the US acted on military expediency, the proclamation stimulated more escapes, as the news slowly spread and especially as Federals captured more territory. Emancipation would also raise new issues. Behind Federal lines, Black refugees would increasingly stretch the principle of liberty toward equal rights. Some reformers would support them, and others would draw limits. Initially after the proclamation's issuance, its consequences varied at least a little between the emancipated zone, the exempted area, and the border slave states.

The Emancipated Region

In the emancipated region, major Federal operations—such as the Chancellorsville, Vicksburg, Meridian, Red River, Virginia overland, Georgia, and Carolinas campaigns—attracted thousands of mostly destitute Black refugee families and abruptly deposited them in contraband camps (the label continued in use after the proclamation). Additionally, some raids into Confederate territory would force that movement, either directly or by stripping plantations of foodstuffs. Not surprisingly, Black troops would eagerly seek to free slaves. All of this added to camp and shantytown populations.[5] Freedmen's departments (a generic label for the small ad hoc bureaucracies in charge of freedpeople) appeared in most of the army's territorial departments. Department superintendents increased the number of camps and staff members. The proclamation's threat to the slave labor force led Confederate troops to start targeting contraband camps.

Along the southeastern coast, the navy opened additional Black refugee settlements. It also closed one on North Island, South Carolina, because of a Confederate advance in 1863. Sometime after the navy captured Fernandina and St. Augustine, General Saxton established nearby plantation camps, probably modeled on the Sea Islands experiment. He built Saxtonville on a South Carolina Sea Island partly as expanded housing for incoming Black refugees and partly as a possible freedpeople's colony or permanent home for Blacks. The older camps at Beaufort and Hilton Head became entry points for new refugees, a common response to increasing arrivals. In such camps, reformers focused first on meeting immediate needs of food, clothing, and medical care (sometimes including a thorough washing). Before aid workers assigned families to a plantation or camp, recruiters tried to enlist the able-bodied men.[6]

In late 1864 and early 1865, Sherman's marches through Georgia and the Carolinas attracted particularly huge waves of Black refugees, whom he sent to the Federally controlled areas on the coast. For a time, overwhelmed aid workers witnessed the deaths of many of the newly freed. After the fall of Charleston, Federals moved thousands to a regained Edisto and other islands near the city. The army shipped one group in a poorly planned and rushed manner that separated some families and caused great suffering.[7]

Earlier in North Carolina, the Emancipation Proclamation had provoked the resignation of Military Governor Edward Stanly, and Lincoln did not replace him. Additional contraband camps opened in Plymouth and Morehead City. The commander of Roanoke Island designated the camp there as a colony. The Reverend Horace James, an evangelical chaplain and the new superintendent of freedmen for the area, developed Roanoke into a highly organized settlement for farmers and craftsmen. In April 1864, a Confederate offensive in the state recaptured Washington and Plymouth. Many freedpeople in those towns escaped to the New Bern, Roanoke, or Beaufort camps. As the enemy briefly advanced toward other Federal posts, James closed two outlying plantation camps near New Bern and temporarily evacuated Roanoke. He subsequently replaced the surviving New Bern camp with a new and more secure Trent River camp.[8]

In the western war theater, Gen. Ulysses S. Grant's 1862–63 Vicksburg campaign penetrated a region with a very large slave population and spawned a new camp at Lake Providence, Louisiana. When its population rose so rapidly as to threaten adequate provision, the general limited entry to able-bodied males. But the fall of Vicksburg attracted a tidal wave of Black families especially into the city and also along the Federally controlled portion of the Mississippi River below Lake Providence. Grant then had to drop his entry restriction. Furthermore, epidemics in Vicksburg forced a hasty dispersal of unemployed refugees to numerous sites to the west and north. The contraband camp in the city became the distribution center as more thousands arrived, and mass suffering ensued. Superintendent John Eaton gradually organized a number of camps, mostly on large abandoned plantations along the river. Goodrich's Landing, Milliken's Bend, Young's Point, Omega Landing, Ralston/Desoto, Concordia, and Vidalia lay on the Louisiana side, while Skipwith's Landing, Palmyra Bend, Natchez, and Fort Adams were in Mississippi. An additional camp arose on Paw Paw Island.[9]

The navy transferred to Eaton the camp it established at Davis Bend, Mississippi, which included Jefferson Davis's plantation. By the end of the war the cluster of settlements on the Bend contained the largest single population of freedpeople in the department. Eaton also gained jurisdiction over upriver camps at Cairo and Columbus, as well as those in Arkansas (Helena, Island No. 63, White River's mouth, Pine Bluff, Little Rock, and De Vall's Bluff). Arkansas' white Unionists set up a new state government without slavery in the Federally occupied portion during 1864.[10]

Confederates in 1863 damaged the prosperous Island No. 63 camp and burned the Helena and Pine Bluff camps. All three reopened. The Holly Springs and Corinth camps evacuated to Memphis in 1863 and 1864, respectively, thanks to approaching Confederates. The Corinth camp had earned praise for its organization and cleanliness, much like Craney Island.[11] Enemy operations forced many residents to move from Goodrich's Landing and Vicksburg to safer sites, including a new one at Island No. 102 in 1864. Vidalia camp closed in 1864 due to various problems. A devastating flood in the Mississippi Valley during the spring of 1865 closed contraband camps at the White River's mouth, Helena, Island No. 63, Paw Paw Island, and Concordia. Flood refugees resettled on higher ground nearby or in other camps (including a new one at Washington, Mississippi). Emergency relocations like these caused the loss of whatever comforts the residents had managed to attain.[12]

During the last years of the war, Eaton's department became by far the largest one, ultimately harboring over one hundred thousand freedpeople. Probably at his request, a regional commander in 1863 ordered camp superintendents wishing to continue in office to apply for commissions as officers in Black regiments. Becoming a colonel himself, Eaton helped to enlist two regiments and scattered detachments to guard camps along the Mississippi

River from Island No. 10 to Natchez. The enemy captured two of these companies guarding Island No. 63 in 1863. Eaton had hoped to gain more security and efficiency for his freedmen's department through stronger military ties, but in practice his initiatives seem to have made little difference. A more practical decision in 1864 was Eaton's division of his jurisdiction into three districts: Arkansas, the Mississippi Valley from Cairo to Memphis, and the valley from Lake Providence to Fort Adams. Each had a district superintendent.[13]

Beyond Eaton's jurisdiction, Black recruiting led to the opening of contraband camps in northern Alabama at Bridgeport, Stevenson, Huntsville, Decatur, and Athens. Some of these came under the Department of the Cumberland's new superintendent of freedmen, who was headquartered in Nashville. Sitting close to an active front, all the Alabama camps were shut down at one time or another, with just Stevenson and Huntsville reopening.[14]

The Exempted Region

Only in the Proclamation's exempted areas and the border states did contraband status technically remain for Black refugees. Virginia's white Unionists, despite controlling little territory, in 1861 had established a new state government, through which most of them hoped to secure slavery. Similarly minded politicians in Tennessee and Louisiana would endeavor to do the same. However, Black refugees in the three exempted states ignored that designation, as Federal occupation had already caused some unraveling of the institution. New Black refugees mostly did not face return to Unionist owners but blended indistinguishably among those already under military protection. Enlistments further accelerated movement towards emancipation.[15]

The exempted western Virginia counties became independent in early 1863 and will be discussed with the border states. Eastern Virginia, partly included in and partly excluded from the proclamation, had a number of contraband camps that continued to attract Black refugees. Right after the proclamation, the army tended neither to uphold the institution nor to interfere with slaveholders there.[16]

However, when Gen. Benjamin F. Butler returned to head a combined Department of Virginia and North Carolina in late 1863, he had evolved into an antislavery Republican. He made Lt. Col. Joseph B. Kinsman the general superintendent of an enlarged freedmen's department with districts under Capt. Charles B. Wilder (area between the York and James Rivers, known during the war as the Peninsula), Capt. Orlando Brown (area south of Chesapeake Bay), Dr. Caleb S. Henry (Virginia's eastern shore, plus southern Maryland), and

Capt. Horace James (northeast North Carolina). Wilder took over the Slabtown laborer camp near Yorktown and possibly another one at Williamsburg. Near Hampton he built the new Mill Creek and Downey Plantation camps. After designating the latter and Fort Monroe as his reception depots for new arrivals, he had as many Black refugees as possible distributed to a number of smaller plantation camps.[17] Brown turned the Norfolk camp into an entry center that placed most of those arriving in new plantation camps. Craney Island closed in the fall of 1863, due to its limited farmland and supply problems. Confederate advances caused the army to evacuate camps around Suffolk. Henry created contraband camps at Townfield, Pawtuxet, and Eastville. A Confederate raid on the last camp seems to have shut it down. Near the end of the war, the freedmen's department in eastern Virginia supervised some 45,000 freedpeople.[18]

General Butler soon placed all Black refugees in the six exempted eastern Virginia counties under Federal protection and initiated extensive Black enlistment. This effectively ended the slave code. Lincoln and the Republican-controlled Congress increasingly made it clear that Unionist reconstruction of state governments must include emancipation, and thereby helped emancipationist Unionists to succeed in the states with exempted areas. In April of 1864, a constitutional convention of Virginia's white Unionists declared slavery abolished.[19]

Louisiana, like Virginia, included both emancipated and exempted portions. As already noted, General Banks continued Butler's semislave/semifree system with wages and no whipping in southern Louisiana. As a matter of public order, he prohibited owners from seizing escapees and directed civil authorities to place all Black refugees in the army's plantation camps to work without wages. The general soon placed Lt. George Hanks in charge of all matters involving Black labor. This gave Hanks a broader jurisdiction than other freedmen's department heads. An increasing number of refugees from both within and beyond the occupied area forced Hanks to establish additional plantation camps at Donaldsonville, Baton Rouge, and Port Hudson. Late in 1862 Butler had slowly begun Black recruitment in the state, and Banks greatly expanded it. Banks suspended the slave code in January 1864, and a Louisiana Unionist referendum ended slavery on September 5, 1864. Chap. Thomas W. Conway, who replaced Hanks around that time, opened additional camps for freedpeople evicted by angry ex-slaveholders.[20]

In western Tennessee, contraband camps already existed, and continued to draw Black refugees. In January 1863, a Confederate force caused the evacuation of refugees from the Grand Junction camp to Memphis. Eaton not only built them several camps near Fort Pickering on the city's south side but also took supervision over the nearby Shiloh camp of military laborers and their families. After the enemy threat passed, new camps opened at Grand Junction, LaGrange, Bolivar, Jackson, and Fort Pillow. Black recruitment began about the same time. Officials relocated many Black refugees from the Cairo and Columbus camps downriver to Island No. 10, Tennessee, to gain farming opportunities and better security, although the move taking them deeper into the South worried the Black Kentuckians. The wider distribution of camps drew more Black refugees, but further Confederate operations had shut down nearly all of them by mid-1864. Many of those living in evacuated or Memphis camps were concentrated close to the city's downtown on President's Island. In the spring of 1865, Island No. 10's residents got plantation jobs in Arkansas, and flooding shut down President's Island, the last contraband camp in western Tennessee.[21]

In middle Tennessee, Military Governor Andrew Johnson, a Tennessee Unionist, originally supported the Department of the Cumberland's policy of excluding Black refugees. Even when he switched positions to favor emancipation, he would not assist aid workers' efforts on behalf of destitute Black refugees. Post commanders, facing constant pressure from Black people seeking refuge at Decherd, Murfreesboro, Gallatin, and Fort Donelson, eventually abandoned exclusion and quietly set up camps. Black recruitment started in the spring of 1863 and drew many of the state's African American men.[22]

In January 1864 a large number of residents from the Stevenson camp arrived by train in Nashville without prior notice. The army's adjutant general, Lorenzo Thomas, soon ordered a contraband camp set up for them. That ended the exclusion policy in the region. The Nashville camp's superintendent soon assumed the role of a freedmen's department superintendent and developed new camps at Clarksville and Hendersonville, as well as taking supervision over the Fort Donelson, Gallatin, and Pulaski camps. Pulaski closed when Confederate Gen. John B. Hood invaded the state. Eastern Tennessee briefly had one camp near Chattanooga. In the fall of 1864, Johnson suspended enforcement of the slave code. Shortly after Congress (with Lincoln's support) proposed a Thirteenth Amendment freeing all the nation's slaves, Tennessee Unionists passed an emancipation referendum on February 22, 1865.[23]

The Border Regions

In the border slave states, most Federal commanders in early 1863 continued exclusion policies, often with active support from the white troops raised there. Some Black refugees managed to gain protection in neighboring free jurisdictions, especially after Congress repealed the Fugitive Slave Act on

June 28, 1864.[24] Once Black enlistment began in border states, it created a legal means of escape from slavery for many enlistees and their families under the Militia Act of 1862. Blacks in Wilmington, Delaware, and St. Louis, Missouri, actually held public Emancipation Proclamation Anniversary celebrations in 1864, probably the only such events in the border states.[25]

The Army shifted jurisdiction over Maryland's southern tip to Butler's department and closed the Point Lookout Hospital in 1864. Many of the laborers there and their families moved to three new and nearby plantation camps along the north bank of the Potomac River in St. Mary's County. These camps also drew enlistees' families.[26]

On November 1, 1864, emancipation occurred in Maryland after its passage in a state referendum. When proslavery whites retaliated by burning several Black churches, Gen. Lew Wallace, the antislavery commander over most of the state, ordered the pro-Confederate families in those neighborhoods to pay for the rebuilding. A Quaker aid association set up an employment agency for evicted freedpeople in Baltimore, and Wallace created a Freedmen's Home for unemployed Blacks in the city. When a former enslaver recaptured a girl residing there, Wallace had troops retrieve her. The general soon turned the Freedmen's Home over to two aid associations. Freedpeople without jobs could also enter Butler's new camps in St. Mary's County. The American Missionary Association got one camp superintendent there fired after he whipped several residents.[27]

Another serious problem occurred in Maryland with apprenticeship by former slaveholders. This legal condition, commonly permitted by states then, enabled the retention of several thousand freed children until adulthood under the guise of training as unskilled laborers. Some ex-owners tricked or pressured some parents into agreement, but most simply obtained a judge's permission on the ground that the parents could not provide for the children. Once alerted to the problem, General Wallace placed destitute freedpeople under military protection in an effort to stop further apprenticeship attempts. However, Secretary of War Edwin Stanton revoked the order on the ground that it interfered too much with a loyal state's laws. Subsequently, a group of Quaker abolitionist lawyers went to court and won release for some apprentices. Many freed children, though, would live as apprentices for years with former enslavers, some of whom felt entitled to whip them. In Missouri, emancipationist Unionists, apparently aware of the problem, wrote a ban on apprenticing any of the freed into the state's referendum on ending slavery (Black laws there did not limit it to minors). Reformers did not mention this problem arising anywhere else during the war, but it would reappear afterward.[28]

Before West Virginia gained statehood, Congress required it to enact gradual emancipation. The program adopted by the state immediately freed only bondspeople born after July 4, 1863; some of the rest would gain liberty years later. The state legislature repealed much of the slave code later in 1863 and then enacted immediate emancipation during February 1865, in the wake of Congress's proposal of the Thirteenth Amendment. The new state with a small slave population had some Black refugees, no contraband camps, and no agents of the freedmen's aid associations, except for an AMA couple who taught briefly at Harper's Ferry.[29]

In Kentucky federal/state tensions over slavery grew. A reformer at Columbus obtained military passes for two sets of Black refugees to leave for the North but could get out no more. Along with the existing Cairo camp, a new Cincinnati Freedmen's Home likely attracted some Black refugees from Kentucky. In April 1863, General-in-Chief Henry Halleck ordered the release of out-of-state freed workers whom Louisville's authorities had removed from Gen. Don Carlos Buell's army months earlier and sold. Federals retrieved most of the group and placed them on military laborer crews.[30]

Slaveholders evicted or otherwise punished the families of men who enlisted in many areas behind Federal lines. This led many relatives to escape to recruiting camps also. In Kentucky recruiters created contraband camps for them at Paducah and Smithland during 1863. One year later, however, Adjutant General Lorenzo Thomas, reacted to many white Kentuckians' anger over Black recruitment by ordering posts to exclude the dependents. At Paducah the recruiter successfully resisted the order, but the Smithland camp probably closed. At other recruiting posts in the state the soldiers' relatives kept coming but suffered repeated ejection. This conflict culminated at Camp Nelson on November 23, 1864, with the destruction of shacks and the expulsion of some four hundred families in freezing weather. Federals transported most of them miles away to Nicholasville without food. Many had thin clothing and no shoes. Most who did not die from exposure eventually returned ill to Camp Nelson. Complaints about this incident moved Thomas to end the expulsions. At least the recruiting stations at Camp Nelson, Covington, Louisville, and Bowling Green could then set up camps for enlistees' dependents. The camps at the last two towns unusually had Black superintendents, both formerly enslaved. If any woman got into the Louisville camp without having a soldier husband, that superintendent arranged a fake marriage to keep her and her children there. Camp Nelson quietly harbored some destitute Black refugees not part of soldiers' families.[31]

In Missouri Black refugees increased in bursts. After a Confederate attack on Helena, Arkansas, Federal officials began in March 1863 to ship many of the freedpeople there to St. Louis. Going from an emancipated area into a slave state, they received free papers and at first were scattered into housing around the city and nearby Brooklyn, Illinois, to avoid attracting attention. For more efficient provisioning, Superintendent Samuel Sawyer subsequently concentrated them in a vacant hotel, later in an army barracks, and finally in a new Contrabands' Home.[32]

General Samuel Curtis, a new Department of Missouri commander in 1863, briefly ended the exclusion policy. As Black refugees began to gather around garrisons, a supporter of exclusion replaced him. The then-enslaved Robert Anderson later recalled: "We did not know what to believe. It was impressed on us indirectly by everyone, that there was little chance of the slaves being set free." The introduction of Black recruiting in the state late in 1863 triggered a new wave of escapes, including Anderson's. When some Missouri enslavers responded by selling their slaves in Kentucky, the army forbad that trade. Exposed sales attempts mostly resulted in liberation of the enslaved. Post commanders tried to protect Black refugees but hired relatively few. Some Black refugees and families of Missouri enlistees wound up in a contraband camp at Quincy, Illinois. In 1863 Missouri Unionists enacted a gradual emancipation plan that freed no one until 1870, but in January 1865, a state constitutional convention enacted immediate emancipation. As in Maryland, a number of angry owners expelled the newly freed. A new camp opened for them in St. Louis, and antislavery Gen. Clinton B. Fisk had some others escorted into Kansas.[33]

Like a border state, the Indian Territory included slaves, and lay outside the Confederacy. When Federals invaded it in 1863, Black refugees gained entrance into the lines. The Civil War had deeply split the allegiances of Cherokees and Creeks. The Unionist portions of both tribes enacted emancipation and repeal of most racially discriminatory laws. Some antislavery Unionists aided slave escapes, though some Black refugees preferred to travel further to Federal posts in Arkansas or Kansas. Many of those remaining in the Territory either enlisted or hired on as military laborers. Their dependents lived in abandoned buildings and received rations. While no contraband camps appeared on this frontier, late in the war the National Freedmen's Relief Association sent aid workers to Fort Gibson.[34] To the north in Kansas the army recruited but did not establish camps for the growing number of the Black refugees arriving from the Indian Territory, Arkansas, and Missouri. Several aid associations operated in the state's towns, and two established homes for destitute freedpeople in Kansas City and Leavenworth.[35]

The District of Columbia increasingly drew Black refugees, especially after its courts stopped enforcing the Fugitive Slave Act. The Department of Washington's new quartermaster, Lt. Col. Elias M. Greene, took on an additional duty as its freedmen's superintendent in early 1863 and quickly decided to create a complex of plantation camps across the Potomac River near Camp Todd. He reassigned Danforth B. Nichols to build the main camp on the Arlington estate of Mary Custis Lee, the wife of Confederate general Robert E. Lee. Due to a wartime direct tax the Lee land soon defaulted to ownership by the United States. Nichols moved a number of Black refugee families from Camp Barker to tents on the site, in order to have the men construct the new buildings. All the Northern Virginia camps would undergo flux because of the periodic movement of Federal and Confederate lines. The most persistent was the one on the vacated Arlington plantation, which also acquired the name of Freedmen's Village. Nichols then superintended it.[36]

As a laissez-faire reformer, Greene intended Arlington as a place to put the freedpeople to work in a step toward the wage labor system. He wanted to relocate all destitute freedpeople in the department there. Because of a lumber shortage during the construction, Greene proposed to disassemble the new Freedmen's Home, a set of barracks opened in February 1863 to replace the makeshift camp in Alexandria. When the town's military governor blocked that plan, Greene dismantled Camp Barker's barracks instead and ordered the freedpeople there to the new camp near the year's end. Having experienced Nichols' authoritarianism, violence, and verbal abuse, a large majority of them (Camp Barker's new superintendent said two-thirds; Wilbur estimated 84 percent) refused to return under his rule. They chose to remain in their old neighborhood by renting rooms, building shanties, or moving in with friends. Camp Barker's hospital continued to operate as the site became a reception camp for new arrivals.[37]

Nichols reinstated his harsh governance at Arlington, and one former slave complained: "Don't feel as if I was free, 'pears like there's nobody free here." Some residents learned to put up with Nichols, because they really liked Arlington's facilities and proximity to well-remunerated government jobs. A year later, Greene transferred Nichols to another new camp and an entry depot on Mason's Island (today called Roosevelt Island). Greene closed Camp Todd and moved the residents to the island. Complaints about Nichols reappeared there.[38]

In Alexandria the military governor appointed Reverend Albert Gladwin, a Baptist missionary, as superintendent of the Freedmen's Home and the army's rental housing for refugees. Gladwin bullied his charges verbally and sometimes physically. He told Julia Wilbur that "if you had been on the plantation as much as I have . . . you would find there is no way to get along with them," which caused her to think he was a former overseer of slaves. In any case, he does not seem to have been an antislavery reformer. When the freedmen's department tried to ship all the unemployed and new arrivals at Alexandria to Freedmen's Village, Harriet Jacobs, who knew about Nichols, interfered by finding many of them shantytown homes. During late 1864 and early 1865, the management of freedpeople in the District of Columbia area underwent a shake-up that replaced Greene, Nichols, and Gladwin. The replacements revised some of their predecessors' practices.[39]

The final Emancipation Proclamation and the expansion of federally con-trolled land generated new, even larger, waves of refugees from slavery. Every freedmen's department had to construct more contraband camps. All tried to improve operations through various innovations. While the Proclamation ex-cluded some areas, this turned out to be impractical, and the Lincoln adminis-tration began to pressure southern white Unionists toward emancipation. The beginning of Black enlistment greatly contributed to the institution's under-mining, especially in the states excluded from the proclamation. Step by step, the Black refugees and the reformers saw the goal of freedom gaining. The new federal commitment to them firmly tied their hopes to that side of the war.

Still, most realities of a Black refugee's life remained unchanged. Too many Federals not only refused to cooperate with emancipation, but also continued to abuse and to disrespect freedpeople. Confederate resistance continued, though it grew futile by 1865. New developments would bring both additional opportunities and challenges. Julia Wilbur feared "that in some way they will be cheated of their freedom." Only the war's outcome and its aftermath would resolve what an anonymous Quaker called "the great uncertainty of their future."[40]

5

Providing Necessities for More

In the wake of the final Emancipation Proclamation, thousands more Blacks entered contraband camps and occupied towns. This called for a major increase in facilities, volunteers, and charitable supplies, as well as improved delivery of necessities. Just four of the northern aid associations collected a total of over a half-million dollars in cash and goods during 1864. Several aid workers contributed to fundraising by undertaking northern speaking tours about their southern experiences. In hopes of raising more funds, many aid societies began to publish leaflets and magazines that often contained letters from relief workers. In the Sea Islands a superior directed Charles Ware to tone down praise for the honesty of his field hands in a report, lest donors think his charges "need no further benefit of benevolent effort." The rising populations of shantytowns did their best to maintain themselves in independence and participate in smaller charitable activities.[1]

Reformers and freedpeople faced opposition from the racially biased, such as Onley Andrus, a Federal soldier who sarcastically commented: "All we have got to do is to go out into the country & pick up all the old crippled and helpless nigger women & children & get them off of *their* [Confederates'] hands & on to our own to feed and raise a big howl over to the people of the North to send them clothing and vegetables . . . and [consequently] the Rebs can't hold out long." Relief societies responded by appealing to both patriotism and charity. They stressed the government's limited ability to meet these needs amid an intensifying war and how many desperate freedpeople would die without enough charitable aid. The freedpeople's support of the Union war effort must have especially encouraged the northern public's positive response, and consequently the Indiana Freedmen's Aid Commission contended that "the future prosperity and happiness of our now afflicted country" was at stake.[2]

More Aid Societies and Workers

To maintain support, as well as to improve operations, the aid organizations sought more efficiency and effectiveness. The leadership now expected aid workers to file reports accounting for distributed goods, special costs, school statistics, and sometimes more. The Northwestern Freedmen's Aid Commission, for example, also desired to hear about a worker's health, activities, hours, difficulties, and encouragements. Associations sent inspectors on tours to assess programs and current needs. The more egalitarian agents made the extra effort to solicit input from the aid recipients, often after passing out small gifts of sewing materials, books, pictures, toys, and candy.[3]

Since the aid associations created for the Sea Islands during 1861 had extended their activities to other sites, the ones in Boston and Philadelphia had broadened their names to New England Freedmen's Aid Society and Pennsylvania Freedmen's Relief Association. The third member of the group, the National Freedmen's Relief Association, obviously did not need renaming. Meanwhile, the American Missionary Association launched a highly successful drive for more donations and volunteers, which enabled its operations to exceed each of the others. Even so, major new aid societies appeared: Northwestern Freedmen's Aid Commission in Chicago, Indiana Freedmen's Aid Commission in Indianapolis, and Western Freedmen's Aid Commission in Cincinnati.[4] Small aid associations formed in more localities, and several of the large organizations encouraged the development of local chapters. By 1864 Black refugees in a number of communities and congregations had small charitable funds of their own. Reformer Mary C. Fletcher observed that "you have no idea how much they contribute, from their scanty earnings." The Contraband Relief Association, already formed by Blacks in Washington, added support for the families of Black soldiers to its activities and so renamed itself the Freedmen and Soldiers' Relief Association.[5]

More religious groups instituted organizations for the aid effort. Both Orthodox and Hicksite Quakers were especially energetic. In addition, the African Methodist Episcopal, African Methodist Episcopal Zion, United Brethren, and several Presbyterian groups dispatched missionaries and aid workers.

Two other organizations founded early in the war to benefit soldiers, the Christian Commission and the Sanitary Commission, now extended services to Black troops and sometimes their families.[6]

The multiplication of relief agencies led to competitive clashes. The conflict between the two organizations in Cincinnati hurt the older Contraband Relief Commission to the point that it reduced activities and then closed down after turning the remaining assets over to the Indiana Quakers' Yearly Meeting.[7] Disparate policies, pay, and leadership quality led to discontent among some workers who subsequently switched sponsoring organizations. At an 1864 meeting in Indianapolis, seven associations convened to discuss their differences, which nevertheless persisted. They only consented to joint supply depots and lobbying for the creation of a federal agency to establish a uniform policy for freedpeople, something that John Eaton had advocated since early 1863.[8]

Several Republican lawmakers had begun working on such a bill in early 1864. Congressional debates raised some of the same conflicting views held by the three groups of reformers, primarily the laissez-faire and paternalistic perspectives. Multiple compromises resulted. The aid associations' support contributed to passage of the Freedmen's Bureau Act in March 1865. The new agency would barely be ready to start operating at the war's end.[9]

The increase in aid organizations, fundraising, and activity brought many new workers into the occupied parts of the South. Much turnover remained, as H. Hyde in the Sea Islands noted that "many of those who put their hands to the work are leaving & returning home partly for reasons of climate and health and partly because of inadequate provision of our temporal necessities." Agents in St. Louis warned the AMA: "With our small salary, it is a great inconvenience to have to wait for it," and "To live without eating has been done, but our faith in it [is] not of that kind." Julia Wilbur complained about being drained by the work's many challenges, despite her basic egalitarianism: "I am getting tired living this way, shut out from society, with so many discomforts to undergo, & the work is so hard & wearing. If I c[oul]d have the society of a few intelligent white people occasionally, it would be such a relief."[10]

With larger staffs came more problematic members. The crusade's emotional appeal and the organizations' eagerness to get more workers resulted in some very unsuitable volunteers. When the Western Freedmen's Aid Commission sent a doctor and his wife, both over 70 years old, to Vicksburg, they quickly became bedridden with serious illness, causing Henry Rountree to comment: "What a pity to send such, they are a care and hindrance to those who can and do work." He worried that "some will be sent merely because they are goodly . . . [though] useless." Colonel Eaton worried more about indiscreet persons, who would "bring down some of the threatening evils & stop all advance." When several very young, uninformed volunteers found the wailing at a freedperson's funeral to be humorous, Julia Wilbur snapped that "I hope no more girls like these will be sent here to teach colored schools." Miss E. A. Lane lost her job in Savannah, Georgia, because she took opium, often used the term "nigger," and—not surprisingly—was "not well liked by the colored people." Serious psychological problems made several individuals very difficult coworkers. The work's stress could lead to overwork and a breakdown, as still happens at today's refugee camps.[11]

Because many of the idealistic reformers were highly judgmental, they were quick to criticize others, especially as interaction increased among the expanding number of workers. Early signs of infighting had appeared in 1862 correspondence from Hampton and the Sea Islands. Subsequently as reformers came to work in groups at many sites, more clashes emerged. Differences of opinion and personality evolved into sharp conflicts that wasted reformers' energy and distressed freedpeople. Samuel Hunt, an American Missionary Association inspector, found that among the reformers at Hampton "there is far more friction than is seemly among brethren, much less among missionary brethren."[12]

The desire to keep growing staffs efficient through more supervision also led to new conflicts. Challenging situations severely tested individuals, and criticism from a manager easily provoked countercharges from a worker. A reformer couple who had difficulties with William H. Woodbury, the AMA's Norfolk manager, claimed that this supervisor took the best donated clothes for his daughter, although nothing came of the charge. Reverend Isaac G. Hubbs, head of the AMA staff in New Orleans, had a particularly messy downfall involving allegations of corruption, bad language, and an affair. In the end, a military commission expelled him from the state for "conduct . . . wholly unbecoming his position."[13]

Allegations of inappropriate romances created touchy situations. The teacher with whom Hubbs allegedly had a liaison asserted her innocence but did not get her contract renewed. The investigator of a charge that another missionary was a "ladies' man" reported that, as far as he could tell, it was false. In a third case, the Reverend M. H. Abbey, after being accused of an affair with a teacher, denied it, resigned, and swiftly departed.[14]

Problems among the reformers only complicated the task, difficult enough in itself, of providing necessities to the rapidly growing body of Black refugees. Modern refugee movements can be much larger, but the challenge during the American Civil War also led to serious problems. So many African Americans poured into Davis Bend with so many needs that they resorted to praying aloud for help. In towns the swelling population of Black refugees contributed not only to shortages but also to rapid price inflation. The army obviously ranked the Black refugees' needs as a lower priority than the troops' but usually above the secessionists,' which likely added to racial tensions.[15]

Food

The rising demand for food led the War Department to establish, in January 1864, a special ration for destitute freedpeople who did not do military labor. It contained significantly less than the generous ration for soldiers. This still may have been adequate, because recorded complaints only referred to rations reduced by a camp's supply shortage or elimination by a commander pressuring adults to take any job. If the freedperson's ration was insufficient, the army seemed immovable on the matter. Along the Atlantic coast, officials began to substitute fish or dried fruit for meat. Although the federal commissaries tried to maintain a stock of rations at contraband camps, they could not always handle sudden population increases. Northern volunteer Lovey Eberhart often bestowed upon the hungry the delicacies sent to uplift her morale. In the extreme case of the new Ralston camp (across the river from Vicksburg), five days passed before the arrival of the first rations. By then some of the desperate residents had threatened to kill Lovey's husband, the camp superintendent, for starving them.[16] Suffering provoked suspicions, justified in some cases when freedpeople did uncover theft and sales of rations by officials.[17]

After 1862 superintendents often founded or relocated camps on plantations, to enable the residents to grow their own food. Black refugees who had family gardens in slavery usually preferred individual plots. Superintendents who focused on individual responsibility might locate a garden by each home, if a new camp consisted of cottages or just had the space. Some superintendents insisted on large communal fields as more efficient. At Arlington, Superintendent Danforth B. Nichols earned money for the government by selling most of the vegetables raised and rarely included them in rations. After elderly residents went begging for money to buy vegetables, shocked reformers secured more of the harvest for the camp. At nearby Camp Todd, Emily Howland had to fight with administrators to get land set aside for vegetable gardens.[18] Ultimately, some camps successfully fed themselves, and some fell short. Others, painfully, had to abandon crops during Confederate offensives.[19]

Superintendents gradually obtained more equipment for food storage and preparation, such as provision lockers to keep insects and the unauthorized out of supplies, large cooking kettles for groups cooking over fires, and wood-burning stoves for common kitchens. Mason's Island had nine large ovens for mass bread-baking. More camps set up mess halls that pooled rations to make meals for all.[20] Camp stores also sold a variety of kitchen wares to freedpeople. Archeological excavations of contraband camp sites have turned up cheap pottery much more often than the valuable tablewares taken from a master's house. At Natchez an aid worker distributed free spoons and knives to the newly arrived.[21]

Black refugees living outside of contraband camps—except for army employees and sometimes their families—had difficulty getting rations, even though the War Department had authorized them for the destitute. Financially successful Blacks pleased reformers with proud assertions, like "I eats *no* government rations! I gets my living by the sweat of my brow." But, those with lower incomes had to pay the rent first and needed help with other necessities. In Washington, Cornelia Hancock visited unemployed Black refugees "living (they say upon the Lord) without bread." When one desperate woman could not afford to feed her children, she turned them over to Hancock, who placed them in Camp Barker's orphanage.[22]

In several towns, Black leaders, mostly ministers, collected food and fuel for the needy. When employment opportunities began to decline in Washington during the winter of 1864–65, the Freedmen's Department there worked with several aid associations to set up three soup kitchens. Large communities of freedpeople at various points along the lower Mississippi River at first lived off food stocked on or growing at deserted plantations until John Eaton established camps with rations at those spots.[23]

Starting in 1863, the reformers generally received free rations, probably the soldier's issue. They greatly benefited if they'd been forewarned to take at least a mess kit with them. Otherwise, they had to borrow equipment until they could get some shipped from the North. A group could hire a cook or prepare their own meals, if sent a cooking stove by their association. Like Black refugees, relief workers had to learn the best ways to prepare rations through experimentation. When Rhoda Smith had major indigestion problems with rations, trading foods with neighbors and financial help from her sponsors enabled her to obtain palatable items. When rations were temporarily unavailable, reformers or their associations had to buy food at prices driven up by wartime inflation. In the absence of free rations, at least one commander allowed the aid workers to buy rations at cost from the army. When Gen. William T. Sherman canceled rations for aid workers along his supply line during his Atlanta campaign, freedpeople at Murfreesboro, Tennessee, shared theirs in order to retain teachers.[24]

Housing

Surges in population greatly strained the availability of shelter at contraband camps. Elizabeth James at Roanoke Island once reported that "every nook and cranny is already crowded to excess." After completely filling existing housing, camp staff usually issued tents to the remainder or placed them in a large hall within a school, church, or public facility.[25] If inspectors found a mass of new arrivals "promiscuously" housed in a hall, they pressured the camp superintendent to at least create separate male and female areas. When Saxtonville's superintendent tried to limit the number in each building, some newcomers let in friends from their old plantations anyway. An influx of new residents also exhausted bedding supplies. At Slabtown in January 1864, half slept upon rags, a fourth had just a bench on which to rest, and the remainder had neither. A Virginia father begged for a blanket for his children whose wintertime suffering "grieves my mind."[26] The worst case of all occurred during the winter of 1864–65, when General Sherman's march through Georgia and the Carolinas brought thousands to the coast. Many, left at the Sea Islands with a little surplus bedding and what charity the resident freedpeople could offer, could only get space beside external walls, where a number died.[27]

Crises pressured camp superintendents to add more buildings, and in some places the construction became constant. More freedmen's departments obtained steam-driven sawmills to speed up construction. Some of the work simply renovated existing structures, especially by adding room dividers to large barns, stables, warehouses, or workplaces. Although quartermaster crews probably erected barracks quicker and cheaper, the Reverend John G. Fee persuaded officials at Camp Nelson to include some of the cottages that freedpeople preferred.[28] Some camps also gained more bedding, wells, and (hopefully) privies.[29]

New buildings often came with better quality. The Alexandria Freedmen's Home had spacious rooms with a stove, cupboard, table, and two benches per unit. Some other new structures had less furniture but included bunk beds. Aid associations also upgraded housing by shipping down doors, windows, and heating stoves. Many residents who lacked experience with glass and stovepipes opposed those furnishings, probably in fear of undermining heat retention.[30] Over time a camp's shelters could acquire increasingly varied appearances.

General Rufus Saxton opened the new Saxtonville camp near Beaufort with dwellings consisting of four one-room units for families. A novel building design at Arlington had four two-story house units built around a large central chimney and dispersed along a suburban-style oval road. Each unit in this showplace camp had cooking stoves and an outside well. During defensive preparations before Confederate general Jubal Early's attack on Washington in July 1864, Federals evacuated and razed the Arlington camp. Afterwards they rebuilt it.[31]

Censuses and estimates of freedpeople done mostly by Freedmen's Department officials suggest that in some locations the majority or at least a large number of Black refugees may have lived on their own by the war's end. It amazed Julia Wilbur that a Black refugee "had rather live by himself & be independent," because many had to scrimp on necessities. A very desperate group of Vicksburg freedmen spent a winter in a gully under a board covering. Unable to afford lumber, many Blacks in Chattanooga built houses out of sod blocks.[32] One historian estimates that rent in wartime Washington especially pinched the resources of the poor, because it underwent more inflation than other necessities. The only place where such housing improved was in Alexandria, after reformers' complaints led to repairs to buildings appropriated and rented by the army. Most of those raising shanties on the city's empty lots or in alleys still had to pay rent to the landowners. Seeing the increased demand for housing, some whites quickly built and leased shanties, which many renters thought had worse quality than their old slave cabins. Shantytowns, as in today's developing nations, could improve, if the inhabitants' income permitted it. Some residents of the Grantville neighborhood near Alexandria's riverfront upgraded their homes and also built a community church/school building.[33]

Shantytowns have long provoked controversy. The army forcibly razed one outside the Arlington camp. Army commanders in Alexandria and Vicksburg tried to limit shanty construction in those towns. However, when Eaton turned multiple shantytowns along the Mississippi into contraband camps, some of the new superintendents worked to upgrade the residents' homes.[34]

At Alexandria in early 1863, the friends Julia Wilbur and Harriet Jacobs clashed with male officials of the Freedmen's Department over charging rent for its appropriated houses. Both had participated in the women's rights movement and lived by the "single blessedness" ideal. They likely shared the common belief of female reformers that women were inherently more moral and compassionate than men. Despite the successful record of women reformers in carrying out prewar charitable projects, many male reformers thought that men provided better leadership and more bureaucratic efficiency. When single women were challenging male authorities, as in this case, they often provided support for one another.[35]

Washington's quartermasters required rent from employed Blacks living in camps or in buildings appropriated by the army. Albert Gladwin, superintendent of the Freedmen's Home, preferred to have only employed refugees there, since part of his pay came from rent collections. The two women instead advocated that the destitute should get priority for government housing and get it for free. Wilbur incidentally sought the position of matron for the Freedmen's Home and noted that "although a *woman* I would like an appointment with a fair salary."[86]

Gladwin, who ran the home in a rough manner, required its employed residents to work on and pay for improvements to the building. They often could not cover all charges by the monthly deadline, because military and private pay came irregularly. The superintendent threatened to kick out those in arrears. This led to heated arguments, and on one occasion "he had to run for his life." He eventually had those not paying locked up in a military jail. Residents like Jasmine Weems felt "as much terrified as if we were with the secesh [secessionists]." The calm and intelligent Jacobs argued with Gladwin, while Wilbur repeatedly filed charges against him. She noted that "Mr. G. says I am out of my sphere, & he does not like to see a woman [symbolically] wear men's clothes." An army investigator who probably supported male dominance upheld Gladwin over what he called "an interfering and troublesome person." When Gladwin kicked Wilbur and Jacobs out of their rooms in retaliation, they appealed to the post commander, who restored all but an extra room Wilbur used for her freedwomen's sewing group. Wilbur never received a salaried position in the camp system.[87]

Aid workers, now more numerous, increasingly found living in a group home or mission house (often with a manager and housekeeper) more economical and efficient than individual arrangements. Aid societies usually relied on the army for an appropriated house and fuel but occasionally built a small home. At times, relief workers had to live with major repairs of the assigned shelter. Because of generally minimal furnishings, several associations started to require volunteers to bring their own bedding. Others shipped it and furniture from the North, since those items tended to be scarce and expensive in occupation zones. An AMA official on one of the Sea Islands reported: "You may think me rather *fussy* about this [bedding], but I am sure there is a *solemn reality* in these things to a young Lady far away from home, comforts, and friends." Charities increasingly covered their workers' most basic requirements in the unspoken awareness that a volunteer deprived of rest, heat, food, or a home medicine chest could not or would not do much good for others.[38]

Some housemates got along well and preferred the company of other relief workers. As Esther Hawks observed: "O how pleasant it seems to have someone *appear* to feel an interest in one's welfare." On the other hand, group living could add to an aid worker's daily tensions. While shared housing made cooperation essential, some individuals were messy, wasteful, irresponsible, or difficult. In a unique case, M. E. Burdick talked the manager at a Norfolk mission house into instituting mandatory prayer services, to suppress what she considered the others' "thoughtless levity."[39]

Interracial mission houses faced special challenges. During 1864, the AMA sent to Norfolk four African American women teachers, who divided over wanting separate or integrated housing. Their manager, William H. Woodbury, at first left them completely by themselves in a bare house for six weeks. After spending their cash and receiving help from others, it took a "plain talk" with Woodbury to get their basic needs met. He decided to move them in with several white teachers. Some, not all, of the whites objected, spoke insultingly, and even expected the Black teachers to do more domestic chores. Mary M. Reed admitted: "Never having been in contact with this race at home, I often find myself in novel and trying positions." Within half a year all of the Black women left that mission house.[40] One of them, Clara Duncan, happily shared her next house with the white Frances Littlefield who "endears herself to everyone." Blacks James Lynch, Charlotte Forten, and Sojourner Truth likewise enjoyed living for a time with white aid workers at Beaufort (South Carolina), St. Helena Island, and Washington, respectively. However, the Reverend J. N. Mars, a northern Black who had an unpleasant experience at another integrated mission house in Norfolk, concluded that "those that come [here] . . . should be free from all prejudice, against Color, or they had better stay at home."[41]

Clothing

The need for clothes during 1863–65 greatly expanded with the Black refugees' population surges, especially during the winters, and exceeded the supply that many contraband camps now tried to keep on hand. During 1863, those in need narrowed mainly to women and children, since enlistees received new uniforms and civilian males now gained access to military clothes rejected by the quartermaster or removed from the deceased.[42]

Periodic short supplies tried the reformers' souls and extended the refugees' distress. Faced with a big influx of Black refugees during cold weather, Minnie A. Hill reported: "I have *seen* and *felt* more of human suffering and degradation since I have been in Norfolk, than I ever *saw* or *felt* or even dreamed of in all my life." When H. S. Beals superintended a plantation camp in eastern Virginia, two weeping mothers asked, "what shall we do for our Dear Little Ones. The nights are becoming chilly. Our houses are open, and our children almost naked." Residents who fled camps attacked by Confederates commonly lost their spare clothes. When those from the Plymouth, North Carolina, camp arrived at Roanoke Island with their aid worker Sarah P. Freeman, she commiserated that "I . . . find them again looking to me for clothing, while I was empty-handed, and nearly as destitute as they. I feel that it was right, that we should be able to sympathize with them in their losses."[43]

When a clothes shipment came, many aid workers, like Esther Hawks, found the mass distribution to be "tiresome work, and sometimes I get very cross over it." The long hours of these events could provoke complaints and rowdiness from disappointed freedpeople. At times, the quantity available only permitted one or two pieces of clothing per person. On Craney Island, Orlando Brown tried limiting the distribution to one barracks at a time, but a "frowning multitude" of the severely destitute from other buildings objected. When an inadequate shipment to one Sea Island plantation went just to those that the distributor judged most worthy, the nonrecipients protested with a work strike. But then a sense of community moved the others to return the goods, and all suffered until enough arrived for everyone. Distributors experimented with different approaches. The main alternatives were the controlled approach of admitting just a few to the storeroom at a time or private meetings with those selected in advance as having priority needs, often issued tickets for goods. Most aid workers now conducted home visits to evaluate the financial status and needs of freedpeople.[44] Lucy Chase also consulted her record of what she had issued to whom and when. Some distributers gave preference to particular groups, typically orphans, school children, mothers, the elderly, workers, soldiers' families, or the most destitute.[45]

Obviously, those in great need intensely appreciated the donated clothes. A freedwoman in Natchez exclaimed that "dis is de best dressin' I's ever had in my life." A group of girls receiving dresses on Island No. 10 gleefully discovered a small rag doll in each one's pocket. However, when Emily Howland departed to visit her northern home and her substitute required recipients to listen to a lecture on morals before receiving clothes, the aggravated started taking clothes from the storeroom at night instead. The return of the empathetic Howland prompted rejoicing in Camp Barker.[46]

To encourage the aid associations' charitable efforts, many commanders granted free or discounted military transportation for their goods and personnel. Also, the associations benefited from services donated by some shipping and railroad companies. Designated persons, often managers of camp stores, received and distributed the goods. In Alexandria, Wilbur and Jacobs pragmatically and cooperatively combined the clothes-distributing operations of their separate sponsors, the Rochester Ladies' Anti-Slavery Society and the New York Yearly Meeting of Quakers. Eaton went beyond all other Freedmen's Department superintendents in his effort to make deliveries more effective by appointing Henry Rountree of the Contraband Relief Commission to supervise clothing issuances in his department. All organizations had to ship garments to Rountree, and he had them transported impartially by need to the local distributors. Eaton even acquired use of a steamer to move materials and personnel along the major Mississippi Valley rivers in his department.[47]

As the Federals drove deeper into the Confederacy, clothes shipments ran into problems. Lieutenant Colonel Kinsman simplified matters by requiring all packages for his department to come to his office for forwarding. Given all his other duties, slow processing resulted, and long storage facilitated robbery, probably by military personnel. Because theft also occurred during shipment, Rountree hired agents to accompany the goods. Of course, purely military materials always had priority in transportation, and nothing could be done about problems arising from storms, ice, or shipwrecks. Aid workers learned that wooden boxes worked best but needed to be built strongly with iron bands, be carefully addressed, and contain a list of contents. A copy of the list, noting the sender, ideally went to the relevant aid association. Tracking down and regaining lost shipments was hard, time consuming, and costly.[48]

Aid associations developed northern sewing circles that produced more textile goods for freedpeople. To expand production in occupied areas during 1863–65, more contraband camps started sewing circles and classes, usually with materials shipped from the North. Women at the Pulaski camp secured spinning jennies and looms for making their own thread and cloth. The seamstresses at Camp Nelson tried reworking discarded federal uniforms into garments for women and children. A few teachers requested that sponsors send them precut fabric pieces, primarily for the beginners. Besides garments, the classes and circles also made bedding ticks, handkerchiefs, quilts, bonnets, and knitted goods.[49]

When Elizabeth Botume's sewing class of Sea Island girls and boys completed their first set of clothes for themselves, "the delight of the possessors was inexpressible. . . . Then their pent-up spirits burst forth; such shouts and guffaws as they gave. They knocked each other in the ribs, rolled over and over, and turned somersaults." By the later war years, most aid workers had learned to honor freedpeople's preferences in clothes, except Superintendent Nichols who still ordered the cheap, durable, but rough "negro cloth" for Arlington's sewing workshop. His camp's store could only issue the resulting clothes to destitute refugees.[50]

Sewing circles and classes created a meaningful alternative to the boredom common in the camps and a community activity for women who were strangers to one another. While working, seamstresses in Fernandina, Florida, had their members or children sing for entertainment. Sometimes a relief worker read to them. The very large Craney Island circle received alphabet lessons during sessions. When a fire in Natchez threatened stored clothing, two women from the sewing class alerted authorities and monitored the situation until the fire was extinguished. Membership in a circle could lead to personal income, as camp stores sometimes purchased a circle's work. Two aid workers in Washington selected a group of seamstresses either recovering from illness or homebound by little children and paid them for making a round of clothes.[51]

Additional camp stores opened, as more Black refugees earned wages. Inventories expanded to include dress clothes, baby clothes, soap, kerosene lamps, and basic furniture. Some reformers now offered to handle transactions or hold money for freedpeople.[52] By 1864 most camp stores only charged employed Blacks for goods. Rountree, though, covered charity cases by marking prices up ten percent. A few freedpeople took pride in paying full price.[53] Some donors and organizations (especially the Contraband Relief Commission) strongly opposed sales. Not all aid workers assigned to evaluating the financial status of Black refugees cared for the task. Rountree suspected that the teachers' "sympathies exceed their judgement," but Lucy Chase observed that "the distracting question to give or not to give is always staring at me and frightening me. . . . Criticism of the Severest, we are subject to from both black and white." Julia Wilbur, though, felt more scandalized when Alexandria's post commander would not buy clothes for his freedman servant but instead sent him to her for free ones.[54]

Some officials now involved stores in other reformer goals. Superintendent Greene, a former merchant, enlarged his freedmen's fund by haggling to get goods for his camp stores at the lowest prices and then selling them at five percent above cost for the fund's benefit. Some camps required clothes recipients to undergo personal washing first; Gladwin insisted on it even during winter. The Natchez camp store required couples to present a marriage certificate before they could buy anything. Several Quaker-operated stores refused to carry tobacco on religious grounds.[55] Various camp store managers praised the good taste that most women shoppers showed in their fashionable selections. Some reformers credited stores for cultivating consumer skills, but others criticized the selling of goods that they considered frivolous. Eaton berated a freedman who bought candy for his ill wife, instead of something more useful. While the freed expected liberty in commercial activity as a right, paternalists judged that the poor needed guidance on exerting self-control over consumption.[56]

Developments affecting the clothes that reformers wore were relatively minor after 1862. During shipment, crates of the reformers' clothes came to suffer occasional pilfering by the same bandits who targeted charitable packages. In a possibly unique incident, the missionary Samuel G. Wright dared to request free clothes, bedding, and utensils from a camp store for his own use. Rountree indignantly refused, and Eaton backed this decision.[57]

Medical Care

Medical care during 1863–65 encountered challenges not only from the large influxes of Black refugees, but also from hasty military evacuations and bad weather. The army assigned more doctors, including those recruited by the aid organizations, to care for the larger freed population, although some camps never got even one. Wilder and Brown, as Pierce had done earlier in the Sea Islands, allotted doctors to provide care to groups of plantation camps in East Virginia, but rural distances slowed their services.[58]

The army established more hospitals for Blacks in the later war years. However, most hospitals for freedpeople were in tents or small buildings, often unsanitary and uncomfortable. Severe weather destroyed flimsy structures at Columbus and Camp Barker in 1863. When an inspector found the Mason's Island hospital filthy, its head appointed a sanitation officer to establish cleanliness. After another inspector noted the lack of a maternity ward there, an aid association funded one. Biased directors of several other hospitals just ignored shortcomings.[59]

Black troops received most treatment in regimental hospitals, if their unit had one, since many lacked a doctor. Few white doctors were willing, and the army commissioned few African American ones. Black soldiers' regimental hospitals tended to lack adequate supplies and staffs. With little immediate medical care and mostly labor assignments, these soldiers had higher death rates from disease than did white ones. The major hospitals for Black troops generally had better facilities.[60] The new, highly rated Freedmen's Hospital in Washington had several northern Black doctors, including Surgeon Alexander T. Augusta, the director for about a year, and another who did outreach care in the shantytowns. That military facility and other large ones in Alexandria, Vicksburg, Memphis, and New Orleans probably had the long barracks-style wings admitting much ventilation and sunlight typical of the major Civil War hospitals. The army designed them for easy cleaning in the hope of avoiding infections.[61]

Staff shortages remained common at all hospitals for Blacks, although a few physicians recruited Black refugees with medical experience. Care quality continued to vary. Julia Wilbur judged the head doctor at the Alexandria Freedmen's Hospital inhumane, especially because he failed to have the sick quarters cleaned and provided with adequate fuel. She and Harriet Jacobs frequently visited patients to distribute more firewood, fresh clothes, soft food, fans, and other amenities. Dr. D. O. McCord, Eaton's very effective medical director, replaced the doctors who performed poorly.[62]

Many aid workers who visited hospitals focused on feeding the patients with farina (a milk and starch mixture), soup, vegetables, and tea—all easily consumed forms of nourishment. At the Island No. 10 and Nashville hospitals, the death rate dropped significantly when such meals replaced the harder-to-digest rations. Reformer and Black visitors to hospitals also offered biscuits, crackers, chocolate, sauerkraut, pickles, sugared concoctions, or fruit in many forms to stimulate the appetite.[63] Due to moral opposition to medicinal liquor, few relief workers would administer it to sick freedpeople. Reformers doing hospital visiting kindly tried to uphold patient morale. Near the end of a chat, a dying woman in the Baton Rouge hospital asked Julia Brown for her name and then closed with, "Farewell, when I go home to Heaven, I will remember that name."[64]

Because of budgetary concerns in the summer of 1864, Secretary of War Edwin Stanton canceled separate medical care for freedpeople. However, Black soldiers' hospitals generally accepted freed civilians who needed major treatment. Eaton's and probably some other freedmen's departments covered a degree of medical care out of freedmen's funds.[65] Eaton had a large enough one, supplemented by aid associations' contributions, to purchase and use a number of recently developed prefabricated structures for hospitals.[66]

Some medical problems required a special response. At one camp in St. Mary's County, Maryland, several mothers who had trouble producing breast milk lost their infants to death, because the proslavery superintendent sold all the milk produced by dairy cattle there. The AMA obtained his dismissal. The Camp Nelson surgeon forwarded three soldiers' wives to a Cincinnati hospital, because owners had whipped them so severely as to require more skilled treatment. As scurvy comes from a lack of vitamin C, aid workers scrambled to acquire more fruits and vegetables to end its outbreaks. A few reformers initiated collections of unused eyeglasses in the north for Blacks with poor sight, especially among the elderly.[67]

During 1863, the dreaded smallpox continued to ravage the southeastern coast and spread into the Mississippi Valley. The army continued to provide free vaccinations, and the Freedmen's Hospital actually inoculated about half of the Black newcomers to Washington. At times officials required Black refugees to have the procedure, but those unfamiliar with inoculation sometimes resisted. When white strangers came to vaccinate Elizabeth Botume's pupils, the children fled in terror. She had to explain the procedure to the mothers to get cooperation.[68] Slowing the epidemic at New Bern required moving the smallpox hospital across a river to stop relatives from visiting contagious patients. While officials commonly burnt victims' clothing, a few also torched their houses.[69]

"Injustice follows these people even after death," according to Julia Wilbur, who attended numerous Black funerals. Her complaints about the overloading of the indigent Blacks' burial plots at Alexandria moved Gladwin to obtain coffins, headboards, and enough land for a new Contrabands' and Freedmen's Cemetery with mostly individual graves in 1864.[70] Rarely did towns have integrated cemeteries, and few camps had well-marked graves for freedpeople, Contraband camps and Black communities required the availability of spare lumber to produce coffins for their dead. Several freedmen's departments, camps, local aid associations, and donors hired Black gravediggers and paid for paupers' burials.[71] Ella Roper, as a novice relief worker, wanted the Roanoke Island camp store to sell shrouding cloth on the grounds that "It will do much to raise the moral tone, if we have the power to teach them to respect the dead," but some freedpeople with earnings did spend significant resources on the interment of family members.[72]

The Federal army quickly put the bulk of its wartime deceased under ground near the place of death, sometimes with a military ritual and sometimes not. In at least Port Hudson, Louisiana, a reformer obtained a full upgrading of the proceedings for Black soldiers. In the Department of Washington, the first Black soldiers to die received interment alongside freedmen in Alexandria with a military ceremony. After Congress created national military cemeteries, patients at L'Ouverture Hospital for Black troops petitioned the army to entomb their comrades at the new one on part of Mary Custis Lee's tax-defaulted Arlington plantation. Supported by the reformer heading the hospital, the petition resulted in a segregated section in the Arlington Cemetery, as well as the reburial there of most Black soldier remains from Alexandria. However, near the year's end Gladwin got the previous arrangement reinstated. When offended Black troops refused to escort military burial processions to the Contrabands' and Freedmen's Cemetery, Gladwin had the group's leader arrested. The matter ended when Alexandria's military governor restored entombment at Arlington and fired Gladwin from his position as

Alexandria Freedmen's Home Superintendent. This conflict's outcome pleased the Black reformer Harriet Jacobs, who judged her longtime opponent Gladwin as one of the "white men who come from the North and pretend to labor among the Colored People."[73]

During 1863–65, the expanded corps of reformers suffered from illness at more places and a death toll of at least twenty-two persons, higher than that during 1861-62.[74] Aid associations strongly encouraged volunteers to visit their northern homes during their work location's sickly season or at least to lighten their workload. Because ill persons in a mission house required much care from the other staff members, sending them home was preferable, when feasible. Other individuals exhibiting emotional illness intensified by the work's stress also required an escorted trip home. It became clear that volunteers not only needed "excellent health," but also "much endurance."[75]

Security

The safety of Black refugees continued to require troops or armed residents. Detachments from several new Black regiments drew the duty of protecting contraband camps. Lacking troops and male residents, one St. Mary's County camp had a female squad of guards.[76] Because determined owners kept trying to snatch camp residents from the Arlington camp, Sojourner Truth noisily drove off some and encouraged the inhabitants themselves to resist slave hunters.[77]

Proslavery whites, particularly in the occupied areas untouched by the final Emancipation Proclamation, increased their verbal and physical aggression. When white boys surprised a Black prayer meeting in Harper's Ferry, West Virginia, with a shower of stones, a reformer reported them, but Federal officials did little. Because proslavery Kentuckians fired shots into the wooden frame houses of the Louisville camp at night, the superintendent and residents had to do without lamps and sleep on floors. Hostile troops from that state would have assaulted the Fort Donelson contraband camp, which attracted Black refugees from Kentucky, if an antislavery Illinois regiment had not stoutly defended it.[78]

After Lincoln's proclamation, Confederates grew much more hostile to African Americans for aiding the enemy. Because the enemy targeted concentrations of freedpeople, Federals directed residents at Helena, Pine Bluff, and Mason's Island in constructing defenses. The Slabtown laborers' camp had a stockade and ditch around it. The lack of a nearby garrison or its withdrawal for a major Federal campaign had a deadly impact in the Mississippi valley. During summer 1863 Confederate troops or guerrillas there attacked and tried to massacre a number of Black refugee settlements.[79] In 1864 they mounted offensives against Federal posts with contraband camps at Pulaski, Tunnel Hill, Fort Pillow, and Nashville, as well as Washington (District of Columbia), Washington (North Carolina), Plymouth, New Bern, and Suffolk. Enemy forces raided Helena, Young's Point, Goodrich's Landing, Davis Bend, Pine Bluff, outlying Sea Islands, and Lawrence (Kansas). Confederates killed or reenslaved numerous freedpeople, and in only a few cases could the security units mount a successful defense. Some superintendents evacuated camps in advance; many residents escaped under assault. The sites lost buildings, property, and crops. After the raid on Lawrence, reformers raised a substantial fund that benefited freedpeople who lost shanties and property there.[80] African Americans who had traversed woods and swamps during a flight from Confederate assault often needed new clothes and medical care afterward. In one unusual case in Arkansas, Confederate guerrillas released captives after stripping them of donated clothes. In the most dangerous parts of the Mississippi Valley, some freedpeople armed themselves, but because this terrified southern white civilians, several Federal post commanders seized the weapons.[81]

During 1863–65, many a reformer, like Lovey Eberhart, "began to realize that my life was very unsafe," after Confederate snipers killed a United Presbyterian missionary couple travelling south aboard a Mississippi River steamboat. Rebels murdered several teachers at Helena and near New Orleans, as well as the doctor at Young's Point camp. They intended the same fate for Superintendent Elkanah Beard, but he chanced to be absent.[82] When briefly staying close to enemy lines, Charlotte Forten and Harriet Ware obtained revolvers. Teachers at Harper's Ferry, Plymouth, Pine Bluff, and Goodrich's Landing managed to flee enemy offensives. The Confederate attack on New Bern so unnerved a new teacher that she promptly returned home. Several months later in the fall of 1864, the pacifist Quaker volunteers at Yorktown decided to stay, when Federals withdrew, and remarkably they suffered no harm.[83]

During the later war years, the greatly increased number of freedpeople faced more challenges in obtaining the necessities. As in the early years, they did what they could with limited resources to help themselves or to contribute to contraband camp life. The destitute sometimes had to endure the preaching and controlling actions of the more biased reformers. Aid associations greatly increased the resources and staff that they provided, as needs rose, but the War Department reduced rations, medical care, and guarding troops, as the lengthening war intensified.[84]

Overall, provision for freedpeople in need was inadequate, but with occasional exceptions. Contraband camps probably had a little more success with meeting the need for food. Supplies of shelter and clothing periodically lagged behind need at many places. Medical care and security were highly inadequate in some camps and towns. In shantytowns only Black refugees with good and regular incomes could live comfortably.

Time and experimentation allowed for the improvement of camp facilities and better methods for care. Well-read reformers could learn about innovative aid efforts made elsewhere through newspapers, magazines, and especially the relief associations' publications, although few made such references in their writings.[85] Common circumstances likely contributed to some of the similar actions. Still, the difficulties encountered by freedpeople required great endurance and cost many lives. Contraband camps and shantytowns became a painful route to freedom for many. Witnessing suffering led to emotional distress for many relief workers, who depended on the flow of supplies from the army and aid associations. Elizabeth Botume admitted that "In times of trouble . . . When I saw their implicit confidence in our knowledge and sympathy, I found it very hard to tell them [that] I could do nothing." While Reverend Wright found his wartime work entailed "self-denial and much hazard of life and health," he added that "this is the most useful part of my life."[86]

Much interaction with Black refugees over a period of time also could have a significant impact on white reformers. It transformed a minority of paternalists into egalitarians, especially if they had strong religious drives for personal as well as social improvement. Fully and informally sharing life with Blacks, this minority of whites slowly underwent the crucial development of seeing varied individual humans, instead of group stereotypes. Most expressed this conversion experience indirectly, like L. D. Burnett: "My respect for the colored people increases every day. When with them, I forget that they are colored." Elizabeth Botume gradually rejected "many theories for the advancement of contrabands" that she and others carried South, because she learned that "this was an unexplored field, requiring a line of action not mapped out in any book." Esther Hawks took nearly the entire war before admitting: "Many is the time when nicely settled in my mind, that I know them well, all my fine spun theories are upset by some entirely new development of character for which I find, I had given them no credit. I am convinced save through love no one can be an efficient laborer among these people."[87] These reformers slowly developed a new identity with Blacks as fellow humans. Beyond rejection of racial oppression and exploitation, this included support for an integrated nation, a radical change. William F. Mitchell most candidly stated: "I have

. . . heretofore pleaded for the Freedmen, for what *they can be made* under the influence of freedom. Hereafter I contend for the colored people of Tennessee for what they *are*." Some other reformers whose outlook at least began to shift during the war were Orlando Brown, Horace James, Edward Pierce, Rufus Saxton, Laura Towne, and Charles Wilder.[88]

It is hard to learn anyone's inmost thoughts, and the process did not necessarily eliminate every trace of racial chauvinism from the minds of these whites. But enough growth did occur that Blacks could consider them as trustworthy and even as friends. Significant good was done sometimes, if not always, and earned appreciation. After positive encounters with reformers, a freedwoman realized that her distrust of the dominant race had been reduced: "I never expected to see such white ladies on this earth."[89]

Obviously, many who briefly served in the South did not revise their attitudes. Paternalist and laissez-faire reformers—committed to a substantial white supremacy—kept clinging to preconceptions by focusing on isolated negative incidents and maintaining as much social distance from the freed as possible. Esther Hawks's reformer associates in a sewing circle rejected her proposal to add freeedwomen to the group. Some reformers failed to learn valuable lessons from their experiences. Meanwhile, Black refugees evaluated each relief worker individually and carefully, on the basis of actions rather than words. Visible proof of worthiness led to degrees of trust, except among those most leery about whites.[90]

6

Wage Labor

During 1863–65 reformers made greater efforts to move freedpeople into the wage labor system. Paternalists mostly wanted them transitioned to employees, while egalitarians and laissez-faire advocates favored free choice in work. The laissez-faire reformers also had concerns about reducing the costs of contraband camps (seen as a drain on the war effort) and of providing necessities (seen as promoting laziness). At this time, the Federal army reshaped the Black civilian workforce by enlisting a larger percentage of adult males and moving many of the remaining men into military labor crews. Officials forced most women and some males into contractual jobs in the private sector. Camp superintendents continued to seek some work for remaining residents. Many independent freedpeople still created their own enterprises, but faced more obstacles.

Independent Work and Business

Freedpeople preferred employment that supported independence and did not resemble slavery. Numerous men and boys in occupied towns became unskilled day laborers in a remunerative but irregular market subject to flooding by too many entrants.[1] Many others copied predecessors by selling various goods and services. By now some had accumulated enough savings to start craftsman shops, delivery services, restaurants, stores, hotels, or undertaking.[2] Some, like Robert Smalls, who commandeered the Confederate supply ship *Planter,* had the talent to do especially well in small business.[3]

Paternalist reformers feared that most of these entrepreneurs would earn so little that they would suffer deprivation and turn to crime. Worrying that those who did reach a subsistence level would stop there and not work any harder, they concluded that the mass of freedpeople needed to be guided back into stable jobs, primarily as agricultural hands. Horace James thought that they naturally must be "a nation of servants" for a time. Obviously, many whites, northerners as well as southerners, benefited economically from cheap and dependent Black labor.[4] This could lead to conflict with Black refugees.

High officials with such views took actions against the self-employed. A commander on a Sea Island placed restrictions on peddling by Blacks. In eastern Virginia, Lt. Col. Joseph B. Kinsman prohibited freedmen-owned stores after making the exaggerated claim that all of them sold unnecessary trinkets to Blacks at high prices. They could hardly have competed with camp stores without filling a market gap.[5] In Memphis in 1863, Col. John Eaton initiated a pass system that required each Black adult living independently to register as an employee under a white person. Federal patrols placed those found without passes in a contraband camp until contracted into acceptable jobs, usually as plantation hands. In 1864 Federals at Pine Bluff, Nashville, and Natchez inaugurated similar systems. When the Natchez system—officially a means to end epidemics—frightened away enough families to shut down most schools, representatives of all five aid associations operating there protested. George Young, superintendent of the Natchez contraband camp, pointed out the obvious: "If individual enterprise among the colored people is going to be thus crushed their condition will be but little changed by their transition from bondage to freedmen." Everywhere many of the seized Blacks quickly escaped from the contraband camps and some paid whites to pose as their employers. When commanders in Vicksburg, Huntsville, and Eastern Virginia adopted similar systems in early 1865, they modified it to include the concession of a limited number of passes for the self-employed.[6]

The United States Treasury included participation by selected freedmen entrepreneurs, when it initiated a leasing program for abandoned plantations. In Eaton's department, funding could come from the lessee's savings, a Treasury loan with a crop lien, or a partnership with merchants. Some just rented ten-acre farms, while others leased large plantations and hired fellow freedpeople. Many Black lessees obtained needed materials from other vacant plantations. In addition, some white lessees sublet plots to their best workers as an incentive. In the Helena area the former contraband camp superintendent, John J. Herrick, managed the freedmen's cotton sales. Confederate raids drove off some lessees in the Mississippi Valley. In 1863 and probably in 1864, most Blacks who engaged in independent farming without being run off did so successfully. However, the army worm, a parasite that damaged the cotton crop, reduced profits. In 1865 the Treasury experimented with leasing all land on Davis Bend to Black co-operatives.[7]

Elsewhere, opportunities for the freed to lease land were limited. In the Sea Islands very few freedmen obtained leases. During 1864–65 the Treasury Department leased some eight-acre farms in the combined Department of Virginia and North Carolina. Lt. Col. Joseph Kinsman and aid associations provided lessees with agricultural advisers, guns, stock animals, farm implements, and tents (many plots lacked houses). Although Confederates killed or captured some lessees outside of New Bern in 1864, most in the department did well enough to renew for 1865. In Louisiana the government encouraged the formation of Black cooperatives for 1865 leases, and a local aid association offered loans to them. Unfortunately, many of these co-ops ran into financial difficulties.[8]

Some freedmen expressed a desire to own at least a small piece of land, and, as freedman Harry McMillan noted, Sea Islanders "would rather have the land than work for wages." Some reformers expected the war to lead to a redistribution of confiscated lands to Blacks. Opportunities for financially successful freedmen did arise from the direct tax law that circumvented constitutional limits on confiscation of traitors' property. Intended to punish Confederate supporters who were unlikely to pay a tax imposed by the United States, the law led to auctions of the defaulters' land in a few places near the Confederacy's east coast.[9]

Although Americans of the time generally idealized family farming, the reformers divided over the matter of land for freedpeople. Egalitarian Mansfield French argued that freedpeople ought to have some privileged access to farmland as a matter of compensatory justice and as a basis for economic independence. Others, like Francis Hinckley, contended that such a policy "would be much like giving our children unlimited means without their knowing the value thereof[;] . . . much of it would soon pass out of their hands and really do them little good." Others pragmatically worried about the future for small-scale farming after high wartime prices for foodstuffs ended.[10]

Before the first auction took place in the Sea Islands on March 9, 1863, the reformer Frederick Eustis disappointed his family's ex-slaves by paying the land tax and regaining ownership of that plantation. Some small farms were reserved for sale to freedpeople, but the auctioning of whole plantations shut out most Black bidders. Harry McMillan and three groups of freedmen who pooled their savings bought their home plantations, totaling a little over 2,000 acres. Several aid workers provided select freedmen with loans, which were paid off within a reasonable amount of time. The new landowners hoped to make profits by growing foodstuffs and cotton. One boasted that on his own land: "I work as long as I kin."[11] However, Edward Philbrick, a laissez-faire reformer, led a set of white investors who cornered the most acreage at the auction. At first, some hands refused to work for the new white landowners, but most on those plantations unhappily renewed contracts rather than leave home. Saxton, originally a paternalist opposing land sales to freedmen, shifted to egalitarian views in late 1863 and supported government plans for the second auction in February 1864, to include the sale of a set of twenty-acre farms to African Americans.[12]

Saxton and Reverend Mansfield French stirred up controversy before the 1864 land sale, when they briefly convinced the Lincoln administration to allow unrestricted preemption sales of plots to freedmen. Preemption would have allowed purchase before the auction and installment payments at a lower price. When the plan's opponents secured its cancellation, furious field hands held work stoppages and resisted planting long-staple cotton. Some protested by obstructively planting corn between cotton rows. An angry African American church elder advocated Black autonomy by urging white teachers at Towne's school to stop attending his church's services. Although Towne and her associates actually supported preemption, they complied all the same. The Reverend Mansfield French advised freedmen to stay on their chosen plots, and some who did so later saw their claims permitted by Congress.[13]

Several of Philbrick's workers formally charged that he had promised to sell them land at cost and then reneged. The Treasury Department's investigation concluded that the allegation could not be proven. Philbrick had considered selling small farms to workers all along, but, due to various factors including a major financial loss from a wrecked ship carrying his cotton, postponed it until after the war.[14]

Most of the new Black landowners kept working on large plantations in the hope of obtaining more acreage in the future. They probably used their employers' equipment to cultivate their own farms. Unfortunately, the smaller plots were less efficient and often lacked all of the various types of land needed to cultivate long-staple cotton. Gen. Rufus Saxton sought to protect them by canceling preharvest sales of cotton to speculators, only to see prices fall after harvest. Despite Philbrick's recent controversy, the Black landowners hired the skilled businessman as agent for shipping and selling their cotton.[15]

Direct tax default auctions moved less land into African American hands in Virginia and Florida. Despite William H. Woodbury's hope that plantation camps would evolve into permanent settlements for freedpeople, many were sold to whites in Virginia. Charles Wilder unsuccessfully tried to organize an investor group to buy land for resale to freedmen. When he bought several plantations by himself for that purpose, he was removed as district superintendent of freedmen in early 1865 under whites' allegations of abusing his powers, but was exonerated at his military trial. Calvin Robinson, superintendent of schools at Fernandina, Florida, bought some land there for resale. Several freedmen assertively complained that he charged them more than his auction bid, but he demonstrated that the higher price came from governmental fees. Blacks' filing of charges based on misunderstandings at times antagonized the white reformers involved.[16]

The largest attempt at land redistribution resulted from a meeting that Gen. William T. Sherman and Secretary of War Edwin Stanton held in Savannah with Black ministers concerned about the disposition of the huge number of African Americans who followed Sherman's march through Georgia. These leaders recommended the creation of an all-Black colony with land allotments so that freedpeople could provide for themselves. On January 16, 1865, Sherman with Stanton's concurrence issued an order implementing the idea in a zone thirty miles deep along the coast from Charleston to the Florida border, excepting only land already confiscated under the direct tax law. Blacks could file for up to forty acres under a possessory title subject to Congressional regulation. The Reverend Mansfield French, who publicly endorsed the colony, assured listeners that the titles would be secure, and he encouraged wide participation. General Saxton would record claims, and the residents could set up their own local governments. They relied heavily on abandoned property, such as food, building materials, seeds, tools, and animals, to start farms. Most settled on Sea Islands near Charleston.[17]

Contraband Camp Work

Throughout the occupied South, contraband camp superintendents found more tasks for unemployed residents. Black men with the skills produced shoes, wheels, furniture, iron goods, leather products, lumber, flour, bricks, and buckets for camp use and sometimes for sale. However, as the army now shifted many freed and fit males into its ranks or work crews, women and children came to predominate in the camps. Military officials tended to consider them as a financial burden for an increasingly expensive war effort.[18] Yet Lucy Chase reported that the women "were clamorous for work," and, if given it, "didn't feel of no account doing nothing." At Craney Island, Lucy and her sister

Sarah organized freedwomen to repair grain sacks for the quartermaster and to make bed ticks for the residents. Some freed women and men continued to draw assignments, now sometimes paid, to the camp crews for cooking, cleaning, farming, building, and firewood collecting or chopping. A few camps put them to work producing simple market products, like mats and fishing nets. However, the market for such goods easily became flooded, as in Norfolk during 1863.[19] Gardening was a common type of work in the camps that had limited spare space. If a superintendent tried to create communal gardens, freedpeople would try to get family plots instead.[20]

Earnings went either into a freedmen's fund or to the workers. Quartermaster General Montgomery C. Meigs endorsed Lt. Col. Elias M. Greene's payments at the Arlington camps, as "only such small wages as would serve as a reward for exertion," because charges there for camp costs and the freedmen's tax absorbed most of a worker's pay. Camp residents could not help but feel deprived by such fees.[21]

Partly to offer work for more of the able-bodied members, many camps were started on or relocated to appropriated plantations during 1863–65. Superintendents also wanted rural camps to move toward self-sufficiency, reduce crowding, and distance residents from abusive Federals. Saxton, James, and possibly some other superintendents hoped that some of these sites would be confiscated and become colonies of the freed. The initial challenge was covering the costs necessary to obtain seeds, implements, and work animals. Gen. Isaac Wistar, commander at Yorktown, sold oystering permits to some entrepreneurial freedmen with savings. Capt. Orlando Brown, a paternalist in the southern Chesapeake Bay area, reduced rations—before the War Department did it—and sold the excess. Lt. Joseph H. Harris hired out some residents of several Tennessee and Alabama camps long enough to earn the funds. Lieutenant Colonel Greene in the Department of Washington relied on the freedmen's tax. A Black regiment conducted raids into Virginia to collect everything that the Maryland plantation camps needed.[22] Superintendents commonly received some materials and animals from the aid associations and the army. They also procured the needed items from abandoned farms, new arrivals, or craftsmen in the camp. In a number of cases, start-up difficulties combined with slow decision-making to delay planting enough to harm harvests.[23]

Some but not all plantation camps succeeded in feeding themselves. Many also tried to grow commercial crops of cotton, sugar, tobacco, grain, sorghum, broom corn, or vegetables. Some camps raised hay and foodstuffs for the army's use. Camps with sawmills at times produced surplus lumber for sale.

Camps along the Mississippi River often cut and sold firewood to steamboats. The Sea Islands model probably led all freedmen's departments, except the Department of the Cumberland, to experiment at some sites with pay for field hands as a transition toward wage labor.[24]

At the Arlington camp Greene provided only a token pay for field hands. At first, he prohibited residents from enlisting or taking other jobs, because of his determination to earn money for the government. He required a full work-day in the fields or shops under supervisors, some of whom had been slave overseers and freely used physical punishments. Because of that, missionary C. B. Webster called the program "modified slavery for these people with the Gov't as a master." Reformer complaints resulted in freedmen receiving the work supervisors' jobs. During 1864, Greene switched his emphasis to pushing most incoming Black refugees toward private employment.[25]

In the Department of the Gulf, the army had always used some abandoned sugar plantations as camps for Louisiana's Black refugees. Lt. George Hanks and later Chap. Thomas Conway, freedmen's department superintendents, experimented with a subset of camps that earned income for the Federal government and paid the Black laborers low wages. When facing resistance from workers demanding more compensation, Edward Stetson, one of the superintendents, found the operation "Most bothersome" and renounced his abolitionism. After state emancipation in 1864, he expelled the dissident hands.[26]

In eastern Virginia during 1863, Capt. Charles B. Wilder launched an extensive plantation camp program, which eventually included 112 abandoned tobacco and grain farms. As in the Sea Islands, most freedpeople would work under supervisors. Depending on the amount of aid received before harvest, workers earned from one-half to three-fourths of the crop. Although some laborers doubted at first that they would get compensated, supervisors carefully recorded work hours for calculating the division of crop proceeds. Given the little territory that the department controlled in its North Carolina district, that area had only a few plantation camps, and Confederate offensives shut most down.[27]

In the Sea Islands, plantation camps adopted Philbrick's task labor system in 1863 and replaced rations with family gardens. Families generally finished their cotton task in the morning. In the evening they tended food crops and domestic animals. They now also had to make or buy their own clothes. One historian estimates that the Sea Islanders' compensation now fell below their subsistence's value in slavery. When some gardens failed to produce enough and pay came late, starvation pressured laborers to steal food. Those caught faced certain punishment at first from their superintendent, and after July

1863, from military commissions composed of several supervisors from government and purchased plantations. Numerous hands responded with a demand for higher wages.[28]

Black refugees, like the enslaved, had a problem in safely keeping money; they generally had to hide or spend it quickly. In the Department of Virginia and North Carolina during 1864, Gen. Benjamin F. Butler set up a military savings bank at Norfolk partly for freedpeople. Savings banks had a good reputation for fiscal security among members of the northern working class. Butler's bank copied a new system of federally chartered national banks by investing deposits in United States bonds to generate interest. By 1865 it had deposits exceeding $9,000.[29]

Rural locations made residents of plantation camps vulnerable to guerrillas, especially in the Mississippi Valley and North Carolina. Confederate partisans captured or killed some camp residents and the survivors went into hiding or flight. Fear lessened work in the fields and reduced harvests. Few or no attacks occurred in the Sea Islands, eastern Virginia, and southern Maryland.[30]

Military Labor

Large numbers of freedpeople continued to serve as civilian workers for the military. The War Department in 1863 authorized payment for all of its Black laborers. More but not all department commanders tried to implement wages. In some cases, supervisors questioned the Emancipation Proclamation's constitutionality and stubbornly persisted in the claim about the laborers' uncertain status through the war's end. Reformers' protests had limited impact. Quartermaster General Montgomery C. Meigs later tried to justify extensive nonpayment with the argument that "Sustenance and freedom given at great cost by the United States has fully compensated such services."[31] As uncompensated laborers escaped crews and the war grew more intense, the army increased the ugly practice of forcibly impressing more Blacks into that service. It occurred even in the Department of Washington, where pay usually was not an issue. In Louisiana, while the semislave, semifree system remained, Banks only impressed Blacks who escaped plantations and sought an independent life. Elsewhere the impressment gangs raided plantations, contraband camps, homes, churches, barbershops, and even a Fourth of July celebration. Some officers set up phony pay and ration distributions to facilitate captures.[32]

Those rounded up included boys, longtime free Blacks, the disabled, the sick, the employed, and caretakers for ill relatives. Families lost income, assistance, and contact from the impressed members. Some supervisors brutally treated the captured men and provided little in the way of provisions. One Federal observed: "My cattle at home are better cared for than these unfortunate persons." The callousness, lies, and violence involved deeply damaged the victims' trust in the Federals.[33]

Impressed workers sometimes filed formal complaints or held work stoppages to demand wages. Reformers protested impressment and occasionally could get one round of payments or improve a few conditions. During a massive 1864 impressment, Orlando Brown, a district freedmen's superintendent and paternalist, went with the men taken from Norfolk and tried to ensure humane treatment. He kept the laborers away from active combat areas and secured necessities for them as well as their families left behind.[34]

Private Sector Jobs

Most freedpeople eventually would need civilian employers. By 1864 most freedmen's departments encouraged or promoted the taking of local jobs by their charges, even though the openings tended to fall below the increased number of Black refugees. The Washington and Virginia Departments cut off rations, if a resident refused a job offer. Freedpeople resented such coercion, filed many substantial grievances about employers, and frequently made appeals for release from contracts along with restoration of rations.[35] The Freedmen's Department in the Washington area first excluded from service employers who failed to pay freedpeople or refused to house a servant's children with her. Eventually it fined those who mistreated workers or refused to pay. Some complaints arose from misunderstandings and minor matters, due to unfamiliarity with contracts and limited literacy.[36]

During 1863–65, more freedmen's departments complicated matters by trying to tax the wages of African Americans as a means of supporting aid programs and promoting civic duty. Saxton's low tax on plantation camp hands came to be paid in corn used to feed military livestock. Eaton's and Banks' taxes were moderate. However, Greene's tax, probably the highest one, stirred up bitter complaints. While taxes and camp charges went into a freedmen's fund, the deductions must have felt predatory to those earning low wages. Neither their collection nor accounting was done systematically.[37]

Programs for moving freedpeople outside the South for work contracts increased. Confederate attacks on Helena, Arkansas, caused the largest number of freedpeople to travel northward for jobs during 1863–65. The post commander issued free papers to each and shipped them to St. Louis. Because Missouri was still a slave state, the operation originally maintained a low profile in an effort to avoid riots or kidnappings. Superintendent Samuel Sawyer printed standard contracts with blanks that allowed the parties to fill in the specific terms. Given the North's wartime labor shortage, he contracted thousands to farmers in Illinois, Iowa, Kansas, and Wisconsin. The St. Louis Ladies Contraband Society paid for their transportation to employers. Similar but smaller programs operated at the Cairo camp and the new Cincinnati Freedmen's Home. However, racist neighbors of contracting parties sometimes drove out the hired Blacks.[38]

In 1864 General Butler directed Lieutenant Colonel Kinsman to advise freedwomen to take servant jobs in the North. The freedmen's departments of both Kinsman and Greene provided free transportation north for such workers. Emily Howland in Washington drew upon her northern contacts to create servant jobs compensated with education or training in skilled crafts.[39] Kinsman used a Philadelphia Quakers' group that arranged for paid jobs, as well as a New York employment organization that only required provision of necessities and some education in its contracts. A relatively small number of freedwomen agreed to go, and Butler soon had to stop Kinsman from using force. The return of some individuals who had gone north and suffered mistreatment discouraged the participation of others.[40]

The entrepreneur Bernard Kock in 1863 obtained Lincoln's support and finally won federal funding to ship 907 freedpeople from Alexandria and Fort Monroe to a lumbering colony in Haiti. This time it seems that no reformer at the two posts opposed it. The unscrupulous and inept Kock's operation quickly collapsed. In 1864 the federal navy brought the miserable survivors, along with 116 discontented emigrants from James Redpath's earlier program, to the Arlington contraband camp.[41]

During the later war years, most freedmen's departments adopted contract labor systems for agricultural hands in a major effort to create jobs and cut camp costs. Officials pressured the adult workforce, increasingly consisting of women, into this private sector work. In the Sea Islands, the 1863 land auction began the move of plantation hands into the private sector, and during 1864, most government plantation jobs ended. Although laborers generally preferred to stay at their ancestral homes, they disliked it when the new landowners sought increased production of long-staple cotton. Additionally, the varying contract terms offered by different white planters caused dissatisfaction. That year Philbrick's laborers received slightly better pay. When many workers and some reformers in early 1864 criticized all wages on the islands as too low, Philbrick retorted that a higher income would create laziness. He did allow his employees' families to take on as many cash-earning field tasks as they wished but started withholding a portion of pay until after the harvest. As the land auctions provoked more labor conflict, he did raise wages a little more in response. As friction continued, T. Edwin Ruggles, a supervisor on one of Philbrick's plantations, felt that his work had become "a thankless task." In the end, damage done by an army worm infestation probably made the islands' cotton crop unprofitable that year. Before the war's end, long-staple cotton production was in decline.[42]

Tense labor relations in 1864 moved Saxton to regulate contracts. His minimal rules required all employers to sign written contracts with workers and to file them with the Freedmen's Department, which soon started to review and enforce contract terms. The general also required payment of workers before the shipping of cotton. He opened a military bank for safekeeping freedmen's savings, similar to Butler's, and required teachers to explain its operation to freedpeople. It had a much larger amount of deposits ($65,000) than Butler's one by the end of the year.[43]

The semislave, semifree labor system in southern Louisiana bore some resemblance to a contract labor system. After the Emancipation Proclamation, slaveholders hoped to turn the state's exemption into a full restoration of slavery, while Blacks struggled for full freedom. General Banks merely modified the system by requiring that planters accept a contract detailing the army's terms, which now allowed either lower wages or a share of crop proceeds paid at the year's end. African Americans abandoned by Confederate owners could farm their home plantations independently but sometimes lacked the cash to do much. The army still put laborers who fled employers into contraband camps where most labored without pay for the army. Through superintendents Hanks and Conway, camp residents could make contracts with Unionist planters and northern lessees of abandoned plantations. Plantation camps mostly with unemployable elderly, orphans, and infirm persons became known as home farms in this and other contract labor systems. Superintendents expected those residents to work as much as they could.[44]

Conflict had characterized the Louisiana labor system from the beginning. Hands often held work stoppages to seek the reinstatement of old privileges and the addition of new ones. Landowners bribed federal officials to overlook whipping and used soldiers (even keeping a few on plantations) to halt employee resistance.[45] Criticism from antislavery Blacks and northerners pushed Banks to revise the program in 1864 to include free choice of employer, signing a written contract, better compensation, use of a garden plot, and a military bank for laborers. However, he also allowed disciplinary pay penalties and preserved some slave code regulations, such as bans on selling goods, possessing guns, or leaving the plantation without a pass. That year most planters would only agree to a post-harvest compensation by crop shares, which Blacks deeply disliked. The rules changed for the minority still on wages by withholding half of their pay until the year's end, while agricultural laborers in the North received full wages monthly. Army officials tried to justify these devices for controlling and exploiting workers with the common white belief in Black laziness.[46]

After Louisiana emancipation in 1864, contention increased over compensation, food, work hours, and privileges. The white Unionist government retained a legal obligation for the freed to have job contracts. However, some wives, copying the gender ideal for white women, refused to do field work. Ongoing military rule enabled Banks to create additional regulations to protect laborers in some ways, but many planters used penalties and charges to eliminate pay. Provost marshals started to have numerous contract issues to resolve, and only a minority sought justice for Black laborers. Superintendents Hanks and Conway claimed to protect Black interests, but the former lost his office due to corruption charges and the latter failed in his effectiveness. The state's freedpeople received little compensation and much oppression. As contract labor to them seemed a means to perpetuate a form of slave labor, sugar production declined.[47]

The army's Adjutant General Lorenzo Thomas, a former slaveholder, went to the Mississippi Valley in 1863 to start both a contract labor system and Black enlistment. He hoped that the two programs would end suffering and rising expenditures in contraband camps. That spring, Thomas ordered as many freedpeople as possible in the area around Milliken's Bend, Louisiana, hired to white Unionists and northerners leasing abandoned cotton plantations. He set low fixed wages and food as their compensation. The adjutant general slowly expanded the project during the year to several other parts of the valley. Sometimes naval vessels collected Black refugees from along the rivers, delivered the men to recruiting camps and the women to contraband camps hiring out contract laborers. While Eaton had focused on developing plantation camps for his charges, he found Thomas hostile to that alternative and bowed to his superior's plan. Some paternalistic reformers, like Abner Olds, enthusiastically favored this large-scale employment opportunity. Whatever camp staff thought of it, they had to support it. Thomas hoped that the camps would shrink into home farms.[48]

The program dramatically worsened many freedpeople's lives in the Mississippi Valley, and likely alienated some from reformers. Many hands feared that the program would lead to reenslavement, especially given the participation of Unionists who had been slaveholders. A number of Blacks abandoned earlier by enslavers lost control of their home plantations and had to apply for employment there or elsewhere. Although a few lessees were reformers, most seem to have only cared about profits.[49] Some hired former slave overseers as assistants. Field hands reported that lessees whipped, overworked, under-provisioned, and outright failed to pay them. Once trouble erupted, some freedpeople fled back to the contraband camps, and some of the men enlisted because that paid better.[50]

Confederate guerrillas targeted leased plantations to reenslave the Blacks and destroy their crops. Thomas ignored freedpeople's and reformers' worries about security. Confederate attacks, Federal appropriation of supplies, labor conflict, army worms, and sometimes late planting ruined many of the white lessees' finances in 1863. Only the minority of workers who received honest treatment and had safe locations willingly renewed contracts.[51]

After a brief interval in 1864, when the Treasury Department took over and reworked the contract labor systems in Eaton's and Hanks' departments, General Thomas reinstated and modified his terms. He also extended his program to the Department of the Cumberland. The new contracts made a small wage increase in response to the Treasury's plan for higher pay. Resolving one issue, adult men's pay rose to the same level as that of soldiers. Employers could offer more than the minimum pay, but that only happened in northeast Louisiana and middle Tennessee. The Adjutant General tried to please freedpeople by requiring compensation to include food, shelter, clothing, medical care, and education. However, Thomas also incorporated Banks's behavioral rules, wage penalties, and option for partial pay withholding until the year's end. The last two provisions created big problems for workers through yearlong dependency and uncertainty about income. Special provost marshals would enforce the terms of the contract labor system on both sides.[52]

Many freedpeople resisted signing up due to unfavorable new terms, a reduction of wages from the level announced by the Treasury, and the continuing guerrilla danger. Col. Samuel Thomas, Eaton's district superintendent for the lower Mississippi, harshly contended that "The best we can do is, to place his labor on an equal footing with white labor, and neither endow him with a fortune, nor open up his road to jump at once to ease and affluence that he does not know how to use or enjoy." Lorenzo Thomas accepted coercion as a means to achieve the freedpeople's transition to wage labor, and Eaton complied by directing camp superintendents to use military force, if necessary, to get the able-bodied to sign contracts. Many superintendents resorted to cutting off rations and using the urban pass systems to force the unemployed into the contract labor system.[53]

Thomas' 1864 system resulted in numerous complaints, involving all the old as well as new issues. At this point the program mostly applied to women, estimated by one historian as 69 percent of the contract laborers in Eaton's department. The forcing of many soldiers' wives into this work worried their husbands and damaged morale.[54] Some of the newly hired did not even have adequate clothing yet, and camp superintendents had to forward shipments upon arrival to employers. Employees shortchanged on necessities resisted by withholding work and devoting more time to independent enterprises. Contract laborers conscripted by overly eager military recruiters felt they'd been duped. Only reformer lessees opened schools, and few teachers agreed to work in rural areas. Workers resisted contracting with their former slaveholders. A girl so contracted later recalled discontentedly that her employer expected to be called "master" and worked her as hard as in the past.[55]

Increased Confederate raiding in 1864 drove numerous hands into garrisoned towns. The Freedmen's Department sometimes tried to force them back to the plantations. By the end of 1864, most laborers again had meager or no earnings, and many resisted signing up again. The 1865 contract labor system in the Mississippi Valley essentially continued the program and its abuses. Eaton disliked the system but could do nothing other than offer more land leases for Blacks. One historian judges the program's advocates as naive about all the difficulties it faced.[56]

In the Department of Virginia, the emphasis on plantation camps allowed relatively few whites to lease abandoned land and contract Black laborers. Only the Eastern Shore district had many freedpeople in a contract labor program. Because numerous labor conflicts arose after the Unionist state government's enactment of emancipation, Col. Frank J. White, the district's new superintendent, required Blacks—except for skilled workers and a limited number of the self-employed—to hire themselves for farm work. White Unionist officials collected job openings and wrote contracts to be enforced by provost marshals. The terms prohibited physical punishment by employers and insubordination by employees. Despite the absence of a wage scale and the presence of a labor shortage, coerced contracting kept wages low. In each of the two Eastern Shore counties Colonel White established a freedmen's home exclusively for the orphans, elderly, and disabled.[57] This program partly resembled the contract labor systems in the western war theater.

The contract labor systems in 1864 involved around 125,000 workers, plus numerous dependents. Fitting best with the laissez-faire reformers' views, the systems shrank paternalistic programs built around contraband camps, although some camps were refilled by new residents. Reformers and the contracted could do relatively little about the program's main problems. These programs often operated at their worst in the Mississippi River Valley with much exploitation and suffering for the African Americans involved. Forced enrollment of freed persons into the system created a fundamental policy contradiction; this fed Black suspicions about the reformers required to carry out the policy. The Lincoln administration seems to have concluded that most freedpeople would become agricultural laborers, not landowning peasantry. Many officials in contract labor systems likely shared Philbrick's belief in "keeping the control of the work, in the hands of white men."[58]

Military Service

The last type of employment, military service, involved around 200,000 Black men during 1863–65. After the final Emancipation Proclamation, the Lincoln administration authorized the raising of numerous Black units. Kansas reformers, who had rushed without permission into recruiting African Americans in 1862 and then could not pay them, now received approval with the stipulation that the regiment eliminate African Americans from positions as commissioned officers. Units created in Louisiana and the District of Columbia also had to make that humiliating change. Many freedmen would have felt more comfortable with Black officers, but the War Department issued few such commissions during the war. The predominately white officers held a range of views about their men. Those who held typical northern prejudices only wanted higher rank and salary. Laissez-faire and paternalistic reformers choosing to serve in the United States Colored Troops (USCT) shared a belief in a degree of Black inferiority but in time might improve their attitudes. Egalitarians probably just composed a minority of officers.[59] Unequal treatment of Blacks would often appear in the USCT.

African Americans who had already reached Federal lines and wanted to fight to end slavery eagerly enlisted. One gave up his well-paid job because "money was worthless to him without freedom." Some paternalistic reformers had long upheld a gender ideal created by militant abolitionists that only fighting for freedom would develop Black manhood and prove it to white doubters. While working in the Sea Islands, William Allen gruffly commented that "I wish sincerely that something would turn up to make these men more willing to fight for their freedom—they have got it altogether too easily." As it happened, some of the enslaved had cultivated a similar ideal of violent defense against oppression. Sergeant Prince Rivers declared that "we sogers are men—de first time in our lives. Now we can look at our old masters in de face" and he sternly looked down on those who avoided enlistment.[60]

Daring recruiters turned to areas outside a post or even Federal lines. The navy found many replacement sailors among Black refugees picked up during patrols. USCT officers often marched their troops into rural areas or isolated Confederate territory to draw enlistees. One recruiter hovered around gristmills beyond Pulaski, Tennessee, to make his pitch to slaves sent there on business. Those desiring enlistment asked him to carry it out in the form of conscription in front of their enslavers in an attempt to prevent retaliation against their families.[61] When an enslaved man escaped to enlist, especially in the zone exempted from the Emancipation Proclamation, his family members frequently suffered for it, such that often they later fled to the Federals. The Militia Act of 1862 freed both the recruits, as well as their wives, children, and mothers, although the families usually had to escape the enslaver first.[62]

Recruiters also commonly met newly arriving freedom seekers at the picket lines. Eaton noted an advantage in making this occur "before their minds have been corrupted by life at private service, or in the cities." Once into new communities, they could prioritize family unity, good pay, and independence over enlistment. They might also have alienating experiences with Federal soldiers. Samuel Johnson in Florida lost his desire to enlist when he saw Black soldiers hospitalized in a filthy horse stable with little care. Another ex-slave summed matters up: "We would like to fight for them, if they would only treat us like men."[63]

At a unique, candle-lit meeting during a night in May 1863, the African American leaders in New Bern, North Carolina, put pistols to a white recruiter's head and forced him to swear agreement to their conditions: equal compensation, provision of necessities for the families, jobs for the wives, education for the children, and a commitment to force the Confederacy to treat captured Black soldiers as legitimate prisoners. Despite the recruiter's inability to guarantee these terms, local enlisting, slow until then, subsequently rose. Perhaps the actual purpose was to send a strong message to his superiors. As other African Americans told Federals what they needed to enlist, Congress responded in 1864 by raising Black soldiers' pay to the same level as whites' as well as granting a $300 enlistment bounty and pensions for those disabled by service.[64]

Many recruiters in federally controlled areas eventually found themselves obliged to provide for recruits' families in contraband camps, often ones exclusively for them. Such a camp at Athens, Alabama, supplied Tom W. Woods's family with "plenty of good food and clothes." In the Department of Virginia and North Carolina, General Butler guaranteed rations, fuel, and housing for the soldiers' families. He also added pressure on men to enlist by lowering unskilled military workers' pay to that of Black soldiers in his army department and limiting those jobs to men unfit to be soldiers.[65]

When army and navy officers could not get enough men voluntarily, many turned to conscription. As noted already, some paternalists held that freedmen should be made to do what was good for them, despite egalitarian and laissez-faire reformers' objections. While the draft could liberate the enslaved from owners, it also coerced the unwilling. White officers often sent Black volunteers, enthusiastic about enlistment and proving manhood, to collect freedmen in a manner similar to impressment patrols.[66] Once again, compulsion caused antagonism and distrust. Press gangs might beat or even shoot those who resisted or fled. If possible, freedmen disappeared into hiding or, if caught, deserted. One probable draftee in the Sea Islands asserted to his colonel that he did not want to fight, even to save others from slavery. Reformers' protests against conscription occasionally obtained the release of the objecting conscripts, but often commanders supported the roundups.[67]

A controversial development in some areas was the conscription or occasionally the voluntary enlistment of entire crews of military workers. Some reformer officers did this seeking to gain wages for unpaid laborers and to return the men to the same or similar duties by placement in a regiment designated just for laboring. In other cases, pressing military laborers into the army disrupted work in progress when the men were reassigned. That moved several commanders to restrict or to prohibit it.[68]

However enlisted, the men had to go through a quick and superficial medical exam. Many whose physical impediments should have discharged them were retained anyway, because unscrupulous officers wanted their units filled up as fast as possible. Military rejection in the border states would too likely have returned a man to an angry slaveholder, yet painful service in an inappropriate job was not desirable either. Examination of severely whipped bodies did modify the racial views of some regimental surgeons.[69]

The military resembled slavery in its demand for absolute obedience to white superiors. It quickly made this clear by giving recruits haircuts, scrubbing them clean, burning old clothes, dressing them in new uniforms, and enforcing strict discipline. The worst white officers acted like the worst slaveholders in roughly treating men whom they considered inferior. Freedmen resented being treated like slaves, such as being ordered to perform menial services for white troops. Most of all, they opposed military punishments that involved being tied up or whipped. Their criticism of the more barbarous military punishments won support from reformer officers. Still, disproportionate numbers of Blacks underwent trials by the army for mutiny and by the navy for insubordination. Elijah Marrs, a freedman enlistee, recognized the special dilemma that he and his comrades faced: "While I felt myself a free man and an U.S. soldier, still must I move at the command of a white man, and I said to myself is my condition any better now than before I entered the army? . . . The time will come when no man can say to me come and go, and I be forced to obey."[70]

Wise USCT officers disciplined with extra care and learned to use light punishment in most cases. They preferred to encourage pride in self-control and military skills. Clear rules, incentives, compassion, respect, working with the men, and modeling good behavior gained a better response than heavy-handedness. An appreciative private commented: "Our old masters would get angry with us and sometimes punish us almost to death, and we not understand why; but here if we are punished, we know why for the officers tell us our duty and never punish us unless we disobey."[71]

Training typically included some marksmanship but focused mostly on drill. Freedmen generally took military service seriously and so did well. Lt. Sam Evans had to admit that they learned the drill "much readier than I anticipated." Novice soldiers also received instruction in the common task of picket duty. Col. Thomas Wentworth Higginson went outside the lines on dark nights and tried to convince guards to let him through the lines without the password. None failed this test.[72]

Some colonels, due to personal preferences and doubts about the men, sought laboring or garrisoning service for their USCT regiments, and the army disproportionately assigned such duties to Blacks. Chap. George N. Carruthers complained in a report that "The regiment is worked too hard." While laboring units significantly aided the Union war effort, they might not do as much for the emancipation cause as those on the front lines. African American soldiers knew the significance of field service. When Pvt. George Hatton's infantry regiment first assembled with Black artillery and cavalry for an operation, he observed: "I felt as though I were in some other country where slavery was never known." Successful combat moved Black soldiers to assert that "We have grown three inches" and "I feel a heap more of a man." The performance of USCT in combat at LaGrange revised the stereotyped views of Lt. Sam Evans. He was not the only such case.[73]

A few white reformers thought that Black troops should take revenge for past abuses. When a Federal raid reached Pvt. William Harris' former home, Gen. Edward A. Wild, a militant abolitionist, presented a whip and directed him to use it on his ex-owner. A few of the enslaved asked the enlisted men to punish their slaveholder, but generally the soldiers preferred to liberate slaves.

After the well-publicized Confederate massacre of USCT at Fort Pillow, Black troops not surprisingly discussed vengeance. Some officers urged their men to give the enemy no quarter, but others opposed such a response as immoral. Most African American soldiers never faced an opportunity for revenge, and some refused to take it. Those who did usually did so on a small scale.[74]

Most of a soldier's or sailor's time went into routine camp and shipboard activities. On the rare occasion that USCT occupied barracks in the same camp as white troops, they usually would be excluded from washing and dining buildings. An egalitarian official of the Sanitary Commission, a soldiers' aid society, opened its facilities at Camp Nelson to them, until the post commander segregated the structure. African American sailors ate in separate messes, and, when friction arose in the close quarters of shipboard life, they generally had either to endure it or to desert.[75]

Some reformers tried to improve the personal lives of African American sailors and soldiers. General Butler required soldiers in the Department of Virginia and North Carolina to deposit one-third of their enlistment bounties in the bank he established. To encourage thrift, he only allowed USCT to withdraw the interest during the war. More commonly, officers managed company banks for the safekeeping of their men's savings. Some performed the service honestly, but others did not.[76]

Many regiments offered a school; some additionally created a library for the unit. Instructors did more than provide education. They enabled the soldiers, who had not yet attained literacy, to stay in touch with distant families by writing and reading letters. Some pressured the military men to give up drinking, smoking, gambling, card-playing, and profanity, as well as to convert to Christianity, on the ground that Black civilians looked up to them as good models. Ending the alleged vices was a tough sell for men in need of recreation. One private told Clara Duncan, a Black northern instructor, that, although he was deeply troubled about his soul, "it is so hard to be good in camp." Col. Thomas Morgan was unusual in requiring participation in prayers connected to most of his regiment's activities. The Reverend Carruthers made attendance at his Sunday services mandatory, but then discovered that the regiment's fatigue duties left many men too exhausted to come.[77]

A major problem for USCT and their dependents was discriminatory pay. At first the Militia Act of 1862 set it at just ten dollars a month minus the cost of clothes, substantially below what white soldiers received. Protests in one unit over the Black soldiers' initially lower pay led to convictions for mutiny. Black troops in several regiments refused to receive unequal pay, but family concerns probably prevented most units from doing so. Many reformer officers strongly supported equalization of their men's wages, and Congress, as already noted, enacted equal pay beginning in 1864. However, equal back pay first required being free before the war and later needed enlistment with equal pay promised. The army paid all soldiers irregularly, which created additional hardship for their families. Three months after General Saxton began recruiting, he borrowed money to provide an advance on unarrived pay but could not keep doing that.[78]

Soldiers with harsh officers, especially if assigned just to heavy labor, likely found the experience miserable. Those with respectful officers could find their service uplifting, as one observed: "This was the biggest thing that ever happened in my life. I felt like a man with my uniform on and a gun in my hand." This encouraged active support for freedom and equal rights. USCT took advantage of their new position to try to help escaping slaves. Some shared rations, tents, and pay with the severely destitute. Many went on private expeditions to assist escapes, especially ones that reunited families. One group in Henderson, Kentucky, even broke captured slaves out of the city jail in an unsuccessful effort to get them to freedom across the Ohio River. Obviously, many of these activities occurred without the officers' knowledge.[79]

During 1863–65, freedpeople encountered more new programs for employment than any other category. They had little input into these programs. Officials and many reformers prioritized helping the larger war effort: recruiting troops, financially aiding the government, lowering contraband camp costs, and maintaining order. Cheap Black labor benefited white employers but not economic development for the freed.[80]

The war had significantly begun the destruction of the southern slave labor system but had not firmly established a replacement. Several of the new models it offered had clear shortcomings. Paying Black laborers wages met with resistance from military and civilian whites. Furthermore, paternalists and many white officials doubted the ability of freedpeople to operate economically on their own, and favored reinstatement as subordinate farm hands. The authorities expanded their control over freedpeoples' work lives with employee passes, taxes, impressments, contract labor systems, and military conscription. These were the Federals' worst violations of freedpeople's liberty, and stirred up opposition from Blacks as well as laissez-faire and egalitarian reformers. Exploitation bred distrust and distance. Some of the freed evaded or resisted. Reformers supporting broader economic opportunities for Blacks ran into adverse decisions from higher officials but occasionally facilitated farm leases, land purchases, and paid military work.

7

Church and Community

The African American congregation at Mason's Island held a series of mass baptism ceremonies in the Potomac River. The seeming fulfillment of the old belief in divine deliverance from bondage probably helped to motivate such picturesque events and the general increase in religious conversions among the freed. The free distribution of Bibles and the expansion of literacy education likely benefited the trend. Both formerly enslaved preachers and northern missionaries eagerly gathered the harvest of souls. Religion played an important role in the new Black communities. In federally occupied towns, Black churches under a southern white minister generally ejected him, as soon as members felt it safe to do so. Some white missionaries sought, by one means or another, appointment as pastors of African American congregations; more served as chaplains in contraband camps. While paternalistic reformers sought to direct and control the lives of Black people, freedpeople increasingly acted on their own and asserted the need for a voice in all matters affecting their religious, family, and community life.[1]

Religion

The objections of the paternalists to the refugees' religion grew more numerous as time passed. Elkanah Beard, a Quaker chaplain and superintendent at Young's Point camp, groused that some residents mocked the sedate style of his prayer meetings. Most northerners who formed or took charge of congregations moved to restrict worship activities. The Reverend G. Greeley, new pastor of a Black Methodist Episcopal church in Portsmouth, Virginia, specifically stopped "wild jesticulations, extravagant noise, and great confusion." Similarly, a number of others, like Joel Baker at Baxter Plantation camp in east Virginia, pontificated: "I control these meetings and keep them respectably quiet." The Reverend William S. Bell, while he appreciated that "many indicated the warmth of the emotions by shouts and responses" during his service, decided that it was hopeless to try to change the parents' worship, and that he should concentrate on forming the children's tastes differently.[2]

The Reverend William O. King tried compromising by prohibiting only a few of what he considered their worst practices, because "if restricted to our modes of conducting meetings, would they not lose their interest in attending?" E. Eliza Lewis added that any objection to traditional religious practices "seems very much like trying to dam up a rushing river." Annie R. Wilkins realized that "they think they cannot worship God any other way . . . [and] we have to be very careful how we approach them, they are very sensitive." Reverend J. N. Mars, a sympathetic northern Black missionary, pointed out that southern white evangelicals had set an example of "jumping, and twisting, and tumbling, and dancing" motions at revivals. Consequently, many southern Blacks thought "we cant get religion without we fall down and rool [roll] and groan, this they call mourning for sin." He thought that only time and more familiarity with scripture could revise "old habits and forms of worship."[3] Several missionaries also complained about beliefs in erroneous doctrines, superstitions, visions, revelations in dreams, and the necessity of a longing (or "worrying") experience for months before conversion. Most freedpeople firmly held to their convictions. As one gently explained to Reverend King: "It doesn't seem as if we poor ignorant Africans could come to the Savior as you educated folks do, we have to worry it out."[4]

Freedpeople found themselves aggravated by the moralistic wrath of the missionaries, by their theological homilies, and by repeated calls for donations. Rhoda W. Smith, a missionary and one of the few female plantation camp supervisors, quickly alienated most residents from attending her Sunday services through sermons in which she criticized them. She then toned down the homilies and allowed those remaining to have control over a portion of the service. Probably without much success, Annie R. Wilkins pressured her adult students to pledge abstinence from smoking and drinking. The Reverend Albert Gladwin, superintendent of the Alexandria Freedmen's Home, uniquely antagonized worshippers by using camp guards to round them up forcibly when his bland services reduced attendance.[5] William H. Woodbury perceived that "to have white preachers still placed over them, is too much like old times, to meet with their approval. Their long silent preachers *want* to preach & the people prefer them." African American congregations soon ended the pastoral role of most northern whites, as the domineering ones tended to drive Blacks into autonomy. The exceptions were probably those who learned to compromise.[6]

Freedmen preachers, particularly the illiterate ones, encountered fault-finding from paternalists. Charles B. Wilder charged that "Such preaching as we get from the Colored Men with very few exceptions is but little better than nothing and in some instances worse." A few northerners, such as E. Eliza Lewis, reported positively on particular preachers, such as one who spoke "touchingly to their past sorrows and degradation, and to the present blessings which God was extending to them."[7] Like southern white churchmen had done, several missionaries ordained selected Black preachers. The Reverend Samuel G. Wright rejected certain applicants, because he claimed that "the Colored men who in days past occupied some position among their people because they could read a little or had the 'gift of gab' as we say are not always by any means the best class as Christians."[8]

Some northerners tried to take constructive steps to aid the preachers' work. Josiah Butler sensitively held a private reading class for Paw Paw Island's preachers so that no one else would observe them making mistakes. The Reverend Charles Strong created the Colored Ministers' Association in New Orleans to reduce rivalry and to offer some training. Northern Baptists organized a seminary for educating freedmen ministers in Washington.[9]

The Black missionaries of the African Methodist Episcopal and the African Methodist Episcopal Zion churches stressed religious independence from whites. Like most northern missionary operations, they only ordained literate freedmen preachers. These two rival denominations often fought each other as well as the predominately white northern Methodists over absorbing the separate Black congregations of the Southern Methodist Church. A church in New Bern invited the two African American churches to send competing candidates for its first Black pastor, and the African Methodist Episcopal Zion minister won it. Both denominations drew open opposition from independent and sometimes nonliterate Black preachers but, despite having very limited mission funds, experienced rapid growth. Simultaneously, northern Baptists also formed a number of southern congregations, usually under local Black presiders.[10]

Most white missionaries, unaffiliated with a Black congregation or a contraband camp, conducted a variety of activities. They typically visited the wounded or ill Black soldiers, held prayer meetings at hospitals, conducted funerals, did religious home visits, passed out tracts, and helped the needy. Several conducted bible study groups, sometimes by reading the bible to illiterates who especially appreciated hearing some passages for the first time. A few missionaries became USCT chaplains.[11]

Marcia Cotton of the American Missionary Association took on a unique assignment as a missionary and matron for Black prostitutes in a miliary prison on Craney Island after the contraband camp there closed. For them she held a daily prayer service, did a little teaching, ran a sewing circle, and wrote letters. She had several military guards removed for sexual relations with her charges. She had the authority to move some of the young women out of incarceration by placing them with supportive families. Cotton did not feel very successful, and after about nine months for unknown reasons the army closed the special prison.[12]

By 1864 many missionaries shifted most of their time to teaching. By then a number of educators, especially those affiliated with the AMA, considered themselves "missionary teachers." The Reverend William D. Harris, a northern Black minister, called on a recent convert among his young students to tell the class about her experience. He hoped to encourage more conversions, and her account moved her fellow students to tears. Missionaries and freedmen preachers opened many more Sunday schools for freedpeople during the latter part of the war. Some had separate classes for children and adults or for males and females; others mixed all the groups in each class. A few included white students. Most classes now relied on Bibles, catechisms, religious textbooks, or newsletters. Some Sunday schools held public programs to demonstrate what members had learned and to attract more participants.[13]

Family

By 1863 many more missionaries and army chaplains conducted weddings for freedpeople, sometimes involving numerous couples at once. All issued certificates, and some kept records in files or registry books. Adjutant General Lorenzo Thomas allowed John Eaton to authorize selected ministers and camp superintendents to perform the ceremony. In a variety of places army officers in Black regiments also did it. However, a division of opinion among the freed over formal marriage now become clear. Some long-married people considered a new ritual unnecessary. Some others considered marriage a private matter freely begun and ended by separation or choice, not the business of any other party. This made it much like its slave form without the enslaver.

They occasionally tried to wed new spouses, while ignoring the old ones, and may have succeeded in some cases.[14]

Eaton and a few other paternalistic officials joined Saxton in requiring formal matrimony of all who lived together in the contraband camps. At Slabtown, a missionary had couples who refused the ceremony tied to trees until they agreed to the ritual and his fee. A new post commander expelled him for it. Some commanders made nuptials a condition for a Black soldier to get family rations and visiting passes. In 1864 several regiments offered furloughs to many soldier-husbands to go to Vicksburg for registered weddings, to ensure that their spouses would receive benefits if they died during service.[15]

Formal matrimony sometimes led to painful choices between past and current spouses as well as in the allocation of children, all while facing varying rules set by officials. Some freed persons entered a wartime marriage with a private agreement that they could return to a previous mate, if located. Elizabeth Botume and some other reformers found these matters baffling, and favored letting those involved work things out.[16] Others, believing in permanent marital obligations, demanded formal marriages solemnizing the first pairing, as necessary to follow divine law and to set the proper example for youth. Some officials used enticements—such as family Bibles, new clothes, and fancy ceremonies—in an effort to encourage participation.[17]

Although Black refugees in the cities faced new temptations that could threaten marital unions in the absence of their old supporting communities, the greatest danger to families during the war was the Federal army. When the military governor of Washington in 1863 revived an effort to apprentice some Camp Barker children to cut costs, families held together by fleeing into shantytowns. Military enlistments and labor impressments took numerous men some distance from their wives and children. The mothers then had to head their families by themselves for the time being. This situation could be hard on women new to it, but even a woman who had her own household during enslavement (due to having a slaveholder different from her husband's) encountered new wartime challenges. Absence tended to foster worries about a partner's well-being and loyalty. A major problem was losing track of a spouse's location without further contact. Destitution and/or loneliness might drive an individual to seek a new partner.[18]

Letters became crucial to preserving family contact and finding lost members. According to reformer Elizabeth James, "each one is a case of *necessity*." Illiterate freedpeople asked aid workers to spend much time writing letters and then reading the responses to the correspondent. Spouses wanted messages to stress their devotion and need for faithfulness. Courting persons only asked young, single reformers to write their love letters. Elizabeth Botume judged that "these letters for the freed people were our best means of becoming acquainted with their characters and needs and of helping them." Aid workers, like Henry Rountree, penned so many that they requested a supply of stationery from their sponsoring organization. The Christian Commission provided USCT chaplains with those materials so as to keep soldiers in touch with their families.[19]

A Black soldier's wife who grew frustrated with separation might take her family long distances in search of her husband. If she found him, she insisted on living in his camp or nearby. A close but separate home resembled the situation of a spouse who lived with a different owner during slavery. Some wives now wanted to adopt the role of white counterparts and expected a spouse to be the breadwinner. However, irregular pay, a local policy denying rations to dependents, or an enlistee's spending habits prevented reliance on his income. Thus, many of these wives, especially if they did not have little children, had to take on paid work. A suffering family could also tempt a husband to leave camp without a pass but with military tools to build a shanty or to obtain food for dependents. Such disciplinary problems contributed to some reformers' opposition to marriage for enlisted freedmen.[20] If a commander forcibly tried to relocate the dependents to a distant contraband camp or job, the troops and reformer officers objected. The wives might return on their own or be retrieved by husbands. The best alternative for all was for reformer officers to set up a contraband camp for the families in a safe area at enough distance to limit yet allow contact. The best of these sites provided the wives with space for large gardens.[21]

The expanded Black refugee population also meant more orphans. A few Black adults allegedly exploited these youths for their rations and for work as beggars or prostitutes. Strong Black families continued to absorb some orphans. Several freedwomen caringly collected groups of orphans that aid workers with more resources later took under supervision.[22]

In 1863 Rachel G. C. Patten left Camp Barker to start a new orphanage in Norfolk, and later moved it to Portsmouth. The orphanage she left at Camp Barker probably moved to Arlington and then to Georgetown under a harsh, new director, whose dismissal other reformers eventually secured. In 1863, when the medical director at Alexandria wanted to collect orphans in a room at the smallpox hospital for Blacks, Wilbur "concluded that it was not my duty to remain quiet & see this outrage go on." She and Harriet Jacobs found this, their first challenge of a male official, became a transformative experience: "We were in such a state of nervous excitement, that we were all of a tremble, & we had such a head ache too!" They successfully convinced the post commander to let them create an orphanage for the youths in the Alexandria Freedmen's Home instead. On several occasions Jacobs took some orphans to the North for adoption. The Alexandria orphanage did not last long, as the Georgetown orphanage became the Washington Department's only one in 1864.[23]

Other new orphanages opened during 1863–65 at Yorktown, Hampton, Fernandina, New Orleans, Natchez, Island No. 63, Helena, Vicksburg, Young's Point, Corinth, Memphis, Nashville, Charleston (South Carolina,) and Richmond (Virginia).[24] An 1864 guerrilla raid led to the relocation of orphans from Vicksburg to Helena, but a new orphanage soon opened back in Vicksburg. At Natchez a federal official unwisely expropriated a mansion and assessed secessionists a large sum to finance an orphanage there. The penalized whites spitefully made the institution's staff fear retaliation, even assassination.[25]

Orphanages focused on basic care at first, since it took some time to build up furnishings and supplies, while the number of young residents rose. Many started with large houses, either appropriated by the army or bought by donors. The army provided rations and sometimes a guard. These institutions required substantial aid from a charitable association and in some cases further fundraising in the North. Local Blacks volunteered services, as well as small donations of cash, sewing, and delicacies. A staff, mostly freedpeople who earned just a subsistence, handled a range of tasks including most childcare, laundry, and maintenance.[26]

Orphanages imposed order and discipline on the children. Older orphans were assigned household chores and sometimes formed into groups for knitting, sewing, or making small market products. A few directors instituted a strict regime by forbidding such things as tobacco use or marble games. The Helena orphanage's director made one girl labor at a contraband camp until her attitude improved. Patten slapped a girl hard enough to cause a bleeding nose because of the child's carelessness that almost killed a baby. William H. Woodbury, the AMA's local manager, reported Patten to the association's leaders, who upon investigation dropped the case. In a time of commonplace physical punishment, Patten loudly complained that Woodbury wrongly treated her as the "vilest of the vile."[27]

During the war, orphanages reunited some juveniles with relatives or placed them, usually with local Black families. A few white reformers, like Emily Howland, adopted one. A small number went to Black orphanages in the North, although Julia Wilbur prevented this in newly fallen Richmond, Virginia, probably because it undermined the children's chance of reconnecting with relatives. Other youths left the institutions through a job, escape, or death.[28]

Social Concerns

Reformer counselors continued to crusade against assumed shortcomings of Blacks, many of whom had and acted upon those same values. Some claimed gains against drinking and cursing but rarely against the very common use of tobacco. Aid workers sometimes gave out brooms in a crusade for higher domestic standards. The determined Esther Hawks, when dissatisfied during home visits, would request a housecleaning on the spot. In Norfolk, Mary M. Reed noted: "When a teacher enters a lane it is the signal for all the brooms to be brought into requisition. . . . There is a show of improvement, at least, and that is much towards securing the desired result." However, little could be done in homes with dirt floors and decrepit structures.[29]

Superintendents could incorporate some of these matters into camp discipline. At Arlington, Lt. Col. Elias M. Greene ordered that idleness, poor work, untidiness, and uncleanliness would lead to a temporary loss of either sugar rations or passes. The "accumulation of filth" near a living area meant expulsion. A civil infraction resulted in a trial; conviction meant major privilege loss, a fine, or imprisonment. Probably by this time, most officials had dropped physical punishments other than incarceration as too reminiscent of slavery.[30]

New social work issues arose in 1863–65. When a distraught mother complained after Lieutenant Colonel Kinsman ordered her daughter and niece to jobs in the North, Patten overlooked the use of force but showed her letters from former orphans who were doing well in the North. At Cairo planters and steamboat captains repeatedly disrupted school in search of servants, most often girls, but Tacy Hadley, suspicious of sexual abuse or reenslavement, consistently refused them. After Wilbur complained for months about the Alexandria military prison for Black offenders, a new administrator had the cells cleaned, regulated the guards' interaction with prisoners, stopped forced showers, placed a screen around the females' shower, and ended enforcement of the town's Black curfew. Maria Lewis, a very muscular teenager who scouted for the Federals, told Wilbur, perhaps after persuasion, that she "wishes to [adopt] womanly ways and occupations." The reformer replaced the girl's masculine clothes with feminine ones and obtained a new job for her.[31]

Community Actions and Politics

Unlike social work, new community-building involved few aid workers. African Americans generally built community through their churches, schools, and activities. A few northern participants, like Wilbur, attended Blacks' events to encourage those "trying to do something for themselves."[32] She noted their pride in the USCT, shown by Freedmen's Home girls, who made a large amount of lemonade for Black troops. In a number of places, both freedpeople and reformers cared for or took special food to the Black soldiers in hospitals. Learning that northern females made regimental flags, freedwomen did likewise for some units in the District of Columbia, North Carolina, South Carolina, Louisiana, Tennessee, and Kentucky. These flags, according to speakers at formal presentations, held special meaning for the community. When Harriet Jacobs gave a flag to the Black troops' L'Ouverture Hospital at an Alexandria ceremony in 1864, she stressed: "Three years ago this flag had no significance for you, but today . . . Soldiers you have made it the symbol for the freedom of the slave." The Emancipation Proclamation had helped to link African Americans to the United States government.[33]

Black urban neighborhoods held their own emancipation anniversary and Fourth of July celebrations with wide participation, despite southern laws against large Black gatherings. Organizers invited northerners to attend. The African Americans dressed in their best clothes or group regalia for parades that included USCT units, military laborers, businessmen, craftsmen, students, clubs, and bands. One procession in New Bern stopped and cheered at the quarters of leading northern reformers along the route. Floats commonly depicted slavery's evils, as well as Miss Liberty. Walkers carried banners that read "Our country, our liberty, and our rights" and "Freedom with Poverty, rather than Slavery with Luxury" as expressions of commitment to patriotism and racial change. When all gathered before a stage, speakers often recalled their experiences in slavery and thanked God for deliverance. The crowd sang hymns with lines like "We must fight for liberty" and "Sound the Loud Timbral over Egypt's Dark Sea, Jehovah Hath Triumphed and My People Are Free." Programs could also involve prayers, readings, dancing, and eating. The celebrations deliberately took place in public spaces that Blacks had rarely, if ever, previously accessed, such as a District of Columbia event on the White House grounds. The participants borrowed some forms from whites' events but presented different content that began to shape a group memory of emancipation connected to American history and ideals.[34]

These events differed from celebrations organized by white reformers in that Blacks presided and predominated on the programs. Ceremonies controlled by reformers during 1863–65 had, at most, small portions designed by Blacks.[35] While the reformers' festivities stressed orderliness, the Blacks' activities sometimes incorporated ribald mockery of the Confederacy. Several parades included slavery's coffin and mock mourners. Banners declared: "Old Massa's Done Gone and Left Us" and "Jeff. Davis, the Great Abolitionist." James Redpath, superintendent of Black schools in Charleston, South Carolina, after the city's fall, asked the pupils in a march not to sing the "Hang Jeff Davis from a sour apple tree" verse of "John Brown's Body," but they did so loudly and repeatedly. Whether northern reformers or southern Blacks organized public gatherings, they generally tried to abide by the laws other than the discriminatory Black codes.[36]

During the war talented freedmen, who rose in income or status joined prosperous freeborn Blacks in the African American community leadership. The two groups began to hold mass political meetings with or without permission. In the North Black leaders had long supported full legal equality and had made some legal gains, including enfranchisement in a few states. Their major newspapers, the *New York Anglo-African* and the *Philadelphia Christian Recorder*, attracted some Black subscribers in the occupied South. During 1863–65, the *Anglo-African's* editor, Robert Hamilton, gave speeches to African Americans while touring federally controlled areas in Virginia, North Carolina, Maryland, Kentucky, and Tennessee.[37]

In November 1863, before Louisiana ended slavery, a meeting of free Black men in New Orleans was the first in the wartime South to advocate the vote but just for themselves. In January 1864, general gatherings of African Americans at Norfolk and Beaufort (North Carolina) endorsed Black male suffrage. The next month, a similar assemblage in New Orleans passed resolutions in favor of full equal rights for their race. During the following summer, freedmen in Leavenworth, Kansas, organized a suffrage club. Advocacy of suffrage and other rights marked a major expansion of freedpeople's view of liberty. Believers in divine deliverance supported the new goal due to their very hopeful outlook. Those with an outlook dominated by pragmatism might see some chance for it but gave more weight to white opposition.[38]

The 1864 Beaufort and New Orleans meetings subsequently sent delegations to lobby for the franchise in Washington. After leaving Washington several Beaufort delegates, including Abraham Galloway, further supported the cause with a speaking tour in the North. The New Orleans group prompted Lincoln's unsuccessful recommendation that white Unionists reconstructing Louisiana's government consider giving certain Blacks the vote. The state constitutional convention in 1864 debated the matter and compromised by allowing the legislature to extend the franchise in the future.[39] Responding to requests, several white teachers did agree to read Republican newspapers to freedmen seeking to develop their political knowledge. A few reformers endorsed Black suffrage, but those believing in romantic racialism, either expressed doubts or kept silent about it.[40]

Freedpeople understood that the 1864 presidential election served as a referendum on emancipation and the war. Several Sea Island Blacks, including Robert Smalls and Sgt. Prince Rivers, tried to win spots on the delegation to the National Republican Convention. Support from some reformers led a local convention in Beaufort to make these individuals, some of whom advocated Black suffrage, alternate representatives, but the national meeting rejected the entire delegation. In Memphis and Nashville, Blacks attended Republican gatherings. Many marched in Nashville to support the Abraham Lincoln and Andrew Johnson ticket. On two occasions when whites threw rocks at them, a brief exchange of gunshots resulted in a few casualties.[41]

A National Convention of Colored Men—called by northern Black leaders to meet on October 4–7, 1864, at Syracuse, New York—drew delegations from the District of Columbia, Virginia (Alexandria, Norfolk, and Portsmouth), North Carolina (New Bern and Roanoke), Florida (Jacksonville), Louisiana (New Orleans), Mississippi (Vicksburg), Tennessee (Memphis and Nashville), and Missouri (St. Louis). The meeting voted for nationwide emancipation and equal rights, including suffrage. It thanked several white and Black organizations for educating freedpeople. Finally, it formed an Equal Rights League to lobby for improvements in race relations.[42]

On election day in Nashville, two African American leaders held a mock vote in which over three thousand Black men voted nearly unanimously for Lincoln. Some freedpeople there joined white celebrations after the Republican victory. In Washington a small group of Blacks attended the post-election presidential receptions, although several White House staffers tried to exclude them. Wilbur noted that the Lincolns treated those who got in the same as the white guests. She also observed fifty young freedmen riding horses in Lincoln's inaugural parade.[43]

Southern Black leaders in North Carolina, Tennessee, Louisiana, and Virginia responded to the National Convention of Colored Men by quickly organizing active Equal Rights League chapters. The North Carolina chapter in 1865 organized New Bern's emancipation anniversary celebration and obtained free railroad transportation for Blacks from nearby towns. Also in January 1865, the Tennessee chapter sent a Black suffrage petition to the white Unionists' state constitutional convention. Sympathetic Unionists introduced the proposal, but the convention, somewhat like Louisiana's, instead allowed the next legislative session to revise suffrage qualifications. In Norfolk, African Americans did try to vote for a candidate at a local Republican convention but had their ballots rejected.[44]

Americans commonly link the right to vote with the right to hold office. In the later war years, some white reformers willingly experimented with the idea of Black officeholders. A few instructors created school boards of appointed freedmen. In the Sea Islands, General Saxton allowed Saxtonville to elect a Black supervisor for community cleanliness. A post commander at Mitchelville subsequently authorized the election of a governing council under the white superintendent. The board had power over schools, sanitation, public order, and taxes. At Davis Bend, Col. John Eaton permitted election of a number of Black officeholders, including the reinstitution of plantation judges begun decades earlier by the Confederate president's brother. Eaton also put the elected officials under the camp superintendent.[45]

Few reformers seem to have recorded an evaluation of the Black officials. Horace James, though, judged the Roanoke camp residents' advisory board, which he appointed, as worthless because of the members' illiteracy, along with what he judged to be too much infighting and too little public support. However, his cousin Elizabeth James thought that a daily meeting on community issues, which she and one board member held, worked very well. Saxton's superintendent on St. Simon's and Sapelo Islands in Georgia, held an election of African American governors, and rated their efforts highly. Robert Smalls and Harry McMillan thought that freedmen should not hold governmental offices until they became educated. Sgt. Prince Rivers, though, felt ready. Freedmen could not help but understand that whites controlled the political system upon which they depended for their legal freedom and rights.[46]

The freedman David D. Williamson wrote that "we have rights that must be respected by this nation." During the war, Black activists focused on rights achievable through sympathetic government officials. Some leaders, like Abraham Galloway, distinguished between political rights desired now and social rights desired in the future. A freedman in Portsmouth upset a white reformer by declaring that he was "as ready to fight the North as the South, if the North denies them the full rights of American citizens." Sergeant Rivers announced in a speech that he "meant to knock at the door of the Union till he got his rights, or die knocking." Several groups passed resolutions or circulated petitions for the repeal of laws restricting Blacks. A mass meeting of Blacks in Alexandria passed a resolution demanding that, until the town repealed its racially discriminatory laws, it should continue under the military government, which had suspended those laws.[47]

Equal access to urban transportation formed a major concern for freedpeople and egalitarian reformers. In St. Louis during early 1864, an abolitionist officer in a Black regiment always had his men sit with him on horse-drawn streetcars and ignore the rule that required Blacks to ride on the outside platform. The Union Aid Society, formed by Black women in that city, secured permission to ride inside the cars on Saturdays when the group visited African American soldiers in hospitals. In Washington, Black soldiers, ministers, and Sojourner Truth protested against segregation on street railways. In response, Congress exercised its jurisdiction over the District of Columbia to ban the practice there. When one line's conductors disobeyed the new law, African Americans mounted "a spirited contest" for equal seating. Wilbur and some other egalitarians, who had previously objected to a segregated ferry, likely supported the campaign.[48]

During 1863–65 some Federal military courts allowed Blacks two important judicial rights: testifying and suing (prohibited by southern state laws). The army pragmatically instituted the first one, because slaves often knew about slaveholders' pro-Confederate activities. Increasing contact with army officials, especially provost marshals who had charge of maintaining order, led Blacks to report whites who owed money to them, physically abused them, or would not release enslaved children. The first issue probably led to the most cases, and many white debtors likely ended the matter by fleeing. Relatively few reformer officials agreed to investigate and sometimes take these issues to a military trial. When freedwomen complained about unpaid wages, the provost marshal in St. Louis ignored state law (which denied property rights to women) and often ruled in favor of the freedwomen. However, superiors overruled a number of those decisions. Reformer officers on military commissions and courts martial made an effort to treat African Americans fairly.[49] Judicial rights to testifying and suing arose from military governance and so would not necessarily last beyond the war.

In 1864 a Black preacher used biblical imagery to declare that "we just got from de Red Sea and wander in de dark wilderness" in order to convey sorrow arising from lost homes and many deaths as well as the ongoing struggle to build new lives.[50] Freedom provided a foundation upon which to seek more rights. Drives to unify families, to undo injustices, and to achieve more rights either required or benefited from whites' cooperation. Many whites, including even some reformers, resisted equal rights for African Americans, especially in politics. As freedpeople's goals only had the support of egalitarians, their efforts regarding religion and community-building aimed for a degree of autonomy in further developing the freedom they wanted.

8

Education

The American Missionary Association started schools in Missouri in 1863, even though military authorities barely tolerated and would not protect Black education. The next year J. L. Richardson, an AMA teacher in St. Louis, created tensions when he tried to entice students from a Black teacher's tuition school to his free one. Another AMA official, George Condee, simultaneously was trying to convince the city's Black leaders to form a supervisory board of education that would raise the funds needed to make all the schools for African Americans free. Although Black teachers expressed fear of losing their living, community leaders eventually formed the board on the basis that the system be "taught by Colored teachers as far as 'practical'" and that all instructors receive equal treatment.[1]

The African American board would not obtain public school funds generated from taxes until after state emancipation and the subsequent repeal of the ban on Black education in early 1865. Because of this, the board initially solicited donations with a notice in the AMA's magazine. Indicating a desire for some of that organization's money and teachers, the board selected an AMA agent as the system's superintendent. At his urging, the AMA provided one Black teacher for St. Louis, though it spent months on the search process. By the time of the hire, proslavery whites had burned down a Black church that housed an AMA school.[2] The case of St. Louis illustrated some of the Black schools' challenges during 1863–65: bulging enrollments, rising costs, the need for more organization, the desire to improve educational experiences, freedpeople's preference for more Black teachers, and rising hostility from southern whites. Despite difficulties, education greatly expanded and improved during the later war years.

New Schools

Swelling numbers of Black refugees caused a proliferation of schools for freedpeople everywhere behind Federal lines. Where the schools already existed, aid associations shipped in more teachers. New ones appeared soon after advancing Federals took towns. In a number of cities, like St. Louis, African Americans created fundraising organizations to provide some support usually for Black teachers. In all border states, northerners now tried to plant schools. The AMA's effort in West Virginia quickly ended. In New Castle, Delaware, one teacher started instruction on her own. In Kentucky aid association efforts seem limited to Columbus, Camp Nelson, and Louisville. After Maryland ended slavery, the Baltimore Association for the Moral and Educational Improvement of the Colored People, created by white emancipationist Unionists, founded schools.[3]

Public education for freedpeople expanded in two peripheral areas. The District of Columbia school board for Blacks opened just one low-budget public school in Washington. The Kansas towns of Leavenworth and Burlingame admitted freed children to their public schools, the former on a segregated basis and the latter with integration. Aid organizations funded additional schools in that state.[4]

Most rural areas under Federal occupation in early 1863, except much of the Sea Islands, lacked freedpeople's schools, but occupied Louisiana and many plantation camps would develop them. Lucy Chase traveled to a number of small plantation camps near Norfolk to distribute textbooks and slates, teach for a few days, and then put the best student in charge. Some rural children would walk or row for miles to attend classes, but damage to a bridge or boat could indefinitely suspend their educations.[5]

Everywhere the larger aid associations, motivated by rising expenditures and the urging of laissez-faire reformers, controversially experimented with shifting some costs to consumers. One approach was to make the opening of a school dependent on the host community's provision of a building and the teacher's pay, board, or fuel. The AMA engaged in lengthy negotiations with the African Methodist Episcopal church in Baltimore, Maryland, over financing a school there. The church felt more comfortable covering the teachers' fuel rather than board, which the association wanted. After approaching other organizations, the congregation decided to go with the AMA, but in the next month canceled the agreement and accepted the Baltimore Association's offer to cover all costs.[6]

Other ways of sharing expenses involved requesting donations or charging for educational materials and tuition, if a parent was employed. Charles P. Day of the AMA worried that selling textbooks would hurt his school's ability to compete with those of associations that gave them to pupils. Laura Towne thoughtfully cut her students' costs by holding texts as school property. Some parents, when asked to start paying, inevitably felt cheated out of free education, and some simply could not do it when small salaries had to go to necessities.[7]

Increasing competition between the multiplying urban schools of aid societies prompted freedmen's department heads to impose supervised systems as a means to greater efficiency and effectiveness. Fixed boundaries for each school's district halted the contention over students, although children grieved over the loss of favored instructors, and vice versa. Education supervisors generally managed buildings, finances, materials, and teachers who now received standardized salaries. They used military appropriation to acquire vacant public schools or other buildings. More schools and equalized equipment benefited many pupils.[8]

The first system appeared in New Orleans. During 1863 the AMA, then other aid associations, started to send instructors there. In the fall Gen. Nathaniel Banks, acting under military governance, appointed a superintendent of public schools for the city's Blacks. Then in March of 1864, the general assigned three reformers to a statewide board of public schools for African Americans and funded it with a property tax. When the tax failed to earn enough, the army contributed some of its revenue from captured cotton. The board hired most northern reformers already present, but also recruited many local Blacks and white Unionist women for the instructional staff. Whether those in the last group supported social change or merely needed a salary, most fellow white Louisianans ostracized them. Proslavery whites ran off some teachers with threats or a refusal to do business with them. Such hostility combined with a lack of support from many provost marshals and especially slowed development of the more vulnerable rural schools. The system started before the state's emancipation referendum in September, but most schools seem to have opened afterward. By the war's end, the program had enrolled a large proportion of Louisiana's freed children.[9]

The Louisiana board, unlike those in other occupied areas, hired inspectors to visit and to improve schools. The best inspectors wisely stressed livelier teaching, maintaining order, and a workable student/teacher ratio. Because of both prejudice and the war's stress on national unity, the board made English the only instructional language, but sensitive teachers held French courses to please the large number of Black French speakers. Since this board only held authority over public schools, it permitted private tuition schools to continue independent operations.[10]

During the spring of 1864, Adjutant General Lorenzo Thomas authorized John Eaton's Freedmen's Department to assume supervision over all schools for African Americans. Like most other freedmen's departments, this one expelled from the region any teacher who refused to submit to the system. Having superintended a school before the war, Eaton standardized textbooks, procedures, and monthly reports for all aid societies' schools. The Reverend Joseph Warren, placed in charge of the whole operation, had subordinate superintendents for Natchez, Vicksburg, Helena, Little Rock, Memphis, and Columbus. William F. Allen, Helena's superintendent, built new schools that included teacher apartments. Levi H. Cobb, the Memphis superintendent, introduced grade levels and a high school there.[11]

Eaton developed a sliding tuition scale based on family income, with the destitute receiving free entry. Allen, aware of the shortage of jobs in Helena, reduced charges below Eaton's scale and added a big discount for children with just a mother present. Still, many students, embarrassed by their poverty, disappeared from the department's schools. A different set of families paid the full rate for their children as a matter of honor and status, despite eligibility for a lower rate. Some instructors in Eaton's department silently refused to collect tuition from any student. The noncooperating individuals could have been fired, but Eaton relied heavily upon a number of associations for screened instructors. Reverend Warren, not surprisingly, reported that the tuition-paying students had better attendance.[12]

In eastern Virginia and North Carolina, Gen. Benjamin Butler in the fall of 1864 gave Orlando Brown and William H. Woodbury additional assignments as co-superintendents of schools for Blacks, except in Virginia's Eastern Shore. That isolated area lacked schools, and Butler left it that way. Rather than charge tuition, the co-superintendents relied on sponsoring associations to continue paying and supplying their teachers. Brown and Woodbury required all schools to establish grade levels, at least a first grade and an advanced class, with different teachers for each grade level, as a minority of schools elsewhere did. The first level learned the alphabet and worked through a basic word primer. The next level focused much time on the second reader, and other levels could center on subsequent readers. Near Hampton, the system experimented with a new boys' school without teachers sponsored by northern societies. A local Unionist was the principal, plus convalescent soldiers volunteered a little teaching, and the better students were trained as monitors (teacher assistants) to lead extensive learning exercises within small groups. An army inspector judged this use of the monitor method "not the best system." Woodbury and Brown, having other duties, seem to have exerted rather light supervision over education in the department.[13]

In Savannah, Georgia, after its surrender in late 1864, the city's Black churches quickly formed a society to raise money for free education. They also secured buildings and hired fifteen Black teachers. The army subsequently appointed T. W. Magill, a white man, as education superintendent for Black students in coastal Georgia. He installed northern teachers from several aid associations in a new set of schools in Savannah. One of Magill's white teachers obtained space in a Black church but quickly got into a fight with the congregation's leaders. The teacher's resignation ended that matter. Magill wanted to restrict Black instructors to assisting white ones, but the African American educational society firmly resisted that during the war's final months.[14]

In early 1865 following the fall of Charleston, South Carolina, the egalitarian reformer and former colonization activist, James Redpath, convinced the post commander to appoint him as the city's public education superintendent. Starting with several thousand students, Redpath employed numerous white and Black instructors, both northern and local. Those lacking experience, mostly the southern ones, received training classes. All began their work without educational equipment. Redpath controversially ordered the school day to open without religious exercises, but protesting staff soon secured the mandate's withdrawal.[15]

The fall of the Confederacy's capital, Richmond, Virginia, in April 1865, prompted a rush of several aid societies to form schools at that symbolic site. After William L. Coan of the AMA secured the education superintendency for Blacks, he led the small group of northern teachers in registering around fifteen hundred pupils for classes held in six African American churches. They had little choice but to identify the children who already had some literacy and appoint them as monitors. Richmond's school system for African Americans completed those instituted by northerners during the war.[16]

Administrative Issues

As school openings multiplied, controversies arose. Freedpeople by 1863 had learned that many of the northern white teachers held less than egalitarian views and that some used oppressive discipline. Like the AMA's Black instructor J. N. Mars, they felt that "I cant for my life see what motive a man or woman can have ... to teach ... with their hearts full of prejudice," and so wanted more Black teachers. From the early war years, a portion of the parents had made great sacrifices to pay tuition to Black instructors with independent schools that generally survived competition with the northern associations' free and better-equipped ones.[17] After the friction between teachers of differing races who briefly shared a house in Norfolk, the AMA slowed down the hiring of Blacks, despite several of its white managers begging for them as valuable models of self-improvement. The National Freedmen's Relief Association, Western Freedmen's Aid Commission, and Northwest Freedmen's Aid Commission acknowledged African Americans' preference by hiring more African Americans. Around the same time, the African Civilization Society, a northern black organization, started to recruit and pay Black teachers to work in the South.[18]

Paternalistic and probably some laissez-faire reformers questioned the availability of enough qualified Blacks. Woodbury argued that only those "with a white person's culture, would be desirable" but added that they "will get nearer to their own race, in a thousand & one ways, than can the same grade of white talent." Some whites wanted to hire African Americans as assistant teachers for training, regardless of experience, before they could eventually rise into the full role. Horace James, who was probably worried that some southern educational restrictions would return after the war, originally opposed using any Blacks on the grounds that whites could "accomplish the most in a short time" before the return of peace. However, William J. Wilson, freed before the war and now heading a school with an all-Black staff in Washington, wrote his sponsor, the AMA, that "colored people must ... do our own work ... [or] we shall be but the same helpless & dependent people, slaves." Sara Stanley, another Black teacher, added that Black teachers had a far better impact on freed pupils than white instructors with biases.[19]

A few Black educators wrote in flawed English, but so did a few of the white ones. Southern Blacks teaching with a limited degree of literacy tended to practice where there were few or no well-educated teachers available. Such an instructor in Arkansas defended herself by saying "I ken cair 'em a heap farther'n they is." The few who did not understand their limitations may have lost their students when enough very literate competitors arrived. George E. Stephens later recalled that after having much difficulty learning from one Black teacher, he made great progress under more experienced white ones. Still, many of the Black instructors had at least satisfactory, if not outstanding, evaluations. Some of the latter changed the minds of several white naysayers, including Horace James.[20]

While most southern Black teachers had established places in African American communities, northern Black instructors had to cope with much white hostility, just to get access to freedpeople. On Clara Duncan's way to Norfolk, a steamboat waiter called her a "nigger wench" and refused food service. When she complained to General Butler, he—in a rare military response—had the server fired and ordered that all steamer passengers within his department should have access to food service. Once arrived in the South, northern Black teachers could face new dangers. Just after Edmonia Highgate had recovered from an emotional breakdown, AMA leaders thoughtlessly assigned her to teach by herself in a small, isolated school on Maryland's part of the Eastern Shore. After reporting several times without effect that she felt unsafe, she quit.[21]

As already noted, friction could occur between competing Black and white instructors. After Blacks in the Alexandria shantytown of Grantsville built their own school, a number of white teachers sought to run it, but the school's trustees picked Harriet Jacobs, then gaining fame for her autobiography, as superintendent. When disappointed whites claimed that the school could not operate without a white person present, Jacobs took her trustees to military officials who explained Butler's suspension of the slave code. She then set up an all-Black staff, based on her firm belief that "It has a good effect upon these people to convince them their own race can do something for their Elevation[;] it inspires them with confidence to help each other." She prudently involved elite free Black women in her school when organizing a fundraising campaign within the African American community. In another case, the Reverend Joseph G. McKee, a northern white teacher who wanted to open a free school in Nashville, clashed repeatedly over facilities with Black educators charging tuition. When this led to a fist fight between a Black pastor and the Black teacher who lost his space in the church to the outsider, the congregation decided, in opposition to their pastor, to eject McKee.[22]

The opening of instruction for Blacks created another conflict as well. Wherever southern white schools had closed for the war, it provoked jealousy, which some northerners believed would end if white children could attend the new schools. However, in three different communities—New Bern, North Carolina; Jacksonville, Florida; and Huntsville, Alabama—social pressure forced white Unionist parents to remove most or all of their children enrolled with Blacks. One white mother admitted, "I should be glad to have them [her children] go, but the neighbors are so hard set I'm afraid I can't do it much longer." In a St. Louis school, J. L. Richardson instead wound up dismissing most white students because of their racist behavior. In Charleston's public schools, Redpath advocated some integration in the belief that it would lead to racial harmony in the future. He drew mostly African Americans, because he put both races in each building, though in separate rooms. The white children only had white teachers, while Blacks had instructors from both races. Redpath had all the youngsters share the playground after notification that he would punish whites who insulted Blacks.[23] Some financially successful free Blacks provoked a different integration issue by asking the new schools to teach their children separately from freed children. Reformers refused to preserve this fading distinction.[24]

Still another organizational controversy for the schools was how to provide effective education for the much larger numbers of freed children wanting it. By 1863 many schools had begun to hold multiple classes simultaneously in large halls, especially in churches. This required booming voices and special techniques from teachers. When only two shared a hall, they could take turns lecturing or holding recitations. Three or four instructors could use different corners in the hall, but more than that posed real challenges. Many divided their pupils into small groups and taught them at different times. Those not under immediate instruction worked on assignments, studied aloud (as southern white children did), or did recitations led by monitors.[25] In all likelihood, the noise made learning more difficult for the pupils.

While some teachers had a talent for managing and engaging large groups, many others found the cacophony of the halls extremely confusing and frustrating. They argued for small rooms, especially for the youngest and most easily distracted students. Some also disliked reliance on monitors. A few schools continued dividing up a large student body to achieve shorter but smaller daily sessions with multiple portions of the pupils.[26]

A last organizational issue involved the traditional practice of school vacations during the summer. While the AMA originally seemed to favor maximizing education with year-round classes, both the societies and many teachers came to favor summer vacations as needed rest and a healthy time to get away from the South. William T. Briggs, district superintendent of Black schools in North Carolina, added that educators during the summer should "declare what they have seen, & perhaps be a light upon a golden candlestick to many dark places in the North." However, to freedpeople the summer departures meant less educational and advocacy service. They worried about forgetting lessons as well as the possibility that an educator might not return in the fall. Aid associations generally allowed instructors a choice, including travel to another occupied area to observe different educational methods.[27]

Improvements

Freedpeoples' education underwent several positive developments during 1863–65. Many defective structures used for schools underwent renovation. If they were African American churches, modifications first required permission from the congregation's leaders. Common improvements included new roofs, external wall shingling, insulation, flooring, ceilings, plastering, windows, and room expansions. Equipment upgrades included ceiling lamps for night classes, summoning bells, heating stoves, desks, and more comfortable seats. At a Louisiana school an inspector also pointed out the need to cover or enclose a well on the playground. The expanded corps of teachers in the later war years included some who had the skills to carry out improvements, which aided the process.[28]

Occasionally, a crew constructed a new building. The Trent River camp built a large hall with milled lumber. When local building materials were too expensive or unavailable, purchasing and shipping a prefabricated building could resolve the problem. In early 1865, Laura Towne secured from her sponsor a three-room school of that type. She had it erected on piles because of her island's vulnerability to flooding. Another alternative not common until 1863 was the appropriation of well-equipped schools that had closed for the war.[29]

With time the schools for Blacks tended to expand their curriculum, to acquire more equipment, and to develop new methods. Several initiated a part-time "infant" or preschool class that might use cards, charts, painted blocks, and counting balls to introduce object names, body parts, colors, and numbers. The group additionally had exercise, singing, and very basic religious instruction. Regular school still began with learning the alphabet, using charts or possibly letter blocks. Learners could eventually begin writing on slates with chalk or the cheaper and quieter tablets with pencils. After mastering letters, pupils advanced to words and sentences in copybooks. That required enough desks, tables, or cobbled together writing surfaces for at least a few students at a time. Practice in writing postal letters had great appeal, because of the exercise's practical usefulness. Instructors sought engagement through competitive spelling bees or a focus on nearby objects for spelling lessons. Music classes benefited from obtaining either a small organ or the more compact melodeon. Mathematics began with what was then called mental arithmetic, basic calculations in the head. Continuing to the more complicated written level required a blackboard or slates. One instructor came up with a very practical and motivating exercise about a store bill. Laura Towne considered math to be the hardest subject for pupils to master.[30]

Lydia Thompson judged religion the easiest subject to teach her pupils: "They listen with more interest to religious instruction than any other. This part of their interest has been most cultivated." Religion classes took place at all levels with students memorizing the Ten Commandments, the Lord's Prayer, other scripture verses, and catechism answers. Some teachers sought to use the lessons to achieve conversions. Protestant elements commonly included in religious lessons, though, disturbed Catholics. Seeking to retain control of religious training, Catholic schools in St. Louis, St. Augustine, and Baltimore for the first time admitted Catholic children who were Black, probably in separate classes. Prudent instructors in New Orleans public schools got more Black Catholics to attend by an open policy of avoiding lessons with a sectarian element.[31]

Reading also remained a central subject. After the primer came the second reader and the rest of the numbered series. Frank H. Green, AMA principal at Baton Rouge, held that his teachers advanced the children too quickly to higher reading levels in order to make themselves look good. But by sending a number of pupils back to lower grades, he stirred up controversy, since "many felt themselves degraded," not to mention discouraged. During the war the American Tract Society printed first and second readers designed for freed children. However, teachers' wartime correspondence rarely refers to using them, unlike the textbooks typically used in northern schools. As the latter readers focused on whites, they said little about race, though what was said fit the stereotypes. The Tract Society's texts presented romantic racialist views, as did geography textbooks of the time. All readers at that time stressed Judeo-Christian values and the work ethic. The standard ones emphasized social mobility in general, while the *Freedman's Readers* only praised rising to farm ownership. All these texts would support many northern educators' desire to spread northern culture.[32]

Jennie Slocum used newspapers and magazines to show children that there was always more to learn. More educators employed children's newsletters and storybooks to pique the pupils' interest. However, many northerners assumed too much about the refugee children's cultural background. Anna A. Carter did come to realize that many of the subjects in educational materials that were "familiar to the youngest of northern pupils, are unknown" to her pupils.[33]

During the war the American Tract Society published the newsletter *Freedman* specifically for southern Black students. The newsletter advocated assimilation of white culture. Like some teachers, it judged Black English as inferior by urging the adoption of white pronunciation and grammar. In an effort to counter the strongly antiracist *New York Anglo-African,* the *Freedman* presented a rosy view of Federal policies. It even made the inaccurate claim that the government treated Black and white soldiers equally.[34] How many or how few students read the newsletter is unknown. Teachers' writings rarely specify a newsletter's source.

Whenever one or more students had well-developed reading skills, a teacher could start an advanced course. Geography, especially when aided by maps and globes, surprised the learners with a much wider world than they had imagined. As an interdisciplinary subject, it helped to reinforce lessons in other classes. Additional advanced courses appearing in the schools late in the war were United States history, zoology, health, and home economics. A few teachers supplemented classroom instruction through guest speakers or field trips. Several introduced competition over class rank to stimulate more motivation.[35]

To encourage student effort and public support, instructors of Black children copied a practice of white schools and periodically held public programs, especially at the end of a term. Dressed in their best clothes, students gained experience in performing before an audience. Typical exercises included speeches, dialogues, group recitations, and singing. The programs showed off the abilities of the students and, by implication, of the educators. At Baton Rouge, according to teacher Frank H. Green, "The *parents* were so delighted that *they wept for joy.*" Refreshments followed for the crowds attending. At Helena, teachers made sure to invite all the post's important whites, and thus successfully collected donations.[36]

Vocational training improved and expanded during 1863–65. Several camps hired skilled workers to offer training for males to become cobblers, blacksmiths, carpenters, wheelwrights, tailors, or broom-makers. The programs seem to have been open to anyone interested except at Arlington, where Superintendent Nichols selected the pupils. As many adult males entered the military, boys filled their slots. So-called industrial schools taught sewing to females but sometimes added reading, writing, arithmetic, domestic skills, spinning thread, knitting, cloth-weaving, basket-making, or straw-weaving (hats, bonnets, and mats).[37] Lydia H. Daggett at Natchez seemed to be a particularly exacting instructor who sometimes made students repeatedly undo and redo work. While a few camps, such as Arlington, had sewing machines, most trainees did their work by hand. Programs always included a workshop in which experienced Black seamstresses often assisted in teaching. The main problem that faced sewing programs was running out of materials before a new supply arrived.[38]

As the future need for Black educators grew more obvious, several more schools created teacher training classes. The sketchy documentation about programs at Washington, Beaufort (South Carolina), Norfolk, and New Orleans hints that they may have only consisted of advanced subject classes for the best pupils. An official of the National Freedmen's Relief Association commented: "With white teachers to supervise, a healthy tone could be given to all the schools" taught by graduates of that organization's training school in Washington. The institution's Black trustees sought to buy it, presumably to install more egalitarian administrative policies. Near the end of the war, Charleston seems to have had the most developed program. Redpath required seventy inexperienced teachers he hired to take two classes. Blacks and whites together took Introduction to Teaching and Discipline, as well as Advanced Reading and Geography. Their instructor, William F. Allen, observed them teaching. The good ones received feedback for improvement; the inadequate ones lost their jobs.[39]

Evening schools continued to proliferate mostly for working adults. An aid association founded by Washington whites instituted night classes at numerous locations, mostly African American churches. A group of whites, mostly government clerks, taught these schools with a few Black assistants. The operation was unusual in that all were unpaid volunteers, except that the needy teachers received free housing. A wide range of adults, including very elderly ones participated in evening schools, when they could. Occasionally, a child who had missed a day class attended as well.[40]

A new type of school appeared within certain Black regiments. Many of the enlistees strongly desired education. Reformers among the officers always wanted it, unlike the unsympathetic ones. Ranking paternalists might even require attendance or assess each soldier for the costs. Typically, the chaplain supervised the operation. He, another officer, an officer's wife, or an aid association worker did the teaching. Teachers, while mostly white, did include some Blacks. At first, many units limited their schools to the noncommissioned Black officers in order to enable them to do paperwork. After accomplishing that goal, classes opened to the privates, although those with a smattering of education might get admitted earlier.[41] Some schools allowed soldiers' family members to attend. The classes usually took place in camps away from the front lines, when attendees were available. Unless a unit stayed at a post long enough to construct a school building, classes likely took place in a large tent or other low-grade shelter. If only a few soldiers had free time, the instructor might hold small tutorials. Most teachers and soldiers prioritized reading and writing, but schools might also cover arithmetic, spelling, geography, history, or science. The men commonly helped one another with the lessons and carried texts for study during work breaks or guard duty. An idealistic soldier-student committed himself "to do all I can to show the white people our race is of some account."[42]

Challenges

All schools for freedpeople faced a number of problems during 1863–65. The most common one was irregular attendance. Many children, especially those over twelve years old, either helped parents with tasks or might obtain a paying job, such that they would disappear or attend infrequently. Elizabeth Botume got a number of baby tenders back in class by hiring a woman to care for the infants. Of course, adults often missed evening classes after hard or long workdays.[43]

Officials' use of force created a variety of problems for schools. They rarely established compulsory attendance for children, as Greene did at Arlington. Superintendent Danforth B. Nichols used his military guards to round up the truants. To an aid society's inspector, this was "proof that there must be something very wrong," and he may have meant the school's management by the condescending American Tract Society. A rumor that Federal officials planned to apprentice children caused parents at Wise plantation camp in Eastern Virginia to withdraw their children from school, until adequately reassured that the story was false. When the army entered Roanoke Island and Beaufort schools to impress older boys for work in the New Bern area, upset parents removed all children for a period of seclusion. When roundups of men for forced enlistment, military work, or labor contracting occurred, most adult male students disappeared.[44]

Schools might temporarily shut down for a variety of reasons. When emergencies turned schoolhouses into hospitals or housing, an energetic teacher might give simple lessons by going door-to-door to homes and writing with chalk or coals on walls. Other children joined in and then reinforced their understanding by following along to hear the lesson at several houses. Several unusual situations completely halted classes for a time. During big revivals neither students nor teachers wished to stay in school. According to the teacher Emily Stuart, "we rather felt it our duty to give our whole time, and our hearts to the [religious] work." Epidemics had a longer effect. Contagious yellow fever in northeastern North Carolina shut down schools from July to December in 1864. Worst of all, Confederate attacks not only terminated schooling, but also could cause the loss of textbooks and other equipment.[45]

A different type of problem was the periodic eruption of talking, fighting, or insubordination, even after a teacher had established a basic level of order in the classroom. Before the war's end, most instructors abandoned whipping, a common punishment in northern schools, because they had realized that the flogging of a Black by a white was a painful reminder of slavery. When Charles P. Day whipped and expelled a Black girl from his school in Hampton, her church excluded him from teaching in its Sunday School. Some educators required guidance regarding alternatives to painful punishment. Many tried forms of shaming, like taking away a slate or textbook, removal to a lower class, a brief lock-up in the post guardhouse, or sending the culprit home (considered by many children as the worst penalty). When on a winter's day several brothers complained that a Mr. Ax's school at the Alexandria Freedmen's Home made their heads sore, he angrily took them outside to pump a large dose of cold water on their heads. Since all the boys subsequently became sick and one died, their mother withdrew her surviving children.[46] More constructive than Ax, the northern Black teacher Clara Duncan effectively added a behavior grade to report cards. Several instructors discovered that, when restlessness first appeared, an interlude of singing could prevent trouble. Alternately, a few teachers found that having an adult Black as disciplinarian in the school greatly improved pupil behavior.[47]

Nonphysical punishments often involved meeting with the teacher after school. Sarah M. Gill completed her scoldings by having the pupil kneel and pray for divine forgiveness and the grace to improve. Charles P. Day required some troublemakers both to write about their misbehavior and to read their confessions in his Sunday School. During a mandatory after-school talk, Isabella McKechie discovered that one miscreant was upset from the loss of all his relatives and "had no one to care for him." She concluded that "kindness is more powerful than severity."[48]

During the later war years hostile white southerners posed an increasing threat to the Blacks' schools. Because the reformers' activities threatened slavery in the border states and areas exempted from emancipation, most trouble took place in those locations. Some southern whites who had hired Black refugees as domestic servants prohibited employees' children from going to school. When one employer locked a schoolchild in the basement, she escaped through a window to get to class. More commonly, the parents left such employers. White boys noisily disrupted Black schools, broke windows, stole textbooks, damaged equipment, knocked over outhouses, or attacked the pupils. A particularly mean incident involved the seizure of two Black schoolboys, blindfolding, and "execution" with blank shots. Southern white civilians threatened or actually assaulted several teachers. Civil authorities in Columbia, Tennessee, publicly whipped a Black instructor. Mary C. Fitch and presumably her pupils hid in the brush, whenever Confederate guerrillas came near her school outside Goodrich's Landing. As already noted, the irregulars even went so far as to kill a handful of educators.[49] Opponents damaged several school buildings, and arsonists destroyed at least six during 1863–65.[50]

Teachers and students endangered by civilians might seek protection from local police, the provost marshal, or a military guard. A provost marshal in Harper's Ferry only lectured stone-throwers, but another one in Norfolk authorized the teachers to make arrests. The Norfolk problem ended after the provost marshal there sentenced two white boys to two months in the guardhouse. Since a Black child who fought them got the same punishment, the teachers urged "patience and long forbearance" on their students. Wilmer Walton, who taught African Americans in Huntsville, Alabama, secured the military arrest of a local white who beat him. He and some other instructors tried to reduce tensions by encouraging school visits from critical whites in order to demonstrate that they taught nothing dangerous and that the freed children would learn skills making them more useful employees. Understandably, the novelty of an observation by critical whites, especially when numerous, could agitate and fluster the pupils.[51]

Good education, as is well known, can make a constructive difference. A freedwoman wrote her former instructor Lucy Chase that slaveholders "have kept us in the dark, but you folks want to put some light into us." Freedpeople showed great respect toward caring teachers. They openly rejoiced when favored instructors came back from summer vacation. An aged freedman prayed that God would bless the northerners who "come way down here for de love [of] us poor niggers, jas as de Lord Jesus Christ leff he home in de hebens for de love of wicked sinners." With time, reformers improved organization, programs, and educational facilities. Freedpeople came to seek more control over their education, primarily through gaining more Black teachers. Both students and teachers—African Americans and whites—suffered from rising southern white opposition to the schools. But despite problems and issues, the gains were real. The newly literate used their skills in reading to others, writing letters, doing the math for financial matters, and tutoring. Subscribing to and reading northern Black newspapers created broader contexts of knowledge. Finding geography fascinating, one adult student decided to buy a world map. Positive educational experiences formed the best part of the interaction between Black refugees and northern reformers. A Portsmouth boy crowed to his teacher: "School is home. I would rather be there than anywhere else."[52] His school represented the future freedpeople desired: freedom to achieve in an environment of respect.

9

Freedpeople and Reformers at the War's End

April 1865 brought the sudden shock of Lincoln's assassination. Many freedpeople put up mourning decorations and wore black-ribboned badges. In Washington, a large number joined whites in the line at the Capitol to view the deceased president laying in state. One viewer called Lincoln "our best friend," and another concluded that "they can't kill his work." A freed person in the Sea Islands told Laura Towne: "Christ saved them from sin and he from Secesh." Some anxious Blacks distant from the capital initially feared that the president's death would result in the collapse of the United States government, the flight of all their northern supporters from the South, and the Confederates' restoration of slavery.[1] A Roanoke freedwoman told Ella Roper: "I cries mighty hard to de Good Lord, to have pity on us, now wese no friend on earth." Reformers tried to reassure them, as H. C. Percy did with his Black students in a Norfolk school, that "it was all a part of God's plan . . . and that it was for us to go on with our duties as before."[2] The end of the war brought uncertainties, new dangers, and changes for freedpeople and reformers.

More Freedpeople, More Refugees

As the major enemy armies surrendered in April and May of 1865, Federal occupation slowly expanded into the dying Confederacy, many of the discontented or evicted Blacks headed for newly garrisoned towns, just as the need for Black military workers and enlistees declined. Furthermore, provisions were inadequate for this surge and great suffering ensued. Besides freedom, many sought lost relatives by traveling about, writing letters, or posting advertisements in newspapers. Thomas Conway had the foresight to create a registry of Louisiana's agricultural laborers to help searchers there.[3]

This mass movement concerned Federal officials who were increasingly worried about the United States' huge war debt. Some implemented reductions in expenditures for freedpeople. The post commander in occupied Richmond, Virginia, required the city's poorhouse to provide for Blacks in need, but that institution had few resources. Julia Wilbur, who had volunteered to work there, stopped its forced hiring of Black paupers at low pay. She then used her connections with aid associations to have charitable aid sent. She also set up an orphanage at the site.[4]

Beginning in February, many military officials tried to move freedpeople into jobs by terminating most or all rations. H. S. Beals noted that in the Norfolk area "Not a week passes, that whole families do not go twenty-four hours without tasting food." Reformers protesting cutbacks sometimes persuaded officials to allow rations for the starving, and some camp stores gave away small amounts of food. So that unemployed freedpeople would have more money for food, Laura Towne gave out clothes for free and bought large amounts of wild fodder that they gathered. The reformer Ellen Wheeler worried: "I fear that the people, whom God has shaken our nation to deliver, must be led through many and deep waters, yet, before they shall be brought to the place He deigns for them."[5]

Commanders urged freedpeople to seek compensated jobs as plantation hands, especially with former owners. They generally upheld any contracts already made. In new contracts, they commonly required a year's commitment, pay, provision of necessities, and Federal enforcement of terms. The contract labor systems of Generals Lorenzo Thomas and Nathaniel Banks show some influence here, except for their fixed wages and behavioral restrictions. In late May, the new Freedmen's Bureau announced similar rules. Some freedpeople reacted again with fear of reenslavement and suspicion of Federal officials.[6]

In Sherman's colony, around 40,000 freedpeople had set up many communal farms, militia units, and local governments by summer. Robert Smalls had hauled in and distributed some farm materials provided by General Saxton, but the majority could only obtain free rations through a long trip. Many there were struggling financially, and consequently relied heavily on other jobs or foraging at abandoned plantations. However, with the Amnesty Proclamation of May 29, 1865, the new President Andrew Johnson—a firm believer in property rights and laissez-faire economics—closed the option of land redistribution. Seeking a rapid return to normal life for the reunified nation, the document guaranteed the return of all abandoned property, except slaves and tax-confiscated land, to ex-Confederates who agreed to take a loyalty oath to the United States.[7]

The Amnesty Proclamation enabled owners to regain many buildings appropriated for northerners' mission houses and schools, as well as African Americans' churches. White congregations that held the deed to structures built at the expense of Blacks, sometimes turned to legal action for repossessing the chapels. During late spring, the army halted provision of rations and transportation to aid workers. It also ended free shipment of donated goods. In some areas, reformers could buy rations from the army; elsewhere the sponsoring association would have to pick up the costs again.[8]

Aid societies rushed teachers into newly occupied cities to start schools. By the war's end, according to one historian's estimate, there were around nine hundred teachers instructing freedpeople. Northern instructors soon realized that they lacked the numbers to teach all southern Blacks who wanted an education. That would require the training of many African American instructors.[9] The public school systems set up by reformers in several cities offered one model for organizing education on a greater scale in the future.

In education and other matters, the reconstruction of southern government would obviously affect Blacks. When freedmen attempted to attend a public meeting on the topic in Charleston, some whites quickly expelled them. Arriving late, the reformer James Redpath ordered the guard to let them go in with him. That caused all whites except Unionists to walk out. The two remaining groups then passed a resolution opposing leading roles in reconstruction for former slaveholders.[10] Some common political ground between freedmen and white Unionists had appeared and would develop further during Reconstruction.

Emancipation's New Context

From the war's beginning to the end of May 1865, at least half a million persons had escaped enslavement.[11] Many had received aid and services from reformers; many others had not. The end of the war created a new phase of Emancipation's story within a context that had changed in three major ways.

The first development was the gradual liberation of the majority of the slaves (around three-and-a-half million). During the war, urban Black populations behind Federal lines had swelled with those seeking safety and opportunity. The process would continue in more southern towns after the war. Yet, as Edward Philbrick had realized, when all the enslaved became free, the reformers would not be able to protect or assist many of that massive number.[12]

Second, returning ex-Confederate soldiers and white refugees in the occupied areas swelled the numbers of those hostile toward reformers and freedpeople. Ex-Confederates in Charleston threatened James Redpath's life. One at Stevenson, Alabama, beat up Wilmer Walton, the principal of the Black school. Educators like Augustus M. Weeks persisted through "trust in Providence for protection." Threats and violence against African American education got some night classes cancelled and occasionally delayed the opening of new schools.[13] In fallen Richmond, former secessionists demanded that the military authorities force freedpeople to work for them and even to exclude Blacks from the audience at public concerts by the USCT band. When Federal authorities refused both requests, local whites snarled about racial equality. Ex-Confederates increasingly became the main employers in the job market. Sarah Chase insightfully commented: "The Negro will suffer more the coming year of Peace, than he has during the War: and no organization can shield him from all the injustice he will be exposed to from the vengeful Southrons."[14] Southern white opposition clearly posed a major obstacle to social change, as the power of sheer numbers began to tilt the local balance away from the freedpeople and reformers, even though Federal military rule continued.

Furthermore, in his Amnesty Proclamation President Johnson directed the establishment of new state governments, which southern whites would obviously dominate. As a slaveholder who had accepted emancipation, the President strongly advised ex-Confederates to do likewise but, as a believer in white supremacy, he did not push hard for anything more.[15] Most southern whites wanted subordination and exploitation of African Americans in some form.

Third, a single Freedmen's Bureau replaced multiple freedmen's departments. General Oliver O. Howard, who had sympathy for freedpeople but little wartime involvement with them, became the Bureau's commissioner in May 1865. Some former freedmen's department officials became regional directors: John Eaton in the District of Columbia, Orlando O. Brown in Virginia, Rufus B. Saxton in South Carolina and Georgia, Thomas Conway in Louisiana, and Samuel Thomas in Mississippi. Charles B. Wilder and Horace James became subdistrict heads. President Johnson pushed the Bureau toward the laissez-faire reformer position. Having belonged to the Democratic Party before the 1864 election, he preferred to minimize government activity. On May 31, 1865, General Howard mandated that the Bureau reduce aid programs, except for education. The Bureau provided some necessities, but it would close most contraband camps. Paternalistic and egalitarian officials in the Bureau soon would either resign or learn to live with the new policies.[16]

A few facilities, such as the Arlington Freedmen's Village and the Washington Freedmen's Hospital, survived longer, because the Federal government had acquired the sites. Rufus Saxton's very successful bank inspired a northern investor group in early 1865 to found the Freedman's Savings and Trust Company. After absorbing both Saxton's and Butler's banks, it would later fail from mismanagement. Aid societies raised more charitable contributions during early Reconstruction and consequently took over a few homes for orphaned, elderly, and disabled freedeople. To partner more effectively with the new bureau, several associations merged into the American Freedmen's Aid Union during May, 1865.[17]

The new Freedmen's Bureau, prodded by Johnson and his Amnesty Proclamation, turned against land redistribution. Black lessees of abandoned land in 1865 sometimes got to stay through the harvesting of their crops and sometimes did not. At least residents in a few locations were able to mount postwar campaigns of delay, with support from some reformers. These included the Sherman colony, the Roanoke colony, Mitchelville, the Trent River Camp, the Peninsula's plantation camps, and Camp Nelson. Economic conditions in the postwar decades were hard on small farmers.[18]

Conclusions

The wartime wave of Black refugees and the response of northern reformers had resulted in extensive experimentation during the war. What difference did that make? Most obviously, the numerous Black refugees from slavery and their northern supporters had helped to bring about the Emancipation Proclamation. By May 1865, slavery legally existed only in Kentucky, Delaware, and pro-Confederate portions of the Indian Territory. Even in those places, Blacks working for the military, their families, and the enslaved belonging to Confederate supporters became free under Federal laws, which, however, lacked full enforcement. Kentucky had the largest population of slaves remaining. The Reverend John G. Fee, an egalitarian, contended at Camp Nelson that the camp's Black refugees confronted whites with the racial problem and the need for change. Ratification in December 1865 of the Thirteenth Amendment ending slavery in the United States and peace treaties with relevant Indian Territory tribes in 1866 would complete the legal process of emancipation.[19]

Since freedpeople could not necessarily count on the continuance of ad hoc rights allowed them in Federally occupied areas during the war, the national government had a pressing need to define the meaning of the liberty that it had established for freedpeople. Otherwise, free Blacks fell under existing state and local laws, which commonly allowed them personal property owner-ship, wage labor, and a degree of free movement, but typically restricted their businesses, education, possessions, use of courts, and some other activities.[20] During the war, most limits on free Blacks were ignored when the slave code was not enforced in an occupied area. The issues of legal marriage for freed-persons, the problems arising from multiple pairings in slavery, and the care of freed indigents would need resolution through new state legislation. In order to maintain wartime changes, Federal action also needed to block state inter-ference. In response to freedpeople and reformers, Republican reconstruction would make a major effort to expand the rights of Black people under freedom.

As in slavery and the wartime contract labor systems, most jobs for south-ern Blacks would involve unskilled agricultural work. While the legacy of slav-ery would extend abuse of Black employees, the contract labor programs also set a problematic example of a twelve-month contract helping to preserve economic exploitation with most—if any—pay delayed until the year's end.

Early in the war, Black refugees' initiation of change led to support from some white reformers. During the war, the two groups, working together and separately, established some precedents for a better Black future. They insti-tuted charities, schools, independent religious congregations, and new Afri-can American neighborhoods. Reformers had the resources to play the larger role regarding the first two, while refugees had the knowledge and skills to shape the greater part of the last two. Some but not all freedpeople supported the reformers who instituted formal marriages and military enlistment for them. Still, new privileges built some momentum that favored continuance or further development.[21]

Freedpeople and reformers had faced challenges in working together for change. Some of the views and behaviors that freedpeople carried over from slavery aggravated the reformers. Life in slavery, of course, had affected peo-ple differently from the middle and upper class lives of northern reformers. Slavery could especially cultivate distrust of whites, which flared up in occa-sional suspicions, sometimes accurate, about reformers' programs. Doubts could be assuaged or erupt in resistance depending on the program's nature.

Reformers serving in or working under the military had to obey orders, whether that resulted in abuse or benefit for their charges. Some of the re-formers' own views and behaviors brought from northern culture antagonized the freed. Too many reformers believed themselves superior, and stereotyped African Americans. The laissez-faire reformers' restrictive approach to char-ity occasionally caused unnecessary suffering. The paternalistic reformers exercised control and guidance, especially in matters of individual character, religion, family life, and work, that caused friction, evasion, and resistance. Criticism of the dearest beliefs of others rarely sits well. Forced subordination restrained the advance of liberty. Additionally, the romantic racialism of reformers other than the egalitarian ones supported negative perceptions that helped to maintain social, economic, and political inequality. Some reformers optimistically had thought that their experiments would change biased whites' minds about the freedpeople's worthiness, but emancipation provoked resistance to the accompanying changes. Years later Lovey Eberhart's romantic racialism led to resignation over Reconstruction's failures, due to her conviction that freedpeople could not adequately think or provide for themselves.[22]

The major obstacle to social change was the entrenched racial prejudice of numerous white people. Some freedpeople and some reformers made heroic efforts to push for change, while navigating many obstacles to African American liberty. Some paternalistic reformers acquired egalitarian views that they held for the rest of their lives. They, especially the teachers, entered into interracial friendships and often won much praise from African Americans during the postwar period.[23] When laissez-faire and paternalistic reformers offended freedpeople by disrespect and attempts to dominate, Blacks increasingly sought more autonomy, especially through community development, congregation creation, and political advocacy. Despite a degree of conflict, the two groups continued to interact, because the reformers' greater resources maintained major benefits for the freedpeople, particularly regarding charity and schools. Furthermore, the Blacks' initial lack of political standing meant that they could only get their new freedom converted into specific legal liberties through whites, some of whom would resist.

Peter, a freed preacher in Washington, prayed: "Oh, Lord, shake thy table cloth Down among us, and may we get some of the crumbs." He sensed that too many whites were too hostile for Blacks to make really big gains. While some readers today may perceive the wartime gains as crumbs, freedpeople then treasured them and hoped for more. Neither freedpeople nor reformers fully agreed on what more was feasible. Freedpeople and reformers would encounter violent opposition from the southern white majority to Black education for a time and to political equality for an even longer time. If large-scale land redistribution had occurred it would have provoked fierce resistance.[24] The Reconstruction period brought the freed and the reformers greater challenges but also solidified gains in religious, educational, and social life.

Appendix A
Contraband Camps

N.B. There may have been more contraband camps, and some of the listed sites may have remained unsupervised laborer camps. Army department territories and names in some cases changed during the war.

Department of the Cumberland

Alabama
Athens
Bridgeport
Decatur
Huntsville
Stevenson

Tennessee
Chattanooga
Columbia
Decherd
Fort Donelson
Gallatin
Hendersonville
Murfreesboro
Nashville
Pulaski
Tunnel Hill

Department of the Gulf
(all in Louisiana)

Algiers
Baton Rouge
Donaldsonville
Jefferson Parish
Lafourche Parish
Port Hudson
St. Charles Parish

District of Kentucky
(all in Kentucky)

Bowling Green
Camp Nelson
Louisville
Paducah
Smithland

Department of Missouri
and Nearby

St. Louis (Missouri Hotel to Benton Barracks to Contraband Home)

Illinois
Brooklyn
Quincy

Department of the South

Florida
Fernandina plantations
St. Augustine plantations

South Carolina
Beaufort
Edisto Island—transferred from the navy
Hilton Head
Mitchelville
Saxtonville
Sea Islands (numerous plantations)

Department of the Tennessee & State of Arkansas

Arkansas
De Valls Bluff
Helena (town and several plantations)
Island No. 63
Little Rock
Pine Bluff
White River's Mouth

Illinois
Cairo

Kentucky
Columbus

Louisiana
Concordia
Goodrich's Landing
Island No. 102
Lake Providence
Milliken's Bend (also several plantations)
Omega
Paw Paw Island
Ralston/Desoto
Skipwith's Landing
Vidalia
Young's Point

Mississippi
Corinth
Davis Bend—Transferred from navy
Fort Adams
Holly Springs
Natchez (city and several plantations)
Palmyra Bend
Vicksburg (bluff camp, Freedmen's Home,
    Van Buren Hospital, and several plantations)
Washington

Tennessee
Bolivar
Fort Pillow
Grand Junction
Island No. 10
Jackson
LaGrange
Memphis (Shiloh, Holly Springs or Camp Fiske,
    President's Island)

Department of Virginia and North Carolina

North Carolina
Beaufort
Hatteras
Morehead City
New Bern (moved from three plantations to Trent River)
Plymouth
Roanoke Island
Washington

Virginia
Eastville
Hampton area (Fort Monroe, Camp Hamilton, Mill Creek,
    Downy Plantation and others)
Newport News
Norfolk area (moved from Fort Norfolk to Ropewalk
    and then to Old Slave Pen); Craney Island;
    numerous plantations
Pawtuxet
Suffolk (Uniontown and several plantations)
Townfield
Williamsburg
Yorktown (Slabtown, and Acreville)

Also
St. Mary's County plantations in Maryland

Department of Washington

District of Columbia

Mason's Island

Washington (moved from Old Capitol Prison to Duff Green's Row
and then to Camp Barker)

Virginia

Alexandria (moved from appropriated buildings
to Freedmen's Home)

Arlington Area (Freedmen's Village, Camp Todd, and several
other plantations)

Appendix B
Superintendents of Freedmen's Departments

Department of the Cumberland

Capt. Ralph Hunt, January–June 1864
Col. Robert Barnard, June 1864–January 1865
Col. Reuben D. Mussey, January–May 1865

Department of the Gulf

Lt. George Hanks, February 1863–August 1864
Chap. Thomas W. Conway, August 1864–June 1865

Department of the South

Edward Pierce, March–May 1862
Gen. Rufus Saxton, May 1862–June 1865

Department of Tennessee

Chap. (later Col.) John Eaton, December 1862–June 1865

Department of Virginia and North Carolina

North Carolina to 1863
Vincent Colyer, March–summer 1862
Chap. James Means, summer 1862–April 1863

Chap. (later Capt.) Horace James, April–December, 1863

Virginia to 1863
Capt. Charles B. Wilder, March 1862–December 1863

Combined Department
Lt. Col. Joseph B. Kinsman, December 1863–November 1864
Maj. George J. Carney, November 1864–June 1865

Department of Washington

Lt. Col. Elias M. Greene, late 1862–September 1864
Capt. Joseph M. Brown, September 1864–June 1865

Notes

Abbreviations

AFIC   American Freedmen's Inquiry Commission Records, National Archives Microcopy 619

AMA   American Missionary Association

AMAA American Missionary Association Archives, Amistad Research Center, Tulane University, New Orleans, LA

FDHE Ira Berlin et al., ed. *Freedom: A Documentary History of Emancipation.* New York: Cambridge University Press, 1985-93), ser. 1, 3 vols., ser. 2, 1 vol.
       Steven F. Miller et al., ed., *Freedom: A Documentary History of Emancipation.* (Chapel Hill: University of North Carolina Press, 2008), ser. 3, vol. 1.

FFAR   Friends' Freedmen's Association Records, Friends Historical Library, Swarthmore College, Swarthmore, PA.

G.O.   General Order

LR   Letters Received

LS   Letters Sent

NA   National Archives

OR   US War Department, *The War of the Rebellion: A Compilation of Official Records of the Union and Confederate Armies,* 131 vols. (Washington, DC: GPO, 1894-1927).

ORN   US Navy Department, *Official Records of the Union and Confederate Navies in the War of the Rebellion,* 31 vols. (Washington, DC: GPO, 1880-1901). All citations are to ser. 1.

RG   National Archives Record Group
       RG 92—Quartermaster General's Office Records
       RG 94—Adjutant General's Office Records
       RG 105—Records of the Bureau of Freedmen, Refugees, and Abandoned Lands
       RG 393—Records of the United States Army Continental Commands, 1821-1920

S.O.   Special Order

USCT   United States Colored Troops

Preface

1. The most useful topical studies are Blum, *Reforging;* Butchart, *Northern Schools;* Butchart, *Schooling;* Gerteis, *From Contraband to Freedman;* Glatthaar, *Forged in Battle;* Harrold, *Subversives;* Manning, *Troubled Refuge; Glymph, Women's Fight.*

2. The model work emphasizing attention to local variations in slavery's breakdown is *FDHE,* ser. 1, 1–3. The most useful case studies are Rose, *Rehearsal;* Ripley, *Slaves and Freedmen;* Engs, *Freedom's First;* Cimprich, *Slavery's End;* Mohr, *On the Threshold;* Horst, *Education for Manhood;* Click, *Time Full;* and Taylor, *Embattled Freedom.*

3. Litwack, *Been in the Storm,* includes a particularly detailed look at wartime slave and slaveholder relations. Manning, *Cruel War,* covers interaction between Black refugees and the Federal army. So far there is no detailed overview of Confederate relations with African Americans.

4. The more recent overviews of emancipation are Ash, *Black Experience;* Williams, *I Freed Myself;* and Reidy, *Illusions.*

1. First Encounters

1. Kaye, *Joining Places,* 177–83; Levine, *Fall,* 157–58; *New York National Antislavery Standard,* May 4, 25, 1861; Oakes, *Freedom,* 74–75, 79, 128–129.

2. *OR,* ser. 2: 752; Engs, *Freedom's First,* 18.

3. Oakes, *Freedom,* 91; Trefousse, *Butler,* 57–63; *New York Tribune,* May 27, 1861; *OR,* ser. 2, 1: 752. A reporter at the fort later attributed the contraband policy to a subordinate officer whom he claimed had won over the general. See *New York Tribune,* May 27, September 27, 1861, and October 15, 1862.

4. Engs, *Freedom's First,* 20–22, 26–27; Pierce, "Contrabands," 628, 632; *OR,* ser. 2, 1: 754; Taylor, *Embattled Freedom,* 28.

5. *OR,* ser. 2, 1: 752; *New York National Antislavery Standard,* June 1, 1861; 754–55; Oakes, *Freedom,* 50, 75.

6. Masur, "Phenomenon," 1058, 1066, 1079–81; *New York Times,* June 1, 1861; Oakes, *Freedom,* 91–92, 99, 102, 216; Pierce, "Contrabands," 626–27; *American Missionary* 5 (November 1861): 258; *FDHE,* ser. 1, 1: 81.

7. Ash, *Black Experience,* 9–10, 14–17; Blassingame, ed., *Slave Testimony,* 567–68; *Friends' Review* 18 (March 26, 1864): 468 (quoted). Most white writers of the time tried to incorporate what they considered a speaker's unusual dialect into a quote.

8. Franklin and Schweninger, *Runaway Slaves,* 210–12, 224–26, 229; Mohr, *On the Threshold,* 72–73; Johnston, *Surviving Freedom,* 135.

9. Emily Howland, 1862 Journal, 89 (Washington quote), Howland Family Papers; Escott, *Slavery Remembered,* 42, 46.

10. *ORN,* 23: 339; Grimke, *Journals,* 396 (Venus quote), 399 (Suzy quote), 408 (Scipio quote); Escott, *Slavery Remembered,* 44; Blight, ed., *Slave No More,* 195; Escott, *Rethinking,* 53–55; Mazzagetti, ed., *True Jersey Blues,* 222 (quoted); Bruce, *New Man,* 108–109.

11. *New York National Antislavery Standard,* May 3, 1862 (quoted); Mohr, *On the Threshold,* 776–78.

12. Manning, *Cruel War,* 76–77; Nanzig, ed., *Badax Tigers,* 80–81; Winkle, *Lincoln's Citadel,* 312; Haviland, *Woman's Life,* 254; Howland 1862 journal, 97 (Graham quote); Edmonia G. Highgate to George Whipple, March 30, 1864 (quoted), Virginia file, AMAA.

13. Fountain, *Slavery,* 93–96; Harper, *End of Days,* 20–25; *American Missionary* 5 (October supplement, 1861): 244; Ann Schofield to Sara Cope, May 6, 1864 (Pollard quote) FFAR; Trumbull, *War Memories,* 400, 405 (freedwoman quote); Rochester Ladies Antislavery Society, *Thirteenth Annual Report,* 5 (Wilbur quote); Pierce, "Contrabands," 638.

14. *Philadelphia Press,* November 3, 1862 (Aleck quote); *New York Times,* December 18, 1861; Mazzagetti, ed., *True Jersey Blues,* 222. For another view of slave response to the war, see Hahn, *Nation,* 68–115.

15. Taylor, *Embattled Freedom,* 32; *FDHE,* ser. 1, 1: 121, 171–72; Brown, *Negro in the American Rebellion,* 31; *Douglass' Monthly* (August 1861): 517; *OR,* ser. 2, 1: 749, 757; *Boston Liberator,* July 26, 1861; *New York Times,* April 10, 1862.

16. US Congress, *Statutes at Large,* 12: 319; Cimprich, *Slavery's End,* 35; Richards, "Dealing with Slavery," 321; *OR,* ser. 1, 14: 332–33, ser. 2, 1: 762, 773; Oakes, *Freedom,* 142, 174–81; Tomblin, *Bluejackets,* 10.

17. *New York Times,* July 20, 1861; Robert Goulding affidavit, September 1, 1865, and David Bird affidavit, September 2, 1865, "Negroes, Employment" consolidated file, LR by Quartermaster General, RG 92, NA.

18. Richardson, *Christian Reconstruction,* 3–4, 20; Benjamin F. Butler to Lewis Tappan, August 10, 1861, E. Sheldon to George Whipple, December 3, 1861, Virginia file, AMAA; Lockwood, *Peake,* 28.

19. *New York Times,* August 6, 1861; Rose, *Rehearsal,* 9, 11–12, 15–1, 20; Dougherty, *Port Royal,* 6–7; *OR,* ser. 2, 1: 803.

20. *FDHE,* ser. 1, 3: 113, 139, 147; Allen, *Yankee,* 102.

21. French, *Slavery,* 162–63; Rose, *Rehearsal,* 17–19; *FDHE,* ser. 1, 3: 128, 131–46.

22. Rose, *Rehearsal,* 34–35, 40–41, 76; Dougherty, *Port Royal,* 28. Port Royal was a major island in the captured area.

23. American Freedmen's Union Commission, *Emancipation,* 14–16; Williams, *I Freed Myself,* 91; Sheridan, "From Slavery in Missouri," 40–42; National Freedmen's Relief Association of the District of Columbia, *First Annual Report,* 3; Berlin, *Slaves without Masters,* 308–13; John Oliver to William E. Whiting, December 5, 1862, Virginia file, AMAA. Because the great majority of references in this book to Washington are to the town in the District of Columbia, it will just be mentioned by its name. References to other Washingtons will include the state.

24. Danforth B. Nichols to Committee, August 8, 1861, LR by Executive Committee, FFAR; *Pennsylvania Freedmen's Bulletin* 1 (February 1865): 13, 18; Contraband Relief Commission, *To the Public* (flyer); Indiana Freedmen's Aid Commission, *Report,* 8; Western Freedmen's Aid Commission, *Second Annual Report,* 19; Convention of Freedmen's Commissions, *Minutes,* 18.

25. Breault, *Howland,* 62; Eaton, *Report,* 13; Danforth B. Nichols to Simeon S. Jocelyn, June 16, 1862, District of Columbia file, AMAA; J. Porter Green to Simeon S. Jocelyn, September 14, 1862, Virginia file, AMAA; Glymph, *Women's Fight,* 182.

26. Towne, *Letters and Diary,* 8; Escott, *Worst Passions,* 1–7, 103; Fredrickson, *Black Image,* 101; McPherson, *Struggle,* 134–37, 143–52; Jimerson, *Private Civil War,* 50–60, 77; Howard et al., "Charles Howard Family Domestic History" (typescript): 88; Reidy, *Illusions,* 244, 349; Glymph, *Women's Fight,* 6–7, 151–62, 166.

27. Pierce, "Contrabands," 632–35; Botume, *First Days,* 30; Wilbur journal, October 17 and December 31, 1862, Wilbur Papers; Whitacre, *Civil Life,* 4–14, 18, 35–41.

28. Breault, *Howland,* 56, 60; Jones, *Soldiers of Light,* 10; Chambers-Schiller, *Liberty,* 18–21, 24, 67–69, 82–88, 111–12, 279; Buss, *My Work,* 42.

29. Higginson, *Journal,* 163; Frederick A. Eustis to Anna Wharton, May 13, 1862, Wharton Papers; Ash, *Firebrand,* 23; Harrold, *Subversives,* 244–47; Glymph, *Women's Fight,* 168. My thinking on the divisions has partly changed from Cimprich, *Slavery's End,* 60–62. For other ways of grouping reformers, see Rose, *Rehearsal,* 217–19; Butchart, *Northern Schools,* 15–34.

30. Rose, *Rehearsal,* 218; Reuben D. Mussey to Joseph Parrish, March 27, 1864, vol. 220/227—DC, 36, LS by the USCT Commissioner for the Department of the Cumberland, RG 393, NA; Indiana Freedmen's Aid Commission, *Report,* 15; Small, "Yankee Schoolmarm," 401–402; Glymph, *Women's Fight,* 168.

31. French, *Slavery,* vii, 28; Lockwood, *Peake,* 54; Julia Wilbur to Sarah Cope, February 7, 1863, LR by Women's Aid Committee, FFAR; Escott, *Rethinking,* 55.

32. Berlin et al., ed., *Free at Last,* 262–63; Laura M. Towne testimony, n.d., South Carolina file, 68–73, AFIC; Higginson, *Journal,* 320; *Friends' Intelligencer* 21 (May 28, 1864): 181; Small, "The Yankee Schoolmarm," 390–92; Allen, *Yankee,* 15; Mann, "Contact," 297, 299. For the debate over the nature of Towne's outlook, see Breitborde, "Discourse," 428–29, 432, 438, 443; Glymph, *Women's Fight,* 163–66, 175–78, 182–83.

33. *FDHE,* ser. 1, 3: 497–99; Maria Mann to Miss Peabody, April 19, 1863, Mann Papers; McPherson, *Struggle,* 168, 173–74; French, *Slavery,* 217–18, 242.

34. *US Statutes,* 12: 354, 599; *OR,* ser. 1, 15: 58; ser. 2, 1: 763, 778, 814–15; *ORN,* 16: 689; *New York National Antislavery Standard,* April 5, 1862; *New York Times,* May 31, July 3, 1862; *New York Tribune,* January 1, 1863.

35. Oakes, *Freedom,* 168–69, 177–84, 190, 323; *FDHE,* ser. 1, 1: 167, 177.

36. Schwalm, *Emancipation's Diaspora,* 68–69; Moore, *Story,* 61; Abby Gibbons to James Gibbons, June 26, 1862, Gibbons Papers.

37. Cimprich, *Slavery's End,* 35; Teters, *Practical Liberators,* 11, 30, 107; *OR,* ser. 1, 16 (pt. 2): 252, 268, 292, 332, 615; Brasher, *Peninsula Campaign,* 175–76.

38. Forman, *Western Sanitary Commission,* 111; W. Perkins to Simeon S. Jocelyn, January 19, 1863, Kentucky file, AMAA; John Eaton, 1863 Report, 40, Tennessee file, AFIC; Magdol, *Right to the Land,* 96–97; Click, *Time Full,* 2.

39. *FDHE,* ser. 1, 3: 88, 113, 147, 675; Cimprich, *Slavery's End,* 48, 77; Rein, *Alabamians in Blue,* 100; Elias M. Greene file, Appointment and Commission Branch, RG 94, NA; *New York Tribune,* November 7, 1862; *New York Anglo-African,* January 11, 1862; Downs, *Sick from Freedom,* 50–51.

40. *FDHE,* ser. 1, 1: 441–43; *OR,* ser. 2, 1: 770; Oakes, *Freedom,* 236–37, 303–7, 335; *US Statutes,* 12: 591, 1267. For a few commanders' issuance of free papers by using a stretched reading of the First Confiscation Act by Secretary of War Simon Cameron, see Oakes, *Freedom,* 138; Berlin et al., ed., *Free at Last,* 72; Romeo, *Gender and the Jubilee,* 29, 51.

41. *FDHE,* ser. 1, 3: 191, 193, 208; Glymph, *Women's Fight,* 175; Higginson, *Journal,* 163, 317; Rose, *Rehearsal,* 52, 83, 152–53; Weicksel, "Fitted up," 157.

42. Lewis C. Lockwood to AMA, January 27, February 5, 1862, Virginia file, AMAA; Blassingame, *Testimony,* 171, 174.

43. *Friends Review* 16 (October 18, 1862): 110; John Oliver to S. S. Johnson, November 12 and December 19, 1862, Virginia File, AMAA; Gerteis, *From Contraband to Freedman,* 25; James, *Annual Report,* 55, 133–34.

44. *New York Tribune,* January 27, 1863; Henry Rountree to Abram M. Taylor, April 30, 1863, Taylor Family Papers; Taylor, *Embattled Freedom,* 88–90; John Oliver to Simeon S. Jocelyn, November 25, 1862, Virginia file, AMAA; Swint, ed., *Dear Ones,* 23, 40–44.

45. *FDHE,* ser. 1, 1: 62; Schafer, *Thunder,* 84, 90; Mohr, *On the Threshold,* 81–82; Tomlin, *Bluejackets and Contrabands,* 67–73, 77–80, 90–91, 180.

46. James, *Annual Report,* 3; Berlin et al., ed., *Free at Last,* 174–75; *New York Tribune,* June 18, 1862; *New York National Antislavery Standard,* June 14, 1862; Reidy, *Illusions,* 217; Greenwood, *First Fruits,* 44–46.

47. Gerteis, *From Contraband to Freedman,* 65–69; Ripley, *Slaves and Freedmen,* 27–38; *OR,* ser. 1, 15: 592; *FDHE,* ser. 1: 3, 356; Conway, *Final Report,* 4; Rodrigue, *Reconstruction,* 36.

48. Cimprich, *Slavery's End,* 35; *Cincinnati Gazette,* April 23, 1862 (quoted); Teters, *Practical Liberators,* 11, 37; *OR,* ser. 1, 7: 595; *Freedmen's Advocate* 1 (May 1864): 18; *American Missionary* 6 (September 1862): 204.

49. *Boston Liberator,* April 11, 1862; *Washington National Intelligencer,* April 1, 1862; Schwalm, *Emancipation's Diaspora,* 59; Walker, "Corinth," 6–7; Cimprich, *Slavery's End,* 37, 48–49; Rogers, *War Pictures,* 110.

50. Spurgeon, *Soldiers,* 41, 52; Epps, *Slavery on the Periphery,* 167–69; Krauthamer, *Black Slavery, Indian Masters,* 105; Littlefield, *Africans and Seminoles,* 181–84; J. W. Fox to AMA, May 10, 1862, Kansas file, AMAA; Rawick, ed., *American Slave,* 1st supp. ser., 12: OK-138–39, 208–10. Indian Territory had tribal governments with a large degree of autonomy defined by treaties with the US.

51. Foner, *Fiery Trial,* 167; King, *Conspicuous Gallantry,* 26 (quoted); Oakes, *Freedom,* 285–86; *FDHE,* ser. 1, 1: 332; *Cleveland Herald,* November 21, 1862.

52. Smith, *On the Edge,* 181; *OR,* ser. 2, 4: 359; Abby Gibbons to her family, August 10, 1862, Abby Gibbons to James Gibbons, August 6, 19 (quoted), 1862, Gibbons Papers; Women's Association of Philadelphia, *Second Annual Report,* 11.

53. Tourgee, *Story of a Thousand,* 87–91; Moore, *Story,* 59–61; Berlin et al., ed., *Free at Last,* 103; G. P. Rilly to John G. Fee, June 17, 1863, Kentucky file, AMAA; Teters, *Practical Liberators,* 54, 57; Fliss, "Wisconsin's 'Abolition Regiment,'" 9–17. Kentucky also had more slaves than three of the Confederate states individually did.

54. Manning, *Troubled Refuge,* 111, 126–27; Warren, ed., *Extracts from Reports,* ser. 2: 40–41; Samuel G. Wright to George Whipple, December 28, 1862, Kentucky file, AMAA.

55. *OR,* ser. 1, 8: 584, ser. 2: 776, 789; Rawick, ed., *American Slave,* vol. 11: MO-6; Schwalm, *Emancipation's Diaspora,* 55, 79.

56. Winkle, *Lincoln's Citadel,* 268–69; Johnston, *Surviving Freedom,* 158.

57. Winkle, *Lincoln's Citadel,* 236–41, 301–3, 307; *FDHE,* ser. 1, 1: 332; Doster, *Lincoln,* 164; McElya, *Politics of Mourning,* 65–66; C. R. Vaughan to George Whipple, December 18, 1861, District of Columbia file, AMAA; C.B. Bean to George Whipple, November 14, 1862, Virginia file, AMAA.

58. Harrold, *Subversives,* 226; Danforth B. Nichols to Simeon S. Jocelyn, July 3, 1862, District of Columbia file, AMAA; *New York Tribune,* November 7, 1862; *FDHE,* ser. 1, 2: 295, 331, 659;

Johnston, *Surviving Freedom,* 121; Laura Towne diary, April 9, 27, 1862, Penn School Papers. Different sources characterized Nichols as either a Baptist or Methodist.

59. *New York Tribune,* June 11, 1861; *FDHE,* ser. 1, 2: 268; Yellin, ed., *Jacobs Family Papers* 2: 402; New York Yearly Meeting of Friends, *Report of a Committee,* 6; Wilbur journal, December 7, 1862.

2. Provision of Necessities

1. Rawick, ed., *American Slavery,* 14: 79–81; Penningroth, *Claims of Kinfolk,* 4; Berlin et al., ed., *Free at Last,* 188, 266–68; *FDHE,* ser. 1, 3: 675; L. E. N. to George Whipple, February 7, 1865, Virginia file, AMAA; French, *Slavery,* 241 (quoted).

2. J. W. Coan to Michael E. Strieby, September 23, 1864 (quoted), District of Columbia file, AMAA; Engs, *Freedom's First,* 77; Glymph, "Black Women and Children," 126–28.

3. Kolchin, *American Slavery,* 253–54; Moore, *In Christ's Stead,* 26; Towne, *Letters and Diary,* 7. White aid workers known to have prewar interracial contact were Daniel Breed, Thomas C. Connelly, Emily Howland, Lorenzo D. Johnson, Julia Wilbur, and William H. Woodbury. See Harrold, *Subversives,* 210, 229–31.

4. Grimke, *Journals,* 3, 8–9, 39, 391 (quoted); Mabée and Newhouse, *Sojourner Truth,* 120; Yellin, *Harriet Jacobs,* 186–87; Cabral, "Letters," 3, 5; Higginson, *Journal,* 320; Pearson, ed., *Letters,* 226; Ash, *Firebrand of Liberty,* 91.

5. Rochester Ladies Antislavery Society, *Thirteenth Annual Report,* 8; Julia Wilbur to Anna M. C. Barnes, November 25, 1862, Rochester Ladies Antislavery Society Papers; Cimprich, *Slavery's End,* 48–49; Butchart, *Northern Schools,* 117; Mabee and Newhouse, *Sojourner Truth,* 139–40; Yellin, *Harriet Jacobs,* 186–87.

6. Wilbur journal, April 2, 1864; Danforth B. Nichols to Simeon S. Jocelyn, September 5, 1862, District of Columbia file, AMAA; New England Freedmen's Aid Society, *Extracts,* ser. 5: 7 (M. H. C. quote); McShane, ed., "Reading, Writing, and War," 109.

7. Ginzberg, *Women and the Work,* 122–23.

8. Kolchin, *American Slavery,* 113; Ramold, *Slaves, Sailors, Citizens,* 95; Nanzig, ed., *Badax Tigers,* 212; Cimprich, *Slavery's End,* 57; Swint, ed., *Dear Ones,* 90; Wiley, *Life of Billy Yank,* 239; Cecelski, *Waterman's Song,* 162. While it could have occurred, I have not seen any record of hunting by a camp member.

9. Wiley, *Life of Billy Yank,* 237–38; William Wakefield testimony, May 10, 1863, Virginia file, 25, AFIC; Taylor, *Embattled Freedom,* 142–44; Charles P. Ware to Emma W. Ware, November 25, 1862, Ware Papers; Rawick, ed., *American Slave,* suppl. ser. 1, 8: 1343; Eberhart, *History,* 215.

10. *Freedman's Friend* (October 1864): 17; New York Yearly Meeting, *Report,* 11; Berlin et al., ed., *Free at Last,* 179–80; John Oliver to Simeon S. Jocelyn, September 1862, report, and Charles P. Day to William E. Whiting, August 22, 1862, Virginia file, AMAA; *FDHE,* ser. 1, 3: 203.

11. Holt, Parker, and Terborg-Penn, *Special Mission,* 6; US Congress, *Africans in Fort Monroe,* 5; Eberhart, *History,* 246; *New York Tribune,* November 14, 1862; *FDHE,* ser. 1, 2: 295; Moore, *In Christ's Stead,* 26–27; William F. Mitchell to Sarah Cope, January 9, 1865, LR by executive committee, FFAR.

12. *FDHE,* ser. 1, 3: 128; *Freedmen's Record* 1 (February 1865): 24; Frederick A. Eustis to Anna Wharton, May 13, 1862, Wharton Papers; *New York Anglo-African,* January 11, 1862.

13. C. H. Hyde to William E. Whiting, February 2, 1864, and Charles B. Wilder to George

Whipple, September 12, 1862, Virginia file, AMAA; Swint, ed., *Dear Ones,* 22, 92; Eberhart, *History,* 247 (quoted); John Eaton 1863 Report, 40, Tennessee file, AFIC.

14. Whitacre, *Civil Life,* 89; Rose, *Rehearsal,* 85; Danforth B. Nichols to Simeon S. Jocelyn, June 16, 1862, District of Columbia file, AMAA; N. Noyes to Michael E. Strieby, May 5, 1865, Maryland file, AMAA; Glymph, *Women's Fight,* 181; Grimke, *Journals,* 399; Pearson, ed., *Letters,* 121, 123; Sherwood, ed., "Journal of Miss Susan Walker," 24, 32.

15. *American Missionary* 9 (March, 1865): 52; Kolchin, *American Slavery,* 114; Wilbur journal, November 8, 14, 1862; Colyer, *Report,* 34; Lewis C. Lockwood to AMA, September 16, 1862, John Oliver to Simeon S. Jocelyn, November 3, December 31, 1862, Virginia File, AMAA; Samuel G. Wright to George Whipple, December 28, 1862, Kentucky file, Danforth B. Nichols to Simeon S. Jocelyn, July 7, 1862, District of Columbia file, AMAA; Nicholson, "Contraband Camp," 138; Tacy Hadley reminiscences, 1; French, *Slavery,* 162–63.

16. Taylor, *Embattled Freedom,* 65–66, 142; Walter T. Carpenter to Abram M. Taylor, January 12, 1864, Taylor Family Papers; *New York National Antislavery Standard,* August 23, 1862; Click, *Time Full,* 65; Rachel G. C. Patten to Simeon S. Jocelyn, June 21, 1863, District of Columbia file, AMAA; *Friends' Review* 16 (October 18, 1862), 109; *New York Anglo-African,* January 18, 1862.

17. *FDHE,* ser. 1, 3: 271; *Freedman's Friend* 1 (June 1864): 11; Ramold, *Slaves, Sailors, Citizens,* 46; Taylor, *Embattled Freedom,* 67, 73–76; Weicksel, "Fitted up," 157–58; New York Yearly Meeting, *Report,* 15; *New York Anglo-African,* January 11, 1862.

18. US Congress, *Africans in Fort Monroe,* 6; Nicholson, "Contraband Camp," 138; *Freedman's Friend* 1 (June 1864): 4; *New York National Antislavery Standard,* May 31, 1862; *Friends' Review* 16 (October 16, 1862): 75; Swint, ed., *Dear Ones,* 24.

19. Engs, *Freedom's First,* 34; Glymph, *Women's Fight,* 234.

20. French, *Slavery,* 163; Haviland, *Woman's Life,* 288; Rochester Ladies Antislavery Society, *Twelfth Annual Report,* 12; *New York Tribune,* August 24, 1863; H. Porter report, March 24, 1865, p. 5, consolidated file V-87 (1865), LR by Adjutant General, RG 94, NA; *Home Evangelist* (March 1863): 10.

21. Click, *Time Full,* 65; Horace James to friends, May 25, 1863, Horace James Papers, American Antiquarian Society, Worcester, Massachusetts; *Freedman's Advocate* 1 (November 1864): 38; Winkle, *Lincoln's Citadel,* 349; Swint, ed., *Dear Ones,* 47; *Friends' Intelligencer* 21 (May 28, 1864): 180; *Friends' Intelligencer* 21 (February 4, 1865): 757; Tacy Hadley reminiscences, 2.

22. *American Missionary* 6 (December 1862): 281; Wiley, *Billy Yank,* 57; *Friends' Intelligencer* 21 (October 22, 1864): 522; *Freedman's Friend* 1 (June 1864): 4; Hancock, *South after Gettysburg,* 41; Wilbur journal, June 10, 1863; William F. Allen journal, September 26, 1864, William F. Allen Papers; Winkle, *Lincoln's Citadel,* 344; *Freedman's Advocate* 1 (November 1864): 35; Committee on Freedmen, *Report,* 5; Manning, *Troubled Refuge,* 31, 37; Berlin et al., ed., *Free at Last,* 188; Danforth B. Nichols testimony, n.d., District of Columbia file, AFIC; Towne diary, August 12, 1862, Penn School Papers; Friends' Association of Philadelphia and Its Vicinity, *Report,* 6.

23. Danforth B. Nichols testimony, n.d., District of Columbia file, AFIC; William F. Mitchell to Sarah Cope, January 9, 1865, LR by executive committee, FFAR; *FDHE,* ser. 1, 2: 289, 460; George M. Peal to T.V. Hayton, March 25, 1865, LR by the Mississippi Freedmen's Department Medical Director, RG 105, NA.

24. Taylor, *Embattled Freedom,* 80–82; Cimprich, *Slavery's End,* 46–47; Wilbur journal, November 8, 14, 1862; Weicksel, "Fitted up," 157; Nelson, *Ruin Nation,* 25–26.

25. Robert Harris to George Whipple, December 29, 1864, Virginia file, AMAA; Pearson, ed., *Letters,* 12; Ames, *New England Woman's Diary,* 10, 12; Pease, "Three Years," 111; James Hawks to Esther Hawks, April 30, 1862, Hawks Papers; Glymph, *Women's Fight,* 167, 172–74, 179.

26. Wilbur journal, November 5, 1862; John J. Linson to George Whipple, March 22, 1862, Lewis C. Lockwood to AMA, April 7, 17, 1862, Virginia file, AMAA; Samuel G. Wright to George Whipple, October 12, 1864, Mississippi file, AMAA; Breault, *Howland,* 55, 61; Eaton, *Report,* 13.

27. Breitborde, "Discourse," 435; Grimke, *Journals,* 393–95; Ames, *New England Woman's Diary,* 11, 13–14, 24; Rochester Ladies Antislavery Society, *Twelfth Annual Report,* 8; Botume, *First Days,* 40.

28. Hawks, *Woman Doctor's Civil War,* 71; Chambers-Schiller, *Liberty,* 72.

29. Botume, *First Days,* 79 (quoted); Hunter, *Bound in Wedlock,* 35; Wilbur journal, November 8, 1862; Ella Roper to AMA, August 5, 1864, North Carolina file, John Oliver to Simeon S. Jocelyn, November 3, 1862, Virginia file, AMAA; *FDHE,* ser. 1, 1: 307.

30. *Freedman's Friend* 1 (June 1864): 11; Charles P. Day to George Whipple, April 1, 1865, Virginia file, AMAA; Samuel G. Wright to Simeon S. Jocelyn, January 2, 1863, Kentucky file, AMAA; Henry Rountree to Abram A. Taylor, May 7, 1863, Taylor Family Papers; *Friends' Intelligencer* 28 (January 9, 1864): 693; Wilbur journal, November 11, 1862; *New York Anglo-African,* January 11, 1862.

31. Eberhart, *History,* 233; Yellin, ed., *Jacobs Family Papers* 2: 594; *Friends' Review* 16 (December 27, 1862), 267.

32. Doster, *Lincoln,* 165; *New York Anglo-African,* January 18, February 8, November 9, 1862; Charles B. Wilder to George Whipple, March 20, 1862, Virginia file, AMAA.

33. Abby Gibbons to Julia Gibbons, September 10, 1862, Gibbons Papers. See John A. Dix, Order, November 19, 1862, Virginia file, AMAA, for a grant of free shipment for donated goods on army steamers.

34. *Freedmen's Bulletin* 1 (September 1864): 19–20; Henry Rountree to Abram M. Taylor, January 1, 11, 1864, Taylor Family Papers; *Freedmen's Record* 1 (April, 1865): 63; Charles P. Day to George Whipple, February report, 1865 and Lilpha R. Harper to George Whipple, April 27, 1865, Virginia file, AMAA.

35. Sherwood, ed., "Walker," 15–16, 30–31; Towne, *Letters and Diary,* 7; *Friends' Review* 16 (December 6, 1862): 201; Friends' Association for the Aid and Elevation of Freedmen, *Extracts from Letters,* 2.

36. Towne, *Letters and Diary,* 18; Lovey Eberhart reminiscences, 29–30, Eberhart Papers; William S. Bell to George Whipple, March 10, 1864, Virginia file, AMAA; Wilbur journal, December 25, 1863.

37. Edward W. Hooper, testimony, n.d., Carolina file, 217, AFIC; Women's Aid Committee minutebook #1, 13, FFAR; *New York National Antislavery Standard,* February 13, 1864; National Freedmen's Relief Association of the District of Columbia, *First Annual Report,* 27; Wilbur journal, December 31, 1862; *Freedman's Friend* 1 (July 1864): 9, 12; Pearson, ed., *Letters,* 33, 46, 57.

38. Hilliard, *Masters, Slaves, and Exchange,* 56, 82; New York Yearly Meeting of Friends, *Second Report of a Committee,* 5; Henry Rountree to Abram M. Taylor, December 6, 1863, Taylor Family Papers; T. Hinckley to Charles P. Ware, September 4, 11, 1862, Ware Papers; Maria Mann to Aunt Mary, May 18, 1863, Mann Papers.

39. *American Missionary* 7 (June 1864): 152 (refugee's quote); Taylor, *Embattled Freedom,* 167–71; *Friends' Review* 16 (November 29, 1862): 201 (investigators' quote), and (December 6, 1862): 218; Towne, *Letters and Diary,* 18, 59; Sherwood, ed., "Walker," 41; Hilliard, *Masters, Slaves, and Exchange,* 47.

40. Rose, *Rehearsal,* 58; Browning, *Shifting Loyalties,* 120; Allen, *Yankee,* 157; *Freedman's Advocate* 1 (March 1864): 9; Eberhart, reminiscences, 31; Buss, *My Work,* 41-42.

41. Downs, *Sick,* 3–4; Coffin, *Reminiscences,* 630; Schwalm, "Surviving," 27; Thomas Thorne & Achilles Pugh, flyer, December 24, 1862, Thorne Papers; James Hawks to Esther Hawks, May 17, 1862, Hawks Papers; Kilham, "Sketches in Color," 208; *FDHE,* ser. 1, 3: 717.

42. Pearson, ed., *Letters,* 213; Women's Aid Committee minutebook #1: 61, FFAR; James Hawks to Esther Hawks, May 16, 1862, Hawks Papers; Hawks, *Woman Doctor's Civil War,* 47–50; Grimke, *Journals,* 399; Rose, *Rehearsal,* 77.

43. Downs, *Sick,* 33; Sherwood, ed., "Walker," 26; Parsons, *Memoir,* 101; Friends' Association of Philadelphia, *Report,* 6; Winkle, *Lincoln's Citadel,* 310.

44. *New York Tribune,* November 10, 1863; John Oliver to Simeon S. Jocelyn, December report, 1862, Virginia file, AMAA; Rachel G. C. Patten to Simeon S. Jocelyn, December 20, 1862, District of Columbia file, AMAA; *FDHE,* ser. 1, 3: 675; Boyer, *Naval Surgeon,* 94, 106, 247.

45. Rose, *Rehearsal,* 77; James Hawks to Esther Hawks, May 16, July 16, 1862, Hawks Papers; Women's Aid Committee minutebook #1: 22, E5, FFAR; Yellin, ed., *Jacobs Family Papers* 2: 401; *Friend* 36 (October 4, 1862): 36, and (October 11, 1862): 47.

46. US Congress, *Africans in Fort Monroe,* 7; Yellin, ed., *Jacobs Family Papers* 2: 401; Danforth B. Nichols to Committee, August 8, 1861 [actually 1862], LR by Executive Committee, FFAR; Wilbur journal, November 8, 1862; Greenwood, *First Fruits,* 44; Wiley, *Billy Yank,* 141; Foster, "Limitations," 355.

47. Schwalm, "Surviving," 24; Kolchin, *American Slavery,* 115; Yellin, ed., *Jacobs Family Papers* 2: 436; Botume, *First Days,* 105–106, 119–20; Women's Aid Committee minutebook #3: 4, FFAR. I did not find these beliefs about Black health in any relief worker's writing, but Long, *Doctoring Freedom,* 50–51, 59–64, holds them as common among whites.

48. *FDHE,* ser. 1, 2: 183; Wilbur journal, October 25, 1862; New York Yearly Meeting, *Report,* 5; James Hawks to Esther Hawks, May 16, 1862, Hawks Papers; Berlin et al., ed., *Free at Last,* 189.

49. Sears, ed., *Camp Nelson,* lii; *Friends' Intelligencer* 19 (July 19, 1862): 302; Holt et al., *Special Mission,* 2–3; Winkle, *Lincoln's Citadel,* 312; J. W. Fox to Simeon S. Jocelyn, July 1, 1862, Kansas file, AMAA; Long, *Doctoring Freedom,* 66; *Freedman's Advocate,* 1 (March 1864): 9.

50. *Friends' Review* 16 (October 4, 1862): 75; John Oliver to Simeon S. Jocelyn, September 30, 1862, Virginia file, AMAA; Rose, *Rehearsal,* 171–72; Foster, "Limitations," 357. The Women's Aid Committee minutebook #1, E-3, FFAR, notes that the Helena camp had a 25 percent death rate in 1864, and McKaye, *Mastership and Its Fruits,* 25, gives the same figure for the Mississippi Valley.

51. Eberhart, *History,* 249; Gerteis, *From Contraband to Freedman,* 121.

52. *Friends' Review* 18 (September 24, 1864): 55; Rochester Ladies Antislavery Society, *Thirteenth Annual Report,* 8 (quoted); Wilbur journal, December 12, 1862; Lewis C. Lockwood to AMA, February 7, 1862, Virginia file, AMAA; Friends' Association for the Aid and Elevation of Freedmen, *Extracts from Letters,* 4; Rose, *Rehearsal,* 171.

53. Terry, *Condemned,* 234; *New York National Antislavery Standard,* June 21, September 27, 1862; Charles B. Wilder to George Whipple, June 9, 1862, and Lewis C. Lockwood to AMA, July 25, 1862, Virginia file, AMAA; Rochester Ladies Antislavery Society, *Twelfth Annual Report,* 8 (quoted); *Cleveland Herald,* October 22, 1862; *FDHE,* ser. 1, 3: 147; Wilbur journal, October 23, 1862.

54. James Hawks to Esther Hawks, June 15, 1862, Hawks Papers; Jones, *Saving Savannah,* 156; Sherwood, ed., "Walker," 39; Rogers, *War Pictures,* 223; Eaton report, 20, Tennessee file, AFIC; Berlin et al., ed., *Free at Last,* 190; *New York Tribune,* November 5, 1862.

55. Towne, *Letters and Diary,* 63–65, 74, 86, 93; Cimprich, *Slavery's End,* 49; Pearson, ed., *Letters,* 42–43, 63–64; Ramold, *Slaves, Sailors, Citizens,* 46; Pierce, "Freedmen," 300–301; Rose, *Rehearsal,* 145, 187.

56. Maria Mann to Elisa [no surname], February 10, 1863, Mann Papers; *Friends' Review* 16 (January 31, 1863): 342 (quoted); Litwack, *Been in the Storm,* 139.

3. Seeking New Privileges

1. Samuel G. Wright to AMA, December 28, 1862, Kentucky file, AMAA.

2. Bremner, *Public Good,* 33; Katz, *In the Shadow,* 59–61, 64; Ginzberg, *Women,* 25; Browning, "Bringing Light," 2.

3. M. Fitch to AMA, May 6, 1862, South Carolina file, AMAA.

4. Engs, *Freedom's First,* 79.

5. Pearson, ed., *Letters,* 113; Botume, *First Days,* 128–32; Towne, *Letters and Diary,* 13–14, 16–17, 30, 126–27; Sherwood, ed., "Walker," 32; Browning, *Shifting Loyalties,* 92; Rochester Ladies Antislavery Society, *Twelfth Annual Report,* 11; US Congress, *Africans in Fort Monroe,* 7; J. M. Broadhead to Montgomery Meigs, August 15, 1863, "Negroes" consolidated file, LR by Quartermaster General, RG 92, NA; Glymph, *Women's Fight,* 176–79.

6. Towne Diary, April 24, 1862, Penn School Papers; Yellin, ed., *Jacobs Family Papers* 2: 402 (woman's quote); Rawick, ed., *American Slave* 16: VA-23; Blight, ed., *A Slave No More,* 194–95.

7. *American Missionary* 7 (February 1863): 37; Livermore, *My Story,* 257; Faulkner, *Women's Radical Reconstruction,* 12–13; *New York Tribune,* November 18, 1862 (quoted); New York Yearly Meeting, *Report,* 21.

8. Lewis C. Lockwood to AMA, January 3, 1862, Virginia file, AMAA; Kolchin, *American Slavery,* 153; *Nashville Banner,* March 9, 1888; Hilliard, *Masters, Slaves, and Exchange,* 23, 33, 46, 108; Hunter, *Bound in Wedlock,* 140–41; Glymph, *Women's Fight,* 91; Penningroth, *Claims of Kinfolk,* 61–62, 98.

9. Browning, *Shifting Loyalties,* 92–95; Lockwood, *Peake,* 27; Maria Mann to Elisa, February 10, 1863, Mann Papers; Boyer, *Naval Surgeon,* 36, 69; Bradford, *Harriet Tubman,* 38; Larson, *Harriet Tubman,* 204–205, 208; Cabral, "Letters," 8; Teters, *Practical Liberators,* 38; Taylor, *Embattled Freedom,* 33–34.

10. *Home Missionary* 35 (July 1862): 710; Charles P. Ware to Emma Ware, August 16, 1862, Ware Papers; Pearson, ed., *Letters,* 37.

11. *FDHE,* ser. 1, 3: 675; Eaton, *Report,* 18; H. S. Beals to Simeon S. Jocelyn, April 28, 1863, Virginia file, AMAA; Towne, *Letters and Diary,* 86.

12. Charles B. Wilder to George Whipple, June 20, 1862, Virginia file, AMAA; Engs and Brooks, ed., *Their Patriotic Duty,* 52, 96; Williams, *I Freed Myself,* 13–14; *FDHE,* ser. 1, 2: 20; *New York Tribune,* January 27, 1863.

13. Engs and Brooks, ed., *Their Patriotic Duty,* 51; J. G. C. Lee to D. H. Rucker, March 31, 1866, "Negroes, Employment" consolidated file (quoted), LR by Quartermaster General, RG 92, NA; Charles B. Wilder to *New York Tribune,* May 1862, Virginia file, AMAA; *New York Tribune,* January 27, 1863; Glymph, "This Species of Property," 63; US Congress, *Africans in Fort Monroe,* 8.

14. *FDHE,* ser. 1, 1: 130–31, 284, 311–32; ser. 1, 2: 113, 364 (quoted); ser. 1, 3: 22–23, 88–89, 98; Cimprich, *Slavery's End,* 65; Rochester Ladies Antislavery Society, *Twelfth Annual Report,* 11; Emancipation League, *Facts,* 9; *American Missionary* 7 (February 1863): 37; Taylor, *Embattled Freedom,* 260; Roediger, *Seizing Freedom,* 37.

15. *Cleveland Herald,* October 22, 1862; Taylor, *Embattled Freedom,* 28; Schultz, *Women at the Front,* 21–22, 41; Larson, *Harriet Tubman,* 210–14, 222; Cecelski, *Fire of Freedom,* 43–57; Bucklin, *In Hospital,* 68-69.

16. Colyer, *Report,* 9, 29; Mohr, *On the Threshold,* 84; Smith, *Corinth 1862,* 290; Lineberry, *Be Free or Die,* 5–28, 88–90, 153–55.

17. *US Statutes,* 12: 599; Cimprich, *Slavery's End,* 65; Engs, *Freedom's First,* 30–31; Ochiai, *Harvesting Freedom,* 58; Lewis C. Lockwood to AMA, October 9, November 16, 1862, Virginia file, AMAA; *New York Tribune,* May 19, 1862; Gerteis, *From Contraband to Freedman,* 20.

18. *FDHE,* ser. 1, 2: 113; Lewis C. Lockwood to AMA, January 3, 6, 1862, and Charles B. Wilder to George Whipple, September 6, 1862, Virginia file, AMAA; Samuel G. Wright to George Whipple, December 28, 1862, Kentucky file, AMAA; Burton, *Penn Center,* 26; *OR,* ser. 1, 7: 628.

19. Wilbur journal, June 7, 1863; *FDHE,* ser. 1, 2: 113 (Lockwood quote); Gerteis, *From Contraband to Freedman,* 20–21; US Congress, *Africans in Fort Monroe, passim.*

20. *FDHE,* ser. 1, 2: 272; Danforth B. Nichols to Sarah Cope, August 8, 1862, LR by executive committee, FFAR; James, "Establishment of Freedmen's Village," 90; *OR,* ser. 3, 2: 589–90, 649; Emancipation League, *Facts,* 4; *Washington National Intelligencer,* September 11, 1862; Rachel G. C. Patten to Simeon S. Jocelyn, November 15, 1862, District of Columbia file, AMAA. *Boston Liberator,* February 7, 1862, reported on an antislavery officer, who similarly created a charity fund for a group of Black refugees by confiscating and selling much of their property upon arrival in Kansas.

21. Ramold, *Slaves, Sailors, Citizens,* 41–43, 46, 50, 63, 83–86, 104–106; *ORN,* 4: 692, 18: 499, 23: 472–73, 475.

22. Lewis C. Lockwood to AMA, October 4, 1862, Virginia file, AMAA; *FDHE,* ser. 1, 2: 150; Eberhart, *History,* 245–46; *New York National Antislavery Standard,* June 7, 1862.

23. Tomblin, *Blue Jackets,* 69–73, 83; Mohr, *On the Threshold,* 80, 82.

24. Lewis C. Lockwood to AMA, April 7, 11, 1862, Virginia file, AMAA.

25. Rose, *Rehearsal,* 24, 126–27; Gerteis, *From Contraband to Freedman,* 52; "Circular of the Port Royal Relief Committee" (1862), Arthur Sumner letters, Penn School Papers; *FDHE,* ser. 2: 174–76, ser. 1, 3: 24, 128; Charles Ware to Emma Ware, August 7, 1862, Ware Papers; Educational Commission of Boston, *Extracts,* ser. 2: 1; Pearson, ed., *Letters,* 180–81. For pay records from the Sea Islands, see "Contraband Fund (South Carolina)" consolidated file, LR by Quartermaster General, RG 94, NA.

26. *FDHE,* ser. 1, 3: 169, 177, 185; Educational Commission of Boston, *Extracts,* ser. 2: 3–4 (Philbrick quote); Pearson, ed., *Letters,* 14; *New York National Antislavery Standard,* May 31, 1862; M. Fitch to AMA, May 6, 1862, South Carolina file, AMAA; Towne, *Letters and Diary,* 9; Ochiai, *Harvesting Freedom,* 67, 70.

27. Charles Ware to Emma Ware, August 16, November 16, 1862, Ware Papers; Rose, *Rehearsal,* 82–83.

28. Frankel, *Freedom's Women,* 29; Pierce, "Freedmen," 309; French, *Slavery,* 106; Rochester Ladies Antislavery Society, *Thirteenth Annual Report,* 22.

29. Pearson, ed., *Letters,* 45, 116, 99–100; *FDHE,* ser. 1, 3: 185, 449; Educational Commission of Boston, *Extracts,* ser. 2: 3. For unusual orders elsewhere creating a tobacco ration for Black laborers, see *OR,* ser. 1, 7 (pt. 2): 13.

30. Pearson, ed., *Letters,* 55–56, 107, 148 (quoted); Towne, *Letters and Diary,* 55; French, *Slavery,* 308.

31. *FDHE,* ser. 2: 50; *OR,* ser. 2, 1: 47–48, 505; *OR,* ser. 3, 2: 346, 695; *Boston Liberator,* August 8, 1862 (Rivers quote); Pierce, "Freedmen," 300–301; Towne, *Letters and Diary,* 29, 44, 94; Rose, *Rehearsal,* 145–48; Wise, Rowland, and Spieler, *Rebellion,* 153.

32. Jones, *Saving Savannah,* 156; *FDHE,* ser. 1, 3: 210; Charles Ware to Emma Ware, October 23, 1862, Ware Papers; Rose, *Rehearsal,* 192; Towne, *Letters and Diary,* 84, 93; Ash, *Firebrand of Liberty,* 35–36.

33. Harrison, *Washington,* 39–40; Yellin, *Harriet Jacobs,* 158; Doster, *Lincoln,* 165; Epps, *Slavery on the Periphery,* 169; Sheridan, "From Slavery in Missouri," 42–43.

34. *Washington National Intelligencer,* April 1, 1862; Schwalm, "Between Slavery and Freedom," 146; *OR,* ser, 3, 2: 569.

35. New York Yearly Meeting, *Report,* 15; New England Yearly Meeting of Friends Executive Committee in Behalf of the Freed People of Color, *Second Report,* 9; Emancipation League, *Facts,* 6; *Cleveland Herald,* April 25, 1862; Conway, *Testimonies,* 104, 108–10, 113–14; Lewis C. Lockwood to AMA, April 11, 1862, Virginia file, AMAA; Schwalm, *Emancipation's Diaspora,* 71.

36. McKivigan, *Forgotten Firebrand,* 77, 82; Lewis C. Lockwood to AMA, April 17, 1862, Virginia file, AMAA; *New York Tribune,* April 2, 1864.

37. *American Missionary* 7 (October 1863): 232; Bruce, *Recollections,* 112–14; Allen journal, December 25, 1864.

38. *New York Times,* February 9, 1862 (quoted); French, *Slavery,* 52, 138.

39. Glymph, *Women's Fight,* 35; Martha L. Kellogg to George Whipple, April 7, 1865, Virginia file, AMAA; Samuel G. Wright to AMA, December 28, 1862, Kentucky file, AMAA.

40. Cabral, "Letters," 65; Rable, *God's Almost Chosen Peoples,* 20; Engs, *Freedom's First,* 56–57, 76; Lewis C. Lockwood to AMA, January 4, 1862, Virginia file, AMAA; Wilbur journal, November 19, 1862; Hawks, *Woman Doctor's Civil War,* 39.

41. Annie R. Wilkins to Michael E. Strieby, April 1, 1865, Virginia file, AMAA; Salemson, ed., "Beard," 22, 25; Arthur Sumner to Joseph Clark, July 7, 1862, Sumner letters, and Towne diary, April 18, 1862, May 28, 1864, Penn School Papers; Sherwood, ed., "Walker," 16; Higginson, *Journal,* 218.

42. John Conant to George Whipple, August 9, 1862, South Carolina file, AMAA; *American Missionary* 5 (October supplement, 1861): 243; *American Missionary* 7 (November, 1863): 254; *New York Tribune,* December 12, 1861; *New York Anglo-African,* January 4, 1862 (quoted); Click, *Time Full,* 35; Moore, *In Christ's Stead,* 29; Kilham, "Sketches," 208–209.

43. Engs, *Freedom's First,* 57; William S. Bell to Simeon S. Jocelyn, August 8, 1863 (quoted), Charles B. Wilder to AMA, November 7, 1862, Virginia file, AMAA; Danforth B. Nichols to Simeon S. Jocelyn, June 9, 1862, District of Columbia file, AMAA; *FDHE,* ser. 1, 3: 148; Coffin, *Reminiscences,* 623.

44. Browning, *Shifting Loyalties,* 104; James A. McCrea to Simeon S. Jocelyn, February 24, 1862, South Carolina file, AMAA; French, *Slavery,* 29; *Home Mission Record* 13 (August, 1862): 31; Chambers-Schiller, *Liberty,* 89.

45. Lewis C. Lockwood to AMA, January 4, May 24, September 29, 1862, J. R. Johnson to AMA, August 22, 1862, Charles B. Wilder to AMA, August 19, 1863, May 8, 1864, Hope Daggett to George Whipple, March 28, 1864, Virginia file, AMAA; W. W. Wheeler to George Whipple, December 2, 1864, Maryland file, AMAA; *Freedman's Friend* 1 (June 1864): 4.

46. Fountain, *Slavery,* 6–7, 16, 97–104; Trumbull, *War Memories,* 389; William O. King to Simeon S. Jocelyn, July 2, 1863, Virginia file, AMAA; James A. McCrea to Simeon S. Jocelyn, December 11, 1862, South Carolina file, AMAA; Edward R. Pierce to Simeon S. Jocelyn, August 7, 1863, Mississippi file, AMAA; Engs, *Freedom's First,* 58; Hawks, *Woman Doctor's Civil War,* 37; Emancipation League, *Facts,* 4, 10–11; *Friends' Intelligencer* 21 (July 9, 1864): 277.

47. Rable, *God's Almost Chosen Peoples,* 292–93, 333; *Anglo-African,* January 30, 1864, quoted in Asch and Musgrove, *Chocolate City,* 129.

48. Mary E. Green to Simeon S. Jocelyn, August 14, 1862, and G. H. Hyde to William E. Whiting, February 21, 1862, Virginia file, AMAA; Engs, *Freedom's First,* 58–65; *Freedman's Advocate* 2 (February 1865): 5 (Smith quote); Trumbull, *War Memories,* 390–91.

49. Lewis C. Lockwood to AMA, December 23, 1861, and John Oliver to Simeon S. Jocelyn, December 19, 1862, Virginia file, AMAA; James A. McCrea to Simeon S. Jocelyn, May 12, South Carolina file, AMAA; Engs, *Freedom's First,* 48; Sherwood, ed., "Walker," 41; *New York Anglo-African,* October 19, 1861, and January 11, 1862; *Boston Liberator,* November 7, 1862; Haviland, *Woman's Life,* 265.

50. Katz, *In the Shadow,* 63; Engs, *Freedom's First,* 48; James A. McCrea to AMA, May 12, 1862, South Carolina file, AMAA; M. L. and H. F. Sheldon to AMA, April 8, 1865, Virginia file, AMAA; *American Missionary* 5 (October supplement, 1861): 246, (October 1862): 232, 277 (February 1863): 39.

51. G. M. Warren to George Whipple, May 20, 1864, South Carolina file, AMAA; Engs, *Freedom's First,* 59; Colyer testimony, n.d., North Carolina file, 27, AFIC; *American Missionary* 6 (September 1862): 210, (February 1865): 26 (Obman quote).

52. Jones, *Soldiers of Light,* 140; *Freedmen's Bulletin* 1 (July 1864): 9–10 (M. J. P. quote); Edwin L. Williams to Simeon S. Jocelyn, December 18, 1862, South Carolina file, AMAA; Samuel G. Wright to Simeon S. Jocelyn, January 2, 1863, Kentucky file, AMAA; Sojourner Truth, *Narrative,* 181–83 (Battle Creek, MI: privately printed, 1878), 181–83; Ginsberg, *Women,* 61, 412; Glymph, *Women's Fight,* 168; Frederick A. Eustis to Anna Wharton, May 13, 1862, Wharton Papers.

53. Kolchin, *American Slavery,* 114; *FDHE,* ser. 1, 3: 206.

54. Moore, *In Christ's Stead,* 26–27; Click, *Time Full,* 99; Lucinda Humphrey to Asa S. Fiske, n.d., 1864, Tennessee file, AMAA; M. Fitch to AMA, May 6, 1862, Edwin L. Williams to Simeon S. Jocelyn, March 25, 1863, South Carolina file, AMAA; M. Noyes to Michael E. Streiby, March 21, 1865, Maryland file, AMAA; Samuel G. Wright to Simeon S. Jocelyn, January 20, 1863, Mississippi file, AMAA; Towne, *Letters and Diary,* 56; Hancock, *South,* 46.

55. Tacy Hadley reminiscences, 3; Jones, *Soldiers of Light,* 40–41; Glymph, *Women's Fight,* 163–66, 170–72; Wilbur journal, June 10, 1863.

56. Magdol, *Right to the Land,* 24; Cimprich, *Slavery's End,* 10–11; *American Missionary* 5 (October supplement, 1861): 247; Hunter, *Bound in Wedlock,* 31–33; *New York National Antislavery Standard,* May 23, 1863; Laura M. Towne testimony, n.d., South Carolina file, 70, AFIC; Mansfield French to George Whipple, March 18, 1862, South Carolina file, AMAA.

57. Colyer, *Report*, 22, 26; *Freedmen's Bulletin* 1 (September 1864): 19; R. J. Hinton testimony, December 14, 1863, Kansas-Arkansas-Indian Territory file, 5, AFIC; Kickler, "Black Children and Northern Missionaries," 31–33, 36; Charles P. Day to Simeon S. Jocelyn, August 11, 1862, Virginia file, AMAA; Charles Ware to Emma Ware, August 16, 1862, Ware Papers; Yellin, *Harriet Jacobs*, 169–70.

58. Hunter, *Bound in Wedlock*, 128–30; *New York Anglo-African*, October 5, 1861; *American Missionary* 5 (November 1861): 248; Abby Gibbons to Julia Gibbons, September 10, 1862, Gibbons Papers; Rhoda Smith to cousin, May 12, 1863 (Black refugee quote), FFAR; Rose, *Rehearsal*, 236; Grimke, *Journals*, 402 (Forten quotes), 406.

59. Abstract of Mansfield French to George Whipple, March 15, 1862, South Carolina file, AMAA; Wilbur journal, November 23, 1863; Whitacre, *Civil Life*, 26; Yellin, ed., *Jacobs Family Papers* 2: 452; James Hawks to Esther H. Hawks, May 17, 1862, Hawks Papers; Swint, ed., *Dear Ones*, 123 (mother's quote); Higginson, *Journal*, 317.

60. Glymph, *Women's Fight*, 229; Yellin, ed., *Jacobs Family Papers* 2: 406; Rachel G. C. Patten to Simeon S. Jocelyn, November 15, December 20, 1862, District of Columbia file, AMAA; James F. Sisson to AMA, July 23, 1863, and Rachel G. C. Patten to Simeon S. Jocelyn, July 28, 1863, Virginia file, AMAA; Rachel G. C. Patten to Anna Wharton, December 20, 1862, Wharton Papers; Pearson, ed., *Letters*, 125–26.

61. *FDHE*, ser. 1, 3: 130.

62. Glymph, *Women's War*, 229–32; Click, *Time Full*, 36; Clifford, *Those Good Gertrudes*, 215; Lewis C. Lockwood to AMA, January 4, 1862, Virginia file, AMAA; Rachel G. C. Patten to Simeon S. Jocelyn, December 20, 1862, and Laurie C. Gates to George Whipple, December 31, 1864, District of Columbia file, AMAA; Horst, *Education*, 186.

63. *Freedmen's Bulletin* 1 (September 1864): 25 (Andrews quote).

64. Trumbull, *War Memories*, 382–83; Williams, *Self-Taught*, 13–21, 41–42; Lucas, *From Slavery*, 140; Butchart, *Schooling*, 4, 10.

65. Butchart, *Schooling*, 4, 18; J. W. Fox to Simeon S. Jocelyn, May 10, 1862, Kansas file, AMAA; Jones, *Soldiers of Light*, 65; Click, *Time Full*, 35; Towne diary, April 18, 1862, Penn School Papers; Rochester Ladies Antislavery Society, *Twelfth Annual Report*, 10; Cimprich, *Slavery's End*, 75–76; Span, *From Cotton Field*, 4, 37.

66. Robert C. Morris, *Reading, 'Riting, and Reconstruction*, 6; *New York Anglo-African*, April 22, 1865 (Letcher quote); Lockwood, *Peake*, 58.

67. Lockwood, *Peake*, 30, 35, 54; Williams, *Self-Taught*, 40; Danforth B. Nichols to Simeon S. Jocelyn, June 9, 1862, District of Columbia file, AMAA; Samuel G. Wright to Simeon S. Jocelyn, January 2, 1863, Kentucky file, AMAA; Cimprich, *Slavery's End*, 76; Ripley, *Slaves and Freedmen*, 127; Pease, "Three Years," 100; James Hawks to Esther Hawks, August 14, 1862, Hawks Papers; Ginzberg, *Women*, 139.

68. *American Missionary* 6 (December 1862): 277–78; Browning, *Shifting Loyalties*, 101; *New York National Antislavery Standard*, June 21, 1862; Colyer quoted in Greenwood, *First Fruits*, 44; Lewis C. Lockwood to AMA, March 11, July 22, 1862, Charles P. Day to Simeon S. Jocelyn, August 22, 1862, and John Oliver to Simeon S. Jocelyn, November 25, 1862, Virginia file, AMAA; *New York Times*, March 9, 1862; Masur, *Example*, 26; *New York Anglo-African*, November 21, 1863. The AMA files for 1861–62 show no activity in Delaware, Maryland, and Missouri.

69. Butchart, *Schooling,* xiii–xv; Towne diary, March 3, 1863, Penn School Papers; *American Missionary* 7 (April, 1863): 114 (Fiske quote); Lewis C. Lockwood to AMA, May 7, 1862, and Charles P. Day to Simeon S. Jocelyn, November 26, 1862, Virginia file, AMAA; Ames, *New England Woman's Diary,* 6 (quoted); Richardson, *Christian Reconstruction,* 12. Butchart found women to be about one half of the teachers in the 1861–76 period, but a different pattern seems likely during wartime, when many men were in the military.

70. Moore, *In Christ's Stead,* 29; Click, *Time Full,* 106, 109; Span, *From Cotton Fields,* 4; Helen M. Dodd to George Whipple, August 3, 1864, and L. R. Harper to George Whipple, May 29, 1865, Virginia file, Emily Gill to Simeon S. Jocelyn, January 1, 1864, North Carolina file, AMAA.

71. Click, *Time Full,* 106–107; Allen, *Yankee,* 77 J. W. Coan to George Whipple, January 2, 1865, District of Columbia file, AMAA; Charles P. Day to Simeon S. Jocelyn, November 26, 1862, and E. Frances Jenks to George Whipple, December 2, 1864, Virginia file, AMAA; Friends' Association for the Aid and Elevation of Freedmen, *Extracts from Letters,* 4; *Friends Intelligencer* 19 (April 5, 1862): 57.

72. Butchart, *Schools,* 117; John Eaton to L. B. Eaton, May 20, 1863, Eaton-Shirley Papers; *Freedman's Friend* 1 (July, 1864): 111; Eberhart reminiscences, 32; Click, *Time Full,* 107; Butler, *Sketch,* 2; E. L. Benton to Simeon S. Jocelyn, August 4, 1863, Robert Harris to George Whipple, December 30, 1864, William S. Bell to George Whipple, March 21, 1865, Virginia file, AMAA; Edward R. Pierce to Simeon S. Jocelyn, April 9, 1863, Mississippi file, AMAA; Isaac G. Hubbs to AMA, January 8, 1864, Louisiana file, AMAA.

73. Indiana Yearly Meeting's Executive Committee for the Relief of Colored Freedmen, *Report,* 39–40; Browning, "Bringing Light," 5; Charles P. Day to William E. Whiting, October 28, 1862, Lewis C. Lockwood to AMA, February 27, 1862, William S. Bell to George Whipple, March 21, 1865, Virginia file, AMAA; James A. McCrea to Simeon S. Jocelyn, February 24, 1862, M. L. Kellogg to Simeon S. Jocelyn, November 20, 1862, James M. Hawks to Simeon S. Jocelyn, May 20, 1862, Edwin S. Williams to Simeon S. Jocelyn, January 28, 1863, South Carolina file, AMAA; Friends' Association for the Aid and Elevation of Freedmen, *Extracts from Letters,* 3.

74. Benjamin Franklin Whitten to Emily Whitten, August 10, 1862 (quoted), Benjamin Franklin Whitten Papers; Butchart, *Northern Schools,* 118; Clifford, *Those Good Gertrudes,* 206; *Friends' Review* 17 (April 9, 1864): 502; *Freedman's Advocate* 2 (January, 1865): 1; *Freedmen's Journal* 1 (January, 1864): 6 (Ball quote); Nicholson, "Contraband Camp," 139 (quoted).

75. Ames, *New England Woman's Diary,* 29; Towne, *Pioneer Work,* 7; Allen journal, December 5, 1864.

76. Clifford, *Those Good Gertrudes,* 206–208; Charles P. Day to William E. Whiting, October 28, 1862, William L. Coan to George Whipple, March 29, 1864, M. E. Burdich to George Whipple, June 26, 1864, Virginia file, AMAA; E. Garrison Jackson to Michael E. Strieby, April 30, 1865, Maryland file, AMAA; *Freedman's Advocate* 2 (January, 1865): 1; Swint, ed., *Dear Ones,* 123.

77. Charles P. Day to Simeon S. Jocelyn, August 11, 1862, Charles P. Day to William E. Whiting, October 28, 1862 (quoted), Harriet Taylor to Simeon S. Jocelyn, March 5, 1863, Charles B. Wilder to AMA, November 2, 1864, Virginia file, AMAA.

78. James Hawks to Esther Hawks, May 22, 1862, Hawks Papers; James M. McCrea to Simeon S. Jocelyn, February 24, 1862, South Carolina file, AMAA; Eberhart reminiscences, 6; Horst, *Education,* 182; *Freedman's Advocate* 1 (September 1864): 29; Educational Commission of Boston, *Extracts,* ser. 2: 1; Morris, *Reading, Riting, and Reconstruction,* 191.

79. "Freedmen's Schools," 1865, 1863–1879 account book, Howland Family Papers; *FDHE*, ser. 1, 3: 205; Lockwood, *Peake*, 32; J. W. Fox to Simeon S. Jocelyn, May 31, 1862, Kansas file, AMAA; Towne, *Letters*, 6.

80. James Hawks to Esther Hawks, June 15, 1862, Hawks Papers; *Freedmen's Bulletin* 1 (September 1864): 26; Grimke, *Journals*, 397.

81. Lewis C. Lockwood to AMA, July 17, 1862, Thomas D. Tucker to Simeon S. Jocelyn, December 24, 1862, Caroline M. Johnson to Simeon S. Jocelyn, May 27, 1864, Virginia file, AMAA; Howard et al., "Domestic History,"(typescript), 176; Port Royal Relief Committee, *First Annual Report*, 7; Butchart, *Schooling*, 13, 147, 271; Allen, *Yankee*, 123; L. Pope to Sara Cope, May 23, 1864, LR by Women's Aid Committee, FFAR.

82. Butchart, *Schooling*, 130–31, 139–41, 150; Jones, *Soldiers of Light*, 140.

83. Clifford, *Those Good Gertrudes*, 32; *Freedmen's Record* 1 (July 1865): 114; *FDHE*, ser. 1, 3: 130, 205; Charles P. Day to Simeon S. Jocelyn, September 30, 1862, Virginia file, AMAA; Educational Commission of Boston, *Extracts*, ser. 1: 4.

84. A. L. Etheridge, June 1864 report, M. E. Burdick to George Whipple, July 20, 1864, Nanny I. Partridge to George Whipple, January 3, 1865, Virginia file, AMAA; Nicholson, "Contraband Camp," 136; Women's Association of Philadelphia, *Second Annual Report*, 4.

85. *Freedmen's Record* 1 (February 1865): 23; Botume, *First Days*, 68; Allen, *Yankee*, 60, 77; Grimke, *Journals*, 393, 420; James A. McCrea to Simeon S. Jocelyn, December 11, 1862, South Carolina file, AMAA.

86. Joel Baker to William E. Whiting, December 1, 1864, Sallie Daffin to George Whipple, March 1, 1865, Virginia file, AMAA; Pearson, ed., *Letters*, 24; Towne, *Letters and Diary*, 19; Ames, *New England Woman's Diary*, 25–26.

87. Forten, "Life," 591; Towne, *Letters and Diary*, 6; *Freedmen's Bulletin* 1 (July, 1864): 9.

88. Blassingame, *Testimony*, 174 (Davis quote); French, *Slavery*, 158 (missionary quote); *FDHE*, ser. 1, 3: 206 (Pierce quote).

89. Browning, "Visions of Freedom," 89; Cabral, "Letters," 12–13; French, *Slavery*, 218; Mansfield French to AMA, June 23, 1862, South Carolina file, AMAA; New York Yearly Meeting, *Report*, 13 (quoted).

4. Emancipation

1. Oakes, *Freedom*, 342; *Boston Liberator*, January 16, 1863; Rachel G. C. Patten to Simeon S. Jocelyn, January 2, 1863, District of Columbia file, AMAA; Franklin, *Emancipation Proclamation*, 86; *American Missionary* 7 (February 1863): 26 (quoted).

2. Jordan, *Black Confederates and Afro-Yankees*, 256; Gerteis, *From Contraband to Freedman*, 23–26; *US Statutes*, 12: 1269. Lincoln's proclamation specifically asked voters within the Confederate states to elect new representatives to the United States Congress, but, after difficulties arose with this, he made some exemptions on his own judgement. Exempted Virginia counties, besides those in the new state of West Virginia, were Accomack, Northampton, Elizabeth City, York, Princess Anne, and Norfolk. For African Americans' celebrations in Hampton and Portsmouth held before learning of their exemption, see Charles B. Wilder to AMA, November 23, 1862, Virginia file, AMAA; *New York Anglo-African*, August 1, 1863.

3. *US Statutes,* 12: 1269; *FDHE,* ser. 1, 1: 231-236. The exempted parishes in Louisiana were St. Bernard, Plaquemines, Jefferson, St. John, St. Charles, St. James, Ascension, Assumption, Terrebonne, Lafourche, St. Mary, St Martin, and Orleans.

4. Ash, *Firebrand of Liberty,* 13-14, 17-19, 23-27. Other nonexempted towns that held celebrations were Alexandria, New Bern, and Key West. See Wilbur journal, December 31, 1862; Greenwood, *First Fruits,* 57; Kachun, *Festivals of Freedom,* 106-108.

5. Teters, *Practical Liberators,* 106; Johnston, *Surviving Freedom,* 129-31; Indiana Yearly Meeting, *Report,* 43; Henry Rountree to Abram M. Taylor, June 14, 1863, Taylor Family Papers; Burton, *Diary,* 6.

6. Ramold, *Slaves, Sailors, Citizens,* 47-48; Tomblin, *Bluejackets and Contrabands,* 94; *New York Tribune,* November 14, 1863; Allen, *Yankee,* 175; *FDHE,* ser. 1, 2: 323; Barnard Freedmen's Aid Society of Dorchester, *First Annual Report,* 7; *Boston Liberator,* January 22, 1864.

7. *Pennsylvania Freedmen's Bulletin* 1 (April, 1865): 33; Joseph R. Hawley to Horace James, April 5, 1865, North Carolina file, AMAA; Allen, *Yankee,* 191; Ellen Murray to Sarah Cope, January 23, 1864 [actually 1865], LR by Women's Aid Committee, FFAR; *Freedman's Friend* 1 (May 1865): 54.

8. Browning, *Shifting Loyalties,* 161; James, *Annual Report,* 3; Click, *Time Full,* 11-12, 38-42, 45-51, 62-63; *FDHE,* ser. 1, 2: 200; New England Freedmen's Aid Society, *Second Annual Report,* 69.

9. *OR,* ser. 1, 24 (pt. 1): 18, (pt. 3): 46-47, 585; Clampitt, *Occupied Vicksburg,* 121; Mann, *"Condition of the Negroes"* (flyer); Glymph, "Black Women and Children," 126-27; John Eaton to Levi Coffin, June 22, 1863, Mississippi Freedmen's Department Letterbook, 44, RG 105, NA; Friends' Association of Philadelphia, *Statistics,* 19; *FDHE,* ser. 1, 3: 716; Warren, *Extracts from Reports,* ser. 2: 11. Ralston and DeSoto were either two names for the same place or very close to one another.

10. Hermann, *Pursuit of a Dream,* 43, 47; D. O. McCord, report, August 3, 1865, Mississippi Freedmen's Department Reports, RG 105, NA; David Todd to George Whipple, February 25, 1864, Arkansas file, AMAA; Friends' Association of Philadelphia, *Statistics,* 19; *American Missionary* 7 (April 1863): 112, (August, 1863): 184; Harris, *With Charity for All,* 84-85, 197-203.

11. Manning, *Troubled Refuge,* 107; Fry, ed., *Following the Fifth Kansas Cavalry,* 59-61; Lovett, "African Americans," 324; Walker, "Corinth," 18-2; Henry Rountree to Abram M. Taylor, October 8, 1863, Taylor Family Papers; Edward R. Pierce to Simeon S. Jocelyn, April 9, 1863, and A. O. Howell to AMA, January 19-February 6, 1864, Mississippi file, AMAA; Cimprich, *Slavery's End,* 49.

12. Reidy, *Illusions,* 181; Butler, *Sketch,* 5; A. O. Howell to AMA, January 19, 1864, Mississippi file, AMAA; Warren, ed., *Final Report,* 11; Warren, ed., *Extracts from Reports,* ser. 1: 30-31; D. O. McCord report, August 3, 1865, Reports for the Mississippi Freedmen's Department, RG 105, NA; *National Freedman* 1 (June 1865), 164; *Freedmen's Bulletin* 1 (June 1865): 115.

13. Gerteis, *From Contraband to Freedman,* 12, 125; Walker, "Corinth," 18; *American Missionary* 9 (January 1865): 6; Henry Rountree to Abram M. Taylor, September 23, 1863, and October 19, 1863, Taylor Family Papers; John Eaton to unknown, February 6, 1864, LS by Medical Director for the Mississippi Freedmen's Department, RG 105, NA.

14. Danielson, *War's Desolating Scourge,* 136-37; *FDHE,* ser. 1, 2: 475-76; Indiana Yearly, *Report,* 50; *National Freedman* 1 (May 1865): 127; *New York National Antislavery Standard,* July 2, 1864; *Pennsylvania Freedmen's Bulletin* 1 (January 1865): 17.

15. Harris, *With Charity for All,* 20-23, 77-79, 100; *FDHE,* ser. 1, 1: 337; Levine, *Fall,* 156.

16. *New York Tribune,* January 16, 1863; Wistar, *Autobiography,* 424; *FDHE,* ser. 1, 1: 67; William H. Woodbury to AMA, December 22, 1863, Virginia file, AMAA.

17. Trefousse, *Ben Butler,* 139–40; Kinsman, *Report,* 2–3; Charles P. Day to Simeon S. Jocelyn, June 16, 1863, and Charles B. Wilder to Simeon S. Jocelyn, September 12, 1863, Virginia file, AMAA; *Freedmen's Friend* 1 (July, 1864): 9; Charles B. Wilder to Rodney Churchill, January 13, 1864, LR by Department of Negro Affairs, Ft. Monroe, VA, Field Office, RG 105, NA; H. Porter, report, March 24, 1865, p. 21, consolidated file V-87 (1865), LR by the Adjutant General, RG 94, NA. The Hampton shantytown and probably some others were also sometimes called Slabtown, but, to avoid confusion, this book will only use that name for the camp near Yorktown.

18. Swint, ed., *Dear Ones,* 88; *Friends' Review* 16 (January 31, 1863): 341; Rhoda Smith to Sarah Cope, LR by Women's Aid Committee, FFAR; *American Missionary* 7 (September 1863): 203; *Friends' Intelligencer* 20 (January 9, 1864): 997; Kinsman, *Report,* 13; C. S. Henry to J. B. Kinsman, March 18, 1864, LR by Department of Negro Affairs, Ft. Monroe, VA, field office, RG 105, NA; H. Porter, report, March 24, 1865, p. 32, consolidated file V-87 (1865), LR by Adjutant General, RG 94, NA.

19. Gerteis, *From Contraband to Freedman,* 38; *OR,* ser, 3, 3: 1140; Butler, *Private and Official Correspondence,* 4: 136; Kinsman, *Report,* 16; Harris, *With Charity for All,* 139–40, 162–63.

20. Conway, *Final Report,* 3; *FDHE,* ser. 1, 1: 98; Rodrigue, *Reconstruction,* 44; Ripley, *Slaves and Freedmen,* 47–49, 54, 61, 105–106; Harris, *With Charity for All,* 181–90.

21. Cimprich, *Slavery's End,* 49–50, 82; Henry Rountree to Abram M. Taylor, April 2, May 12, 1863, Taylor Family Papers; Haviland, *Woman's Life,* 246; Indiana Yearly Meeting of Friends, *Minutes,* 45.

22. Cimprich, *Slavery's End,* 50, 82; New York Yearly Meeting of Friends, *Third Report of a Committee,* 13.

23. Cimprich, *Slavery's End,* 44, 50–52, 104–106, 116.

24. Oakes, *Freedom,* 435; Manning, *Troubled Refuge,* 129; *American Missionary* 9 (February, 1865): 30; Smith, *On the Edge of Freedom,* 181.

25. Kachun, *Festivals of Freedom,* 111–12; Longacre, *Regiment of Slaves,* 14–15; Williams, *Slavery and Freedom,* 242–43; *FDHE,* ser. 1, 1: 338, 410, 514; Lucas, *From Slavery,* 160.

26. *FDHE,* ser. 1, 2: 492, 502; C. S. Henry to J. Burnham Kinsman, May 16, 1864, LR by the Department of Negro Affairs, Ft. Monroe, VA, field office, RG 105, NA; Bryant, *36th Infantry,* 221.

27. Oakes, *Freedom,* 467; *FDHE,* ser. 1, 2: 525–26; Stephens, *Shadow of Shiloh,* 165–70; Fuke, *Imperfect Equality,* 118; W. W. Wheeler to Michael E. Strieby, November 6, 1864, and W. W. Wheeler to George Whipple, November 18, 1864, Maryland file, AMAA.

28. Foner, *Reconstruction,* 201; Fuke, *Imperfect Equality,* 69–82; Andrew Stafford to Henry H. Lockwood, November 21, 1864, consolidated file M-1932 (1864), LR by Adjutant General, RG 94, NA; Stephens, *Shadow of Shiloh,* 169–70; *Friends' Intelligencer* 21 (February 25, 1865): 810; *New York Anglo-African,* February 4, 1865.

29. Stealey, *West Virginia's Civil War Era Constitution,* 105, 118; Woods, "Mountaineers Becoming Free," 37–44, 58; Ellen P. T. Wheeler to George Whipple, June 22, 1864, West Virginia file, AMAA.

30. W. Perkins to Simeon S. Jocelyn, January 19, 1863, Samuel G. Wright to Simeon S. Jocelyn, January 27, 1863, Kentucky file, AMAA; Indiana Yearly Meeting, *Minutes,* 49; *FDHE,* ser. 1, 1: 558–59, 562, 573, 591; *OR,* ser. 2, 5: 536.

31. Lucas, *From Slavery,* 154, 160; Coffin, *Reminiscences,* 643; Sears, ed., *Camp Nelson,* 89–93, 118–19, 134–42, 153–54, 194; Indiana Yearly Meeting, *Minutes,* 45; Marrs, *Life and History,* 61–62; James, *Wonderful, Eventful Life,* 4, 15–17.

32. Maria Mann to William L. Ropes, March 16, April 13, 1863, Mann Papers; George Condee to Simeon S. Jocelyn, March 26, 1863, J. L. Richardson to Simeon S. Jocelyn, April 18, 30, 1863, Katherine Dunning to George Whipple, September 20, 1864, Missouri file, AMAA.

33. Romeo, *Gender and the Jubilee,* 50–53; Anderson, *From Slavery to Affluence,* 42–44; *FDHE,* ser. 1, 1: 411–12, 489, 2: 610; J. Copeland to Charles H. Langston, July 25, 1864, and L. A. M. Montague to George Whipple, September 7, 1864, Freedmen's Relief Society flyer, January 24, 1865, Missouri file, AMAA; *OR,* ser. 1, 34 (pt. 4): 93; *New York National Antislavery Standard,* July 11, 1863; S. H. Wilcox to Newton Flagg, June 21, 1863, "Negroes" consolidated file, LR by Quartermaster General, RG 92, NA; Oakes, *Freedom,* 478; Epps, *Slavery on the Periphery,* 184.

34. Littlefield, *The Cherokee Freedmen,* 15–17; Littlefield, *Africans and Seminoles,* 184; R. J. Hinton testimony, December 14, 1863, Kansas-Arkansas-Oklahoma file, 7, AFIC; Rawick, ed., *American Slave* 7: OK-117; *Freedmen's Advocate* 1 (May 1864): 18; Warren, ed., *Final Report,* 17.

35. Haviland, *Woman's Life,* 361–74; *Boston Liberator,* January 29, 1864; J. F. Norris to George Whipple, December 28, 1864, and J. Copeland to Michael E. Strieby, October 29, 1864, Kansas file, AMAA.

36. *New York Anglo-African,* August 1, 1863; Elias M. Greene file, Appointment and Commission Branch, RG 94, NA; *New York Tribune,* August 3, 1863; McElya, *Politics of Mourning,* 28, 39, 62, 79; Emerson, *Life of Abby Hopper Gibbons,* 2: 74; C. B. Webster to George Whipple, July 16, 1863, District of Columbia file, AMAA; Wilbur Diary, June 20, 1863.

37. Wilbur journal, February 27, 1863; Winkle, *Lincoln's Citadel,* 347; *FDHE,* ser. 1, 2: 323, 329; Julia Wilbur to Anna M. C. Barnes, December 27, 1863, Rochester Ladies Antislavery Society Papers; Hancock, *South,* 35–36, 40; James B. Feree to William E. Whiting, January 13, 1864, District of Columbia file, AMAA.

38. *FDHE,* ser. 1, 2: 310, 329, 331; New York Yearly Meeting, *Report,* 5 (quoted); Bestebreurtje, "Beyond the Plantation," 342–43; McElya, *Politics of Mourning,* 351; "Freedmen's Schools," 1863–1879 account book, Howland Family Papers; Association for the Aid and Elevation of the Freedmen, *Report,* 12.

39. Whitacre, *Civil Life,* 110, 120, 157; Yellin, ed., *Jacobs Family Papers* 2: xxv, 453 (quoted), 619; Julia Wilbur to Anna M. C. Barnes, February 20, 1863 [actually 1864], Rochester Ladies Antislavery Society Papers; Danforth B. Nichols to George Whipple, February 4, 1865, Virginia file, AMA; *FDHE,* ser. 1, 2: 260, 360.

40. *Freedmen's Friend* 1 (July, 1864), 8 (quoted); Julia Wilbur to Sarah Cope, February 7, 1863, LR by Women's Aid Committee, FFAR.

5. Providing Necessities for More

1. *Freedmen's Record* 1 (March, 1865): 41–42; *Freedmen's Bulletin* 1 (September, 1864): 26; *New York Tribune,* November 10, 1863, February 27, 1864; Northwestern Freedmen's Aid Commission, *Minutes of the First Annual Meeting,* 13; T. Hinckly to Charles P. Ware, May 21, 1865, Ware Papers.

2. Andrus, *Civil War Letters,* 75; Women's Aid Committee minutebook, #1: 12, E2–3, FFAR; Indiana Freedmen's Aid Commission, *Report,* 9, 15.

3. Coffin, *Reminiscences,* 627–45; Samuel G. Wright to George Whipple, January 4, 1865, Mississippi file, AMAA; Convention of Freedmen's Commissions, *Minutes,* 19; Eberhart reminiscences 17–18; Women's Aid Committee minutebook, #1: 62, 3: 12, 20, FFAR.

4. Dougherty, *Port Royal,* 41–44; New England Freedmen's Aid Society, *Second Annual Report,* 5–6; Convention of Freedmen's Commissions, *Minutes,* 13–14, 18, 23; Indiana Freedmen's Aid Commission, *Report,* 13.

5. Abby Gibbons to Julia Gibbons, February 12, 1863, Gibbons Papers; St. Louis Ladies Contraband Society statement, n.d., Missouri file, 161, AFIC; Women's Association of Philadelphia, *Third Annual Report,* 9; Whitacre, *Civil Life,* 156; Warren, ed., *Final Report,* 19; *Freedmen's Journal* 1 (March, 1865): 6 (quoted); Freedmen and Soldiers' Relief Association, *Second Annual Report,* 6.

6. Horst, *Education,* 162; Walker, *Rock in a Weary Land,* 48–49; Warren, ed., *Final Report,* 16–18; Harper, *End of Days,* 29; Harriet E. Townsend to Simeon S. Jocelyn, March 22, 1864, Missouri file, AMAA; Maria Mann to Elisa, February 10, 1863, Mann Papers.

7. Sears, ed., *Camp Nelson,* xlv–xlvi; Henry Rountree to Abram M. Taylor, May 1, 7, 18, 1863, Taylor Family Papers; George Condee to Simeon S. Jocelyn, March 26, July 31, 1863, Missouri file, AMAA; Contraband Relief Commission, *To the Public* (flyer); Indiana Yearly Meeting, *Minutes,* 44.

8. Butchart, *Schooling,* 96; Convention of Freedmen's Commissions, *Minutes,* 3, 7–9; John Eaton to Henry Wilson, n.d., 1863, John Eaton to Robert W. Carroll, March 10, 1863, Mississippi Freedmen's Department letterbook, 16–19, 28, RG 105, NA.

9. Michael E. Strieby to George Whipple, February 24, 1865, District of Columbia file, AMAA; Belz, *A New Birth of Freedom,* 70–88, 94–106. For Eaton's and Greene's attempts to influence the law's content, see Eaton, *Grant, Lincoln and the Freedmen,* 221–22, 226, 238–41; Elias M. Greene to Mr. Whiting, January 9, 1864, "Bureau of Emancipation" consolidated file, LR by Quartermaster General, RG 92, NA.

10. H. Hyde to AMA, June 3, 1863, South Carolina file, AMAA; Lydia A. Hess to George Whipple, June 28, 1864 (quoted), and George Condee to Michael E. Steiby, July 2, 1864 (quoted), Missouri file, AMAA; Wilbur journal, February 21, 1864.

11. Henry Rountree to Abram M. Taylor, October 31, December 20, 1863, Taylor Family Papers; John Eaton to M. Boynton, n.d., 1863, Mississippi Freedmen's Department Letterbook, 38, RG 105, NA; Wilbur journal, May 24, 1864; W. T. Richardson to George Whipple, January 31, 1865 (quoted), W. T. Richardson to E. A. Lane, April 29, 1865, South Carolina file, AMAA; Terry, *Condemned,* 225.

12. Browning, "Bringing Light," 2; Sherwood, ed., "Walker," 16, 18; Charles B. Wilder to George Whipple, September 12, 1862, William L. Coan to Simeon S. Jocelyn, May 9, 1863, James P. Stone to AMA, July 20, 1863, Samuel Hunt to AMA, November 16, 1864, Virginia file, AMAA.

13. T. W. Magill to George Whipple, April 5, 21, 1865, J. N. Coan to George Whipple, February 15, 1864, William L. Coan to George Whipple, February 15, May 3, 1864, William S. Bell to George Whipple, June 9, 1864, William H. Woodbury to George Whipple, October 7, 1864, Virginia file, AMAA; E. Andrews to George Whipple, September 24, 1864, Department of the Gulf, S.O. 280, October 15, 1864 (quoted), Louisiana file, AMAA.

14. Josiah Beardsley to Edwin M. Wheelock, January 24, 1865, LR by the Louisiana Board of Education for Freedmen, RG 105, NA; John Phillips to AMA, July 23, 1863 (quoted), Mississippi file, AMAA; M. H. Abbey to George Whipple, October 14, 1864, Virginia file, AMAA; S. A. Bartlett to George Whipple, September 25, 1864, March 6, 1865, Louisiana file, AMAA.

15. Indiana Yearly Meeting, *Report,* 32; Ash, *When the Yankees Came,* 79–81.

16. *OR,* ser. 3, 4: 44–45; Cimprich, *Slavery's End,* 57; Eberhart reminiscences, 31; H. Porter, report, March 24, 1865, pp. 7, 22, 31, Charles B. Wilder to Edward O. C. Ord, January 23, 1865, consolidated file V-87 (1865), LR by Adjutant General, RG 94, NA; Mann, *Condition* (flyer); Eberhart, *History,* 243–46; *Washington National Intelligencer,* October 8, 1863.

17. Click, *Time Full,* 136, 142–44; *FDHE,* ser. 1, 2: 202; Larson, *Harriet Tubman,* 218.

18. Weicksel, "Fitted up," 157; *FDHE,* ser. 1, 2: 202; New England Yearly Meeting of Friends, *Report to the Executive Committee,* 5; Breault, *Howland,* 63; *New York Tribune,* May 14, 1864; Coffin, *Reminiscences,* 636.

19. Manning, *Troubled Refuge,* 80; *National Freedman* 1 (March 1, 1865): 51, (May 1, 1865): 127.

20. Henry Rountree to Abram M. Taylor, May 1, 7, 10, September 19, 1863, Taylor Family Papers; Committee on Freedmen, *Report,* 5; *FDHE,* ser. 1, 2: 700; New England Freedmen's Aid Society, *Second Annual Report,* 30, 70; Friends' Association of Philadelphia, *Report,* 8; James, *Annual Report,* 8.

21. Ellen Murray to Sarah Cope, November 14, 1863, LR by Women's Aid Commission, William F. Mitchell to Sarah Cope, January 9, 1865, LR by Executive Committee, FFAR; *Freedmen's Bulletin* 1 (July 1864): 8–9; H. Porter report, March 24, 1865, p. 11, V-87 (1865) consolidated file, LR by Adjutant General, RG 94, NA; Weicksel, "Fitted up," 162–165.

22. Wilbur journal, January 28, 1865; Robert M. West to Anna Wharton, January 4, 1862 [actually 1863], Wharton Papers; Ripley, ed., *Black Abolitionist Papers,* 5: 285; Yellin, ed., *Jacobs Family Papers* 2: 618; *Freedmen's Advocate* 1 (June, 1864): 22 (quoted); *FDHE,* ser. 1, 2: 356; Hancock, *South,* 35, 47.

23. *FDHE,* ser. 1, 2: 586–87; George E. H. Day et al. to Edwin Stanton, December 30, 1864, "Freedmen's Relief Association" consolidated file, LR by Quartermaster General, RG 92, NA; Wilbur journal, January 28, 1865; Rochester Ladies Antislavery Society, *Twelfth Annual Report,* 16, *Fourteenth Annual Report,* 11; Friends' Association of Philadelphia, *Statistics,* 19; Hermann, *Pursuit,* 47.

24. Richardson, *Christian Reconstruction,* 14; *Freedmen's Journal* 1 (January 1865): 7–8, 15; Buss, *My Work,* 42; Ella Roper to George Whipple, August 5, 1863, Elizabeth James to George Whipple, August 23, 1864, and Helen Lyman to George Whipple, December 20, 1864, North Carolina file, AMAA; H. S. Beals to Simeon S. Jocelyn, May 9, 1863, Rhoda W. Smith to Simeon S. Jocelyn, May 25, 1863, William H. Woodbury to George Whipple, February 6, 1865, Virginia file, AMAA; Samuel G. Wright to Simeon S. Jocelyn, February 4, 1863, Kentucky file, AMAA; daily record book, 9, New England Freedmen's Aid Society Papers; *Friends' Review* 17 (June 25, 1864): 682.

25. William T. Briggs to George Whipple, May 4, 1864, and Elizabeth James to George Whipple, December 19, 1864, North Carolina file, AMAA; Abner D. Olds to George Whipple, June 7, 1863, Mississippi file, AMAA; J. M. McArthur, S.O. 76, March 22, 1864, Mississippi Freedmen's Department Orders, RG 105, NA; *Freedmen's Record* 1 (March, 1865): 40.

26. Friends' Association of Philadelphia, *Statistics,* 27; S. D. Seymour to J. Burnham Kinsman, May 18, 1864, LR by Department of Negro Affairs, Ft. Monroe Field Office, RG 105, NA; *FDHE,* ser. 1, 2: 339 (inspector quote); Friends' Association for the Aid and Elevation of Freedmen, *Extracts from Letters,* 4; Botume, *First Days,* 80–81; Swint, ed., *Dear Ones,* 100 (father's quote).

27. James, *Annual Report,* 56–58; Joseph R. Hawley to Horace James, April 5, 1865, North Carolina file, AMAA; Barnard Freedmen's Aid Society, *First Annual Report,* 6–7; Ellen Murray to Sarah Cope, January 23, 1864 [actually 1865], LR by Women's Aid Committee, FFAR; *FDHE,* ser. 1, 1: 155.

28. *FDHE,* ser. 1, 2: 465; Walker, "Corinth," 18; William S. Bell to George Whipple, June 9, 1864, Virginia file, AMAA; Samuel F. Porter to George Whipple, July 1, 1863, Tennessee file, AMAA; Click, *Time Full,* 68–70, 91; Eaton, *Report,* 10; Cope, *Report,* 14–16; Sears, ed., *Camp Nelson,* 171, 175–76, 180.

29. Women's Aid Committee Minutebook #1: E8-E9, FFAR; *Friends' Intelligencer* 21 (October 22, 1864): 522; Western Yearly Meeting of Friends, *Minutes,* 100; Friends' Association of Philadelphia, *Extracts from Letters,* 4; H. Porter, report, March 24, 1865, pp. 5–6, consolidated file V-87 (1865), LR by Adjutant General, RG 94, NA.

30. Rochester Ladies Antislavery Society, *Twelfth Annual Report,* 12; Botume, *First Days,* 51; *Freedmen's Friend* 1 (June 1864): 4; Friends' Association of Philadelphia, *Statistics,* 7, 10; Wilbur journal, March 29, 1864; Taylor, *Embattled Freedom,* 72; Weicksel, "Fitted up," 158–59.

31. Botume, *First Days,* 51; *Friends' Intelligencer,* 20 (January 9, 1864): 692–94; *Friends' Review* 17 (January 2, 1864): 282; Bestebreurtje, "Beyond the Plantation," 341; "Freedmen's Schools," in 1863–79 account book, Howland Family Papers.

32. Julia Wilbur to Anna M. C. Barnes, March 14, 1863, Rochester Ladies Antislavery Society Papers; *Freedman's Advocate* 1 (March, 1864): 9; Cimprich, *Slavery's End,* 47; Lyman W. Ayer to Michael E. Strieby, February 18, 1865, Tennessee file, AMAA; *FDHE,* ser. 1, 2: 357.

33. Johnston, *Surviving Freedom,* 163; Rochester Ladies Antislavery Society, *Thirteenth Annual Report,* 18; James Webster to Albert Gladwin, December 26, 1863, Unregistered LR by Alexandria, VA, field office, RG 105, NA; *Freedmen's Record* 1 (February 1865): 17; New England Yearly Meeting, *Report to the Executive Committee,* 3, 5; Wilbur journal, July 3, 1863; *American Missionary* 9 (March 1865): 52.

34. *FDHE,* ser. 1, 2: 312–13; Wilbur journal, June 12, 1864; Warren, ed., *Extracts from Documents,* 25.

35. Wilbur journal, February 25, 28 (quoted), 1864; Yellin, ed., *Jacobs Family Papers* 2: xxxvi; Yellin, *Harriet Jacobs,* 101–2, 164, 166; Faulkner, *Women's Radical Reconstruction,* 16, 20; Ginzberg, *Women,* 12, 60, 65–66; Katz, *In the Shadow,* 66; Chambers-Schiller, *Liberty,* 155.

36. Yellin, *Harriet Jacobs,* 169; Greene, *Regulations* (poster); *FDHE,* ser. 1, 2: 281, 282 (quoted), 285, 301; Yellin, ed., *Jacobs Family Papers* 2: xxv, 462, 525.

37. Whitacre, *Civil Life,* 117, 120; *FDHE,* ser. 1, 2: 281, 285, 286 (quoted); Yellin, ed., *Jacobs Family Papers* 2: 450 (quoted), 526; Yellin, *Harriet Jacobs,* 170–71; Wilbur journal, June 2 (quoted), 14 (quoted), October 2, 1863; Chambers-Schiller, *Liberty,* 176.

38. *Freedmen's Journal* 1 (January 1865): 14; *Freedman's Friend* 1 (June 1864): 11; Weicksel, "Fitted up," 168; Taylor, *Embattled Freedom,* 74; daily record, 9, New England Freedmen's Aid Society Papers; Daniel W. Knowles to Simeon S. Jocelyn, May report, 1864, Louisiana file, AMAA; George N. Greene to William E. Whiting, June 22, 1863, J.R. Johnson to AMA, September 25, 1863, Joel Baker to George Whipple, October 5, 1864, Anne Wilkins to George Whipple, October 20, 1864, William S. Bell to George Whipple, October 21, 1864, William S. Bell to William E. Whiting, February 24, 1865, Sarah A. Macdonald to William E. Whiting, February 25, 1865, Virginia

file, AMAA; W. T. Richardson to Michael E. Strieby, October 27, November 4, 1864 (quoted), South Carolina file, AMAA; Ames, *New England Woman's Diary,* 32–33, 35, 40.

39. Hawks, *Woman Doctor's Civil War,* 75; James P. Stone to George Whipple, December 26, 1863, October 18, 1864, M. E. Burdick to George Whipple, April 6, 1864, M. L. Sheldon to George Whipple, January 20, 1865, Fannie Gleason to George Whipple, May 1, 1865, Cyrus Jordan to George Whipple, May 4, 1865, Virginia file, AMAA.

40. Perkins, "Black Female," 127–29; Rachel G. C. Patten to George Whipple, June 3, 1864 (quoted), Sara G. Stanley and Edmonia G. Highgate to William H. Woodbury, July report, 1864, Mary M. Reed to George Whipple, July 18, 1864, Sallie L. Daffin to William H. Woodbury, August 29, 1864, Sara G. Stanley to George Whipple, October 6, 1864, William H. Woodbury to George Whipple, September 24, 28, 1864, January 19, 1865, Virginia file, AMAA.

41. William S. Bell to George Whipple, Oct. 21, 1864, William D. Harris to George Whipple, October 4, 1864, Clara Duncan to George Whipple, April 1, 1865, J. N. Mars to George Whipple, July 1, 1864, Virginia file, AMAA; Lynch, *A Few Things,* 34; Sterling, ed., *We Are Your Sisters,* 253; Glymph, *Women's Fight,* 180.

42. Cimprich, *Slavery's End,* 55; Committee on Freedmen, *Report,* 13; Indiana Freedmen's Aid Commission, *Report,* 4, 32.

43. Cimprich, *Slavery's End,* 56; *Freedmen's Advocate* 1 (December 1864): 42 (Hill quote), (July/August 1864): 25 (Freeman quote); Western Freedmen's Aid Commission, *Second Report,* 30; H. S. Beals to William E. Whiting, September 27, 1864, Virginia file, AMAA.

44. Hawks, *Woman Doctor's Civil War,* 136; *Freedmen's Bulletin* 1 (November 1864 supplement): 44; Educational Commission for Freedmen, *First Annual Report,* 30; Swint, ed., *Dear Ones,* 45–46 (quoted), 66; *Freedman's Friend* 1 (December 1864): 22; Friends' Association of Philadelphia, *Report,* 14; H. Porter report, March 24, 1865, p.8, V87 (1865) consolidated file, LR by Adjutant General, RG 94, NA.

45. Swint, ed., *Dear Ones,* 66; Indiana Yearly Meeting, *Report,* 4, 42; [Pennsylvania Freedmen's Relief Association], *Report of the Proceedings,* 19.

46. Rachel G. C. Patten to William E. Whiting, March 10, 1864, Virginia file, AMAA; Indiana Freedmen's Aid Commission, *Report,* 5; Haviland, *Woman's Life,* 253, 294 (freedwoman quote); Breault, *Howland,* 57.

47. Coffin, *Reminiscences,* 626; Indiana Freedmen's Aid Commission, *Report,* 6; P. H. Watson to G. Whipple, March 31, 1863, District of Columbia file, AMAA; Convention of Freedmen's Commissions, *Minutes,* 21, 27; Julia Wilbur to Anna M.C. Barnes, December [actually January] 15, 1863, Rochester Ladies Antislavery Society Papers; Henry Rountree to Abram M. Taylor, November 4, 29, December 6, 1863, Taylor Family Papers; *Freedmen's Bulletin* 1 (July, 1864): 6.

48. Henry Rountree to Abram M. Taylor, November 10, 12, December 16, 1864, Taylor Family Papers; John Eaton to H.W. Cobbs, November 9, 1863, LS by the Mississippi Freedmen's Department, RG 105, NA; P. Mixer to George Whipple, January 19, 1864, Mississippi file, Rachel G.C. Patten to William E. Whiting, September 11, 1863, James P. Stone to William E. Whiting, February 8, 1864, Charles B. Wilder to George Whipple, November 28, December 13, 1864, May 25, 1865, Virginia file, AMAA; Indiana Freedmen's Aid Commission, *Report,* 32; *Freedmen's Bulletin* 1 (July, 1864): 7; Botume, *First Days,* 70.

49. Friends' Association of Philadelphia, *Statistics,* 3–4; Susan Drummond to Miss Dodge, December 21, 1863, Virginia file, AMAA; New York Yearly Meeting, *Second Report,* 56;

Freedmen's Bulletin 1 (July, 1864): 8, (September, 1864): 20, (March, 1865): 78; Western Freedmen's Aid Commission, *Second Report,* 30; Ellen Murray to Sarah Cope, January 26, 1863, LR by Women's Aid Committee, FFAR; Swint, ed., *Dear Ones,* 29, 32–33; Wilbur journal, October 2, 1863.

50. Botume, *First Days,* 64, 69; *New York Principia,* December 31, 1863.

51. Teed, *Joseph and Harriet,* 114; Swint, ed., *Dear Ones,* 29; *Freedman's Advocate* 1 (May, 1864): 18, (June, 1864): 23, (June, 1864, supplement): 29; *Freedman's Friend* 1 (May, 1865): 52; *Friends' Review* 18 (July 8, 1865): 709; *American Missionary* 8 (April, 1863): 193.

52. *Friends' Review* 17 (May 7, 1864): 571; James, *Annual Report,* 14; Port Royal Relief Committee, *First Annual Report,* 6; Henry Rountree to Abram M. Taylor, December 13, 1863, Taylor Family Papers; Maria Mann to Aunt Mary, May 18, 1863, Mann Papers; *Freedmen's Friend* 1 (October, 1864): 15; Edwin S. Williams to Simeon S. Jocelyn, March 25, 1863, South Carolina file, AMAA.

53. William S. Bell to George Whipple, March 10, 1864, Virginia file, AMAA; Henry Rountree to Abram M. Taylor, December 6, 1863, Taylor Papers; New England Yearly, *Second Report,* 3–4, 7; *Freedman's Advocate* 1 (March, 1864): 9–10; *Freedman's Friend* 1 (June, 1864): 2; Knox, *Startling Revelations,* 5.

54. Rhoda W. Smith to George Whipple, November report, 1863, Virginia file, AMAA; Swint, ed., *Dear Ones,* 131; Henry Rountree to Abram M. Taylor, December 21, 1863, Abram M. Taylor to Henry Rountree, January 4, 1864, Taylor Family Papers; Lucy Chase to Sarah Cope, November 28, 1863, LR by Women's Aid Committee, FFAR; Wilbur journal, June 6, 1863.

55. *New York National Antislavery Standard,* November 7, 1863, E.A. Holman to Elias M. Greene, January 28, 1864, "Contraband Tax" consolidated file, LR by Quartermaster General, RG 92, NA; P. B. Nickerson to George Whipple, January 9, 1865, North Carolina file, AMAA; Elias M. Greene file, Appointment and Commission Branch files, RG 94, NA; Yellin, ed., *Jacobs Family Papers* 2: 439; *Friend* 37 (June 25, 1864): 341.

56. Maria Mann to Aunt Mary, May 18, 1863, Mann Papers; Wilbur journal, November 16, 1863; Higginson, *Journal,* 320; Henry Rountree to Abram M. Taylor, December 6, 13, 25, 1863, Taylor Family Papers; Cimprich, *Slavery's End,* 74; Taylor, *Embattled Freedom,* 172; Stanley, "Slave Emancipation," 275–277.

57. N. Noyes to Michael E. Strieby, April 27, 1865, Maryland file, AMAA; Henry Rountree to Abram M. Taylor, December 13, 1863, Taylor Family Papers.

58. D.O. McCord, report, August 3, 1865, Mississippi Freedmen's Department Reports, RG 105, NA; Kinsman, *Report,* 20; *Freedman's Advocate* 1 (March, 1864): 9; *Freedmen's Friend* 1 (July, 1864): 9, (October, 1864): 17; Foster, "Limitations," 350; H. Porter report, March 24, 1865, p. 15, consolidated file V-87 (1865), LR by Adjutant General, RG 94, NA.

59. Cimprich, *Slavery's End,* 58; Henry Rountree to Abram M. Taylor, April 10, 1863, Taylor Family Papers; Friends' Association of Philadelphia, *Report,* 6, 9, 12; Rachel G.C. Patten to Simeon S. Jocelyn, January 21, 1863, District of Columbia file, Samuel G. Wright to Simeon S. Jocelyn, January 20, 1863, Kentucky file, AMAA; *New York Tribune,* January 23, 1863; Selleck, *Gentle Invaders,* 69. D.O. McCord report, August 3, 1865, Mississippi Freedmen's Department reports, RG 105, NA, notes that the freedmen's hospital in Memphis was relocated to a building of poor quality in May, 1865.

60. Ramold, *Slaves, Sailors, Citizens,* 105; Foster, "Limitations," 350–352; Allen journal, September 29, 1864; Schwalm, "Surviving Wartime Emancipation," 23.

61. *FDHE,* ser. 1, 2: 461; Holt et al., *Special Mission,* 7; D. O. McCord, report, August 3, 1865, Reports of the Mississippi Freedmen's Department, RG 105, NA; Foster, "Limitations," 355; Friends' Association of Philadelphia, *Report,* 3, 5; Kisacky, *Rise of the Modern Hospital,* 23–25, 41.

62. Friends' Association of Philadelphia, *Report,* 11; D. O. McCord, report, August 3, 1865, Mississippi Freedmen's Department reports, RG 105, NA; Swint, ed., *Dear Ones,* 23; *FDHE,* ser. 1, 2: 460; Wilbur journal, April 19, October 13, 29, 1863, January 1, 17, March 29, May 23, 28, 29, June 9, July 2, 1864, January 25, 1865; Yellin, ed., *Jacobs Family Papers* 2: 584; Warren, ed., *Extracts from Reports,* ser. 1: 17, ser. 2: 43, 48.

63. New England Freedmen's Aid Society, *Extracts,* ser. 5: 18; *Friends' Intelligencer,* 21 (July 23, 1864): 315; Manning, *Troubled Refuge,* 102; Allen journal, November 6, 21, 1864; Eberhart reminiscences, 29.

64. Allen journal, November 6, 1864; Wilbur journal, June 2, 1864; *Freedmen's Bulletin* 1 (November, 1864 supplement): 43 (quoted).

65. Cimprich, *Slavery's End,* 58; Eaton, *Report,* 95; D.O. McCord, report, August 3, 1865, Mississippi Freedmen's Department reports, RG 105, NA; Foster, "Limitations," 355; *National Freedman* 1 (April, 1865): 78; Rochester Ladies Antislavery Society, *Thirteenth Annual Report,* 14.

66. Warren, ed., *Extracts from Reports,* ser. 1: 17, ser. 2: 43, 45–48; Rein, *Alabamians in Blue,* 93.

67. W. W. Wheeler to Michael E. Strieby, October 27, 1864, W.W. Wheeler to George Whipple, November 21, 1864, Maryland file, AMAA; Sears, ed., *Camp Nelson,* 171; *FDHE,* ser. 1, 2: 186; *Freedman's Advocate,* 1 (June, 1864): 22; *Freedmen's Bulletin* 1 (September, 1864): 28, (July, 1864): 1.

68. *FDHE,* ser. 1, 3: 730; J.C. Richardson to Simeon S. Jocelyn, April 7, 1863, Missouri file, George N. Greene to George Whipple, January report, 1864, North Carolina file, AMAA; Manning, *Troubled Refuge,* 48; Downs, *Sick,* 111; Sears, ed., *Camp Nelson,* 174; Botume, *First Days,* 44–45; Hancock, *South,* 31.

69. Horace James, *Annual Report,* 16; H.L. Beals to George Whipple, January 30, 1864, Virginia file, AMAA; Finley, "In War's Wake," 139.

70. Wilbur journal, May 15, September 28, 1863, January 21 (quoted), February 13, 1864; Rochester Ladies Antislavery Society, *Thirteenth Annual Report,* 11–12; Whitacre, *Civil Life,* 170.

71. Downs, *Sick,* 194; James F. Sisson to William E. Whiting, August 13, 1863, March 9, 1864, Virginia file, W. W. Wheeler to Michael E. Strieby, November 6, 1864, Maryland file, AMAA; Elias M. Greene to Montgomery C. Meigs, August 9, 1864, "Contrabands" consolidated file, LR by Quartermaster General, RG 92, NA; Augustus L. Chetlain et al., flyer, October, 1865, Tennessee file, AMAA; *Freedman's Advocate* 1 (October, 1864): 34; Warren, ed., *Extracts from Documents,* 27.

72. Ella Roper to AMA, August 5, 1864, North Carolina file, AMAA; *Freedmen's Record* 1 (July, 1865): 119; Wilbur journal, February 23, 1864; Taylor, *Embattled Freedom,* 172.

73. McElya, *Politics of Mourning,* 5, 97, 103, 106; Howard et al., "Domestic History," (typescript), 178; Wilbur journal, May 5, June 13, December 26, 1864 (Jacobs quote); Yellin, ed., *Jacobs Family Papers* 2: 563; Rochester Ladies Antislavery Society, *Fourteenth Annual Report* 8 (Rochester, NY: William S. Fall, 1865); Yellin, *Harriet Jacobs,* 170; Whitacre, *Civil Life,* 183.

74. Charles P. Day to George Whipple, February 23, 1865, Virginia file, AMAA; W. F. Eaton to George Whipple, October 31, 1864, South Carolina file, AMAA; *Freedman's Advocate* 1 (July/August, 1864): 26–27, (December, 1864): 41; Towne, *Letters and Diary,* 117; James, *Annual Report,* 17, 43; *Freedmen's Record* 1 (July, 1865): 119; Walker, "Corinth," 18; *Home Evangelist* 15 (April, 1864): 15; *American Missionary* 8 (September, 1864): 212; *New York Tribune,* February 27, 1864.

75. E. Congden to Sarah Cope, September 28, 1864, LR by Women's Aid Committee, FFAR; W. T. Richardson to George Whipple, June 14, 1864, South Carolina file, AMAA; Mary Reed to George Whipple, July 15, 1864, S. A. Walker to George Whipple, July 15, 1864, M. H. Abbey to George Whipple, August 2, 1864, William D. Harris to George Whipple, October 4, 1864, Virginia file, AMAA, D.O. Allen to C. H. Fowler, January 1, 1864 (quoted), Arkansas file, AMAA.

76. W. W. Wheeler to George Whipple, December 2, 1864, Maryland file, AMAA; "Mason's Island," November 27, 1864, in 1863–79 Account Book, Howland Family Papers; Hermann, *Pursuit,* 43; *FDHE,* ser. 1, 2: 200, 237; New England Freedmen's Aid Society, *Second Annual Report,* 28; Magdol, *Right to the Land,* 102; *New York Anglo-African,* May 21, 1864.

77. Mabee and Newhouse, *Sojourner Truth,* 141; Truth, *Narrative,* 182–183.

78. Ellen P. T. Wheeler to George Whipple, June 22, 1864, West Virginia file, AMAA; James, *Wonderful, Eventful Life,* 17; Thompson, *Dear Eliza,* 76.

79. J. W. Locke, July report, 1864, Helena, AR, field office reports, RG 105, NA; Lovett, "African Americans," 323–324; *Boston Liberator,* September 16, 1864; Kilham, "Sketches," 207; *OR,* ser. 1, 24 (pt. 2): 517.

80. *Freedman's Friend* 1 (June, 1864): 3; Cimprich, *Fort Pillow,* 76, 95, 100; *FDHE,* ser. 1, 2: 475; Hermann, *Pursuit,* 43; James, *Annual Report,* 7, 37; *Boston Liberator,* January 29, 1864; Western Freedmen's Aid Commission, *Second Annual Report,* 29–30; *Home Missionary* 37 (May, 1864): 10–11; *Friends' Intelligencer* 21 (June 11, 1864): 219; *New York Anglo-African,* December 24, 1864.

81. Friends' Association of Philadelphia, *Second Report,* 11; *Freedmen's Bulletin* 1 (September 1864): 27–28; Taylor, *Embattled Freedom,* 133–34.

82. Eberhart reminiscences, 32, 44; James Sisson to AMA, July 16, 1863, Virginia file, AMAA; Isaac Thorne, Report for 1863, Thorne Papers; McGranahan, ed., *Historical Sketch,* 20; Indiana Freedmen's Aid Commission, *Report,* 6–8; Salemson, ed., "Beard," 46.

83. Grimke, *Journals,* 477; J. R. Johnson to AMA, August 5, 1863, W. W. Wheeler to George Whipple, July 5, 1864, Maryland file, AMAA; Eliza Austin to George Whipple, May 10, 1864, Arkansas file, AMAA; *Freedmen's Bulletin* 1 (September 1864): 44; Friends' Association of Philadelphia, *Second Report,* 8–9.

84. Browning, "Vision," 89.

85. Oakes, *Freedom,* 396; *New York Principia,* July 16, 1863.

86. Botume, *First Days,* 88; Samuel G. Wright to Simeon S. Jocelyn, January 30, February 4, 1863, Kentucky file, AMAA.

87. L. D. Burnett to George Whipple, December 3, 1864, Virginia file, AMAA; Breault, *Howland,* 55–57, 63–65; Beecham, *As if It Were Glory,* 168; Towne, *Letters and Diary,* 146; Botume, *First Days,* 91; Hawks, *Woman Doctor's Civil War,* 116; McShane, ed., "Reading, Writing, and War," 109; Blum, *Reforging,* 60–66.

88. Blum, *Reforging,* 52–54, 60–61, 70; *New York Anglo-African,* August 6, 1864; *Freedman's Friend* 1 (April 1865): 45 (Mitchell quote); Towne diary, May 1, 1862, Penn School Papers; Escott, *Worst Passions,* 106. Glymph, *Women's Fight,* 172, and Breitborde, "Discourse," 429, discuss more critical views of the degree of change in the reformers' thinking.

89. *Freedmen's Record* (April 1865): 63 (freedwoman quote).

90. Blum, *Reforging,* 60; Glymph, *Women's Fight,* 161, 172; Hawks, *Woman Doctor's Civil War,* 115; Perkins, "Black Female," 129; Rose, *Rehearsal,* 270.

6. Wage Labor

1. Warren, ed., *Extracts from Reports,* ser. 2: 53–54; Eaton, *Report,* 217; S. S. Smith to George Whipple, May 30, 1864, Virginia file, AMAA; Allen journal, October 6, 1864; *American Missionary* 7 (October 1863): 232.

2. James, *Annual Report,* 12; New England Yearly Meeting, *Report to Executive Committee,* 3; Boyer, *Naval Surgeon,* 69, 102; Indiana Freedmen's Aid Commission, *Report,* 17; Cimprich, *Slavery's End,* 71; *Philadelphia Christian Recorder,* April 29, 1865.

3. Kaye, *Joining Places,* 204–5; James, *Annual Report,* 19; *National Freedman* 1 (April, 1865): 91; Educational Commission of Boston, *Extracts,* ser. 3: 3; Cimprich, *Slavery's End,* 71; Rose, *Rehearsal,* 314.

4. Frankel, *Freedom's Women,* 35; Dougherty, *Port Royal,* 56, 58, 67; James, *Annual Report,* 45–46; Gerteis, *From Contraband to Freedman,* 184; Glymph, *Women's Fight,* 171, 193.

5. *Friend* 38 (December 10, 1864): 117; Schwalm, *A Hard Fight,* 100; *FDHE,* ser. 1, 3: 319; Cimprich, *Slavery's End,* 66–67; *Freedman's Friend* 1 (July 1864): 12; Kilham, "Sketches," 26.

6. Eaton, *Report,* 70–71; *FDHE,* ser. 1, 3: 814–15 (quoted), 817–19; Warren, ed., *Extracts from Documents,* 25–27; Warren, ed., *Extracts from Reports,* ser. 1: 47; *Pennsylvania Freedmen's Bulletin* 1 (August 1865): 30; E. O.C. Ord, G.O. 26, February 22, 1865, District of Columbia file, AMAA; Samuel Thomas endorsement, January 31, 1865, on George N. Carruthers to John P. Hawkins, January 27, 1865, LR by Mississippi Freedmen's Department, RG 105, NA.

7. Ross, "Freed Soil, Freed Labor," 220–22; Eaton, *Grant, Lincoln, and the Freedmen,* 163–64; David Todd to George Whipple, February 25, 1864, Arkansas file, AMAA; Gerteis, *From Contraband to Freedman,* 179; Allen journal, September 26, October 2, 4, 1864, and January 1865; Warren, ed., *Extracts from Documents,* 29; *Freedman's Advocate* 1 (January 1864): 3.

8. *American Missionary* 8 (February 1864): 37; *Freedman's Friend* 1 (June 1864): 12; *Freedman's Friend* 1 (July 1864): 8; J. B. Kinsman to Isaac J. Wistar, March 31, 1864, LR by Department of Negro Affairs, Ft. Monroe, VA, field office, RG 105, NA; Browning, *Shifting Loyalties,* 90; Charles B. Wilder to George J. Carney, December 30, 1864, consolidated file V-87 (1865), LR by Adjutant General, RG 94, NA; *New York Anglo-African,* May 28, 1864; Eiss, "A Share in the Land," 68, 71, 74.

9. Elias M. Greene to Mr. Whiting, January 9, 1864, "Bureau of Emancipation" consolidated file, LR by Quartermaster General, RG 92, NA; Contraband Relief Commission Committee, *Report,* 16; "Freedmen's Schools," 1863–79 account book, Howland Family Papers; Rose, *Rehearsal,* 200–201; Harry McMillan testimony, n.d., South Carolina file, 130–31, AFIC; United States Constitution, article III, section 3.

10. *FDHE,* ser. 1, 3: 15; Dougherty, *Port Royal,* 110; Rufus Saxton, A. D. Smith, W. K. Lee Jr., Laura M. Towne, and Elbridge Gerry Dudley testimony, n.d., South Carolina file, 25–27, 35, 54, 74, 118–19, AFIC; Richard J. Hinton testimony, December 14, 1863, Kansas file, 12–13, AFIC; James F. Sisson to William H. Woodbury, December 30, 1863, Virginia file, AMAA; Pearson, ed., *Letters,* 148; Towne diary, February 45, 1863, Penn School Papers; Towne, *Letters and Diary,* 106; Allen, *Yankee,* 15; *Boston Liberator,* June 17, 1864 (Hinckley quote).

11. Rose, *Rehearsal,* 214–15; Charles P. Ware to Harriet Ware, February 8, 1863, Ware Papers; *Friends' Review* 17 (May 7, 1864): 570; Allen, *Yankee,* 112 (freedman quote); *Freedman's Advocate* 1 (April 1865): 13.

12. Rose, *Rehearsal,* 213, 215, 272–74; Saville, *Work of Reconstruction,* 43; *Friends' Intelligencer* 21 (June 11, 1864): 219.

13. Rose, *Rehearsal,* 276–77, 284–95; Towne, *Letters and Diary,* 129–30; Wise et al., *Rebellion,* 269, 272; Dougherty, *Port Royal,* 119–20; *Friends' Intelligencer* 21 (June 11, 1864): 219.

14. Rose, *Rehearsal,* 309–12; Edward S. Philbrick to Charles P. Ware, June 30, 1865, Ware Papers.

15. Francis Hinckley to Charles P. Ware, May 21, 1865, and Charles P. Ware to Edward S. Philbrick, May 29, 1865, Ware Papers; Dougherty, *Port Royal,* 113–14; *OR,* ser. 3, 4: 1023; Pearson, ed., *Letters,* 295.

16. William H. Woodbury to AMA, September 18, 1863, and Charles B. Wilder to AMA, February 24, 1865, Virginia file, AMAA; Charles B. Wilder to Edwin Stanton, March 8, 1865, District of Columbia file, AMAA; Taylor, *Embattled Freedom,* 214; Robinson, *Yankee in a Confederate Town,* 106, 108, 110.

17. Rose, *Rehearsal,* 325–27; *New York Tribune,* February 13, 1865; *FDHE,* ser. 1, 3: 338–40; T. W. Magill to AMA, April 5, 1865, Georgia file, AMAA; *Boston Liberator,* March 10, 1865; *Pennsylvania Freedmen's Bulletin* 1 (April 1865): 32–33; Saville, *Work of Reconstruction,* 73, 75. Congress would need to come up with an alternative basis for confiscation that would avoid limits in the US Constitution's treason clause.

18. *FDHE,* ser. 1, 3: 318; Cope, *Report,* 7; William S. Bell to George Whipple, March 4, 1864, Virginia file, AMAA; Cimprich, *Slavery's End,* 64; *Friends' Review* 17 (April 1864): 486, (November 7, 1864): 154–55; Glymph, "This Species of Property," 64; *Pennsylvania Freedmen's Bulletin* 1 (March 1865): 15, 17.

19. *FDHE,* ser. 1, 2: 152 (Chase quotes): 338; Indiana Freedmen's Aid Commission, *Report,* 17; *Friends' Review* 17 (November 7, 1864): 154–55; *American Missionary* 8 (August 1864): 193; Cimprich, *Slavery's End,* 64; Superintendents of Freedmen for the State of Arkansas and District of West Tennessee, *Reports,* 13.

20. New England Freedmen's Aid Society, *Second Annual Report,* 69–70; Cimprich, *Slavery's End,* 64–65; Henry Rountree to Abram S. Taylor, April 14, 1863, Taylor Family Papers.

21. Indiana Freedmen's Aid Commission, *Report,* 17; Friends' Association of Philadelphia, *Second Report,* 25; Montgomery C. Meigs, memo, August 9, 1864, "Contraband Camp" consolidated file, LR by Quartermaster General, RG 92, NA; Winkle, *Lincoln's Citadel,* 348; Whitacre, *Civil Life,* 117; Yellin, ed., *Jacobs Family Papers* 2: 538.

22. Rufus Saxton testimony, n.d., South Carolina file, 12, Orlando Brown testimony, n.d., Virginia file, 32, AFIC; Click, *Time Full,* 12; Wistar, *Autobiography,* 419; *New York National Antislavery Standard,* July 2, 1864; *FDHE,* ser. 1, 2: 320; Bryant, *36th Infantry,* 90–96.

23. Orlando Brown testimony, n.d., Virginia file, 29, AFIC; *Friends' Review* 17 (May 13, 1865): 587; Henry Rountree to Abram M. Taylor, April 8, 1863, Taylor Family Papers; Warren, *Extracts from Reports,* ser. 2: 36–38; Burton, *Diary,* 6; Reidy, *Illusions,* 245; Coffin, *Reminiscences,* 628.

24. Women's Aid Committee minutebook #1: 6–12, FFAR; Committee on Freedmen, *Report,* 6–12; *National Freedman* 1 (June, 1865): 41; *Friends' Review* 17 (January 2, 1864): 282; US Congress, *Colored Refugees,* 12; *Freedman's Advocate* 1 (May, 1864): 20; *Freedmen's Friend* 1 (July, 1864): 11; *Freedmen's Bulletin* 1 (May, 1865): 109; *FDHE,* ser. 1, 2: 700.

25. Greene, *Regulations* (poster); C. B. Webster to George Whipple, July 16, 1863, J. R. Johnson to Simeon S, Jocelyn, October 13, 1863, District of Columbia file, AMAA; Wilbur journal, January 7, 1864; *New York Tribune,* May 14, 1864; Yellin, ed., *Jacobs Family Papers* 2: 568.

26. Gerteis, *From Contraband to Freedman,* 84; Edward Stetson to mother, August 25, October 26, 1864, and March 3, 1865, Stetson Papers.

27. Gerteis, *From Contraband to Freedman,* 40, 43; Edwin Stanton, order, January 28, 1863, "Contrabands at Fort Monroe" consolidated file, LR by Quartermaster General, RG 92, NA; Kinsman, *Report,* 3–4; Thomas P. Jackson to George Whipple, April 22, 1863, Virginia file, AMAA; *FDHE,* ser. 1, 2: 214–15; New England Freedmen's Aid Society, *Second Annual Report,* 72; H. Porter, report, March 24, 1865, p. 33, consolidated file V-87 (1865), LR by the Adjutant General, RG 94, NA.

28. Pierce, "Freedmen," 308; Educational Commission, *First Report,* 37; New England Educational Commission, *Extracts,* ser. 4: 6; Ash, *Firebrand of Liberty,* 20; Saville, *Work of Reconstruction,* 60, 67–68; Mann, "Contact," 297; Pease, "Three Years," 110.

29. H. Porter, report, March 24, 1865, p. 33, consolidated file V-87 (1865), LR by the Adjutant General, RG 94, NA; Penningroth, *Claims of Kinfolk,* 97; Swint, ed., *Dear Ones,* 133; Osthaus, *Freedmen, Philanthropy, and Fraud,* 3, 9.

30. Engs, *Freedom's First,* 41; *Friends' Review* 17 (January 2, 1864): 282; Friends' Association of Philadelphia, *Statistics,* 12; Indiana Yearly Meeting, *Report,* 29, 35.

31. *FDHE,* ser. 1, 2: 24, 364 (quoted), 410, 665; Reuben D. Mussey to George Mason, April 11, 1864, Records of Capt. R. D. Mussey, RG 393, NA; Click, *Time Full,* 133–34; Cimprich, *Slavery's End,* 65–66; *OR,* ser. 3, 4: 773; John B. Howard to J. C. Slaught, April 7, 1865, Abraham Wells affidavit, September 22, 1865, James Banks affidavit, September 16, 1865, and numerous similar statements in box 720, "Negroes" consolidated file, LR by Quartermaster General, RG 92, NA. Because the disordered "N" section of RG 92's consolidated files was undergoing reorganization when I went through it, some documents related to Black military workers could end up under nearby files.

32. Teters, *Practical Liberators,* 109–10; *FDHE,* ser. 1, 2: 157, 392, 666, 3: 629; Wilbur journal, May 31, 1863; D. C. Houston to Orville Leonard, February 26, 1863, Leonard Military Papers; Click, *Time Full,* 130, 136–37; Cimprich, *Slavery's End,* 65; *OR,* ser. 1, 24 (pt. 2): 306.

33. *OR,* ser. 3, 3: 841; Click, *Time Full,* 136–38; Charles P. Day to Simeon S. Jocelyn, July 8, 13, 1863, Virginia file, AMAA; George L. Stearns to Robert Dale Owen, November 25, 1863, Tennessee file, 74, AFIC; Asa Prescott to Edwin Stanton, July 11, 1863, "Negroes, Fort Monroe" consolidated file, LR by Quartermaster General, RG 92, NA; *FDHE,* ser. 1, 2: 21 (Federal's quote), 157–58, 202, 416, 667–68.

34. Wilbur journal, July 13, 1864; Click, *Time Full,* 131–34, 136, 138; New York Yearly, *Third Report,* 8; Orlando Brown to J. Burnham Kinsman, May 12, 1864, LR by the Department of Negro Affairs, Fort Monroe, VA, field office, RG 105, NA.

35. Johnston, *Surviving Freedom,* 157; Rochester Ladies Antislavery Society, *Twelfth Annual Report,* 16; H. Porter, report, March 24, 1865, 4–5, 23, 29, 31, consolidated file V-87 (1865), LR by Adjutant General, RG 94, NA; McElya, *Politics of Mourning,* 90–91, 93.

36. *Pennsylvania Freedmen's Bulletin* 1 (March, 1865): 37; Elias M. Greene to Danforth B. Nichols, March 19, April 26, 1864, Nichols Papers; Reidy, *Illusions,* 238; Winkle, *Lincoln's Citadel,* 348.

37. Cimprich, *Slavery's End,* 69; Rose, *Rehearsal,* 225; Conway, *Final Report,* 11; Elias M. Greene to Montgomery C. Meigs, February 22, 1864, Robert A. Stanley et al., to Edwin Stanton, December, 1863, "Contrabands" consolidated file, LR by Quartermaster General, RG 92, NA; *FDHE,* ser. 1, 2: 251, 256, 307; H. Porter report, March 24, 1865, pp. 38, 45, V-87 (1865) consolidated file, LR by Adjutant General, RG 94, NA; Terry, *Condemned,* 36.

38. *FDHE,* ser. 1, 2: 565, 568, 572–73; George Condee to Simeon S. Jocelyn, March 26, 1863, J. L. Richardson to Simeon S. Jocelyn, April 30, 1863, Samuel Sawyer to Simeon S. Jocelyn, April 21, 1865, Missouri file, AMAA; St. Louis Ladies Contraband Society statement, n.d.,

Missouri file, 161, AFIC; *OR,* ser. 2, 5: 521; Schwalm, *Emancipation's Diaspora,* 81; Coffin, *Reminiscences,* 647; *Cleveland Herald,* August 12, 1863.

39. Benjamin F. Butler to Charles Wilder, April 13, 1864 (with Wilder endorsement, April 29, 1864), LR by Department of Negro Affairs, Ft. Monroe, VA, field office, RG 105, NA; *Pennsylvania Freedmen's Bulletin* 1 (March, 1865): 37; Breault, *Howland,* 56.

40. Joseph B. Kinsman to Benjamin F. Butler, July 14, 1864 (with Butler endorsement, July 18, 1864), Joseph B. Kinsman, "List of Colored People Taken North," August 2, 1864, J.M. Truman, Jr. to Joseph B. Kinsman, August 11, 1864, Oliver P. St. John to Joseph B. Kinsman, November 19, 1864, LR by Department of Negro Affairs, Ft. Monroe, VA, field office, RG 105, NA.

41. Thomas D. Peake to AMA, March 26, 1863, and Charles P. Day to William E. Whiting, April 3, 1863, Virginia file, AMAA; *Cleveland Herald,* April 6, 1864; *New York Tribune,* April 2, 1864; Winkle, *Lincoln's Citadel,* 350–51; McKivigan, *Forgotten Firebrand,* 82.

42. *OR,* ser. 3, 4: 1024; *FDHE,* ser. 1, 3: 106; Ochiai, *Harvesting Freedom,* 95–96; Pearson, ed., *Letters,* 245–46, 250, 286–87; Rose, *Rehearsal,* 310, 313; *Friends' Review* 17 (April 2, 1864): 486; Edward S. Philbrick to Charles P. Ware, August 24, and November 29, 1864, Ware Papers; T. E. Ruggles to Charles P. Ware, May 6, 1865, Ware Papers.

43. *OR,* ser. 3, 4: 1022–23; *FDHE,* ser. 1, 3: 323; Osthaus, *Freedmen, Philanthropy, and Fraud,* 3.

44. Ripley, *Slaves and Freedmen,* 47–50; Rodrigue, *Reconstruction,* 48–49; Gerteis, *From Contraband to Freedman,* 75–77; *FDHE,* ser. 1, 3: 371, 416, 438–39, 449, 573; Thomas W. Conway to T. M. Bentley, September 1, 1864, Records of Miles Taylor Plantation, Donaldsonville, LA, field office, RG 105, NA; James Bowen to Provost Marshals, February 2, 1863, Nathaniel P. Banks to S. W. Sawyer, February 4, 1865, L. S. by Jesuit Bend field office, RG 105, NA.

45. Ripley, *Slaves and Freedmen,* 50–51, 62–63; Rodrigue, *Reconstruction,* 47; Gerteis, *From Contraband to Freedman,* 77, 84; Eiss, "Share the Land," 48, 53, 56–57, 60; *FDIC,* ser. 1, 3: 356, 416; William Eastman to mother, October 13, 1863, Eastman Letters.

46. Gerteis, *From Contraband to Freedman,* 77–78; Rodrigue, *Reconstruction,* 45–46; Ripley, *Slaves and Freedmen,* 56–57; *New York National Antislavery Standard,* October 3, 1863; Osthaus, *Freedmen, Philanthropy, and Fraud,* 3.

47. Rodrigue, *Reconstruction,* 52–54; *FDHE,* ser. 1, 3: 536; George H. Hanks testimony, n.d., Louisiana file, 36, AFIC; Ripley, *Slaves and Freedmen,* 66–67, 99–101; Eiss, "Share in the Land," 52; Gerteis, *From Contraband to Freedman,* 86–87, 92–93, 104–5.

48. Eaton, *Grant, Lincoln, and the Freedmen,* 159; Cimprich, *Slavery's End,* 39, 68–69; Gerteis, *From Contraband to Freedman,* 122–26, 130, 154–55; McCurry, *Women's War,* 99.

49. Taylor, *Embattled Freedom,* 123; Eaton, *Grant, Lincoln, and the Freedmen,* 207; Bercaw, *Gendered Freedoms,* 33; Phillip Bacon to friends, June 19, 1864, January 22, 1865, Bacon Papers; *FDHE,* ser. 1, 2: 47.

50. Yeatman, *Report,* 7–8; Barnickel, *Milliken's Bend,* 53; *FDHE,* ser. 2, 1: 149; Thomas Gibson to W. G. Sargent, January 17, 1864, LR by Little Rock, AR, field Office, RG 105, NA.

51. McCurry, *Women's War,* 100; *FDHE,* ser. 1, 3: 633; *New York National Antislavery Standard,* December 12, 1863; *New York Times,* November 28, 1863.

52. Gerteis, *From Contraband to Freedman,* 140–49, 157; *OR,* ser. 3, 4: 123–24, 166–68; Allen journal December 25, 1864; Cimprich, *Slavery's End,* 68–69.

53. Warren, ed., *Extracts from Reports,* ser. 2: 30, 32 (Thomas quote); *FDHE,* ser. 1, 3: 809, 813, 825, 827–28; *Freedman's Advocate* 1 (June 1864 supplement): 25.

54. Bercaw, *Gendered Freedoms,* 34; Carruthers journal, 1: 113 (November 1864), 116 (December, 1864); Thomas Gibson to W. G. Sargent, January 17, 1864, LR by Little Rock, AR, field office, RG 105, NA; Barnickel, *Milliken's Bend,* 73.

55. *Freedman's Advocate* 1 (June 1864): 22; Phillip Bacon to friends, June 19, 1864, Bacon Papers; Gerteis, *From Contraband to Freedman,* 158–61; *FDHE,* ser. 1, 2: 68, 3: 861, 871–73; Allen journal, October 16, December 25, 1864; *American Missionary* 8 (April 1864): 102; Bercaw, *Gendered Freedoms,* 38; Rawick, ed., *American Slave,* 19: 214.

56. Gerteis, *From Contraband to Freedman,* 162–166; Warren, ed., *Extracts from Reports,* ser. 1: 17, ser. 2: 27; Bercaw, *Gendered Freedoms,* 39; *FDHE,* ser. 1, 3: 871–872; Frankel, *Freedom's Women,* 52.

57. James, *Annual Report,* 5; Charles B. Wilder to Edward O.C. Ord, January 23, 1865, V-87 (1865) consolidated file, LR by Adjutant General, RG 94, NA; *New York Tribune,* March 21, 1865; Gerteis, *From Contraband to Freedman,* 59–61.

58. *FDHE,* ser. 1, 2: 65–66; Gerteis, *From Contraband to Freedman,* 154, 160; Edward S. Philbrick to Charles P. Ware, September 24, 1863, Ware Papers; Berlin et al., ed., *Free at Last,* 263 (Philbrick quote).

59. Glatthaar, *Forged in Battle,* 10, 36, 39–44, 65, 176; Spurgeon, *Soldiers,* 54–61, 106, 110–111; Winkle, *Lincoln's Citadel,* 330–333; Reidy, *Illusions,* 53–56.

60. Churchill, "When the Slave Catchers Came," 529; *Chicago Tribune,* October 9, 1863; W.K. Lee, Jr., testimony, n.d., South Carolina file, 57 (soldier quote), 173, AFIC; Allen, *Yankee,* 71; Doddington, *Contesting Slave Masculinity,* 16–36; *New York Anglo-African,* July 16, 1864; *New York Tribune,* November 9, 1863 (Rivers quote).

61. Glatthaar, *Forged in Battle,* 72–75; *US Statutes,* 13: 6–9; Cimprich, *Slavery's End,* 84; Rein, *Alabamians in Blue,* 120; *FDHE,* ser. 2, 1: 137; Buker, *Blockaders, Refugees, & Contrabands,* 45, 55.

62. Thompson, *Dear Eliza,* 92; Glatthaar, *Forged in Battle,* 70; Romero, *Gender and the Jubilee,* 61–66; Stealey, "West Virginia," in *Dictionary of Afro-American Slavery,* ed. Miller and Smith, 808; Crane, "The Demise of Slavery," 625–626.

63. *Boston Liberator,* January 22, 1864; Charles B. Wilder to George J. Carney, December 30, 1864, consolidated file V-87 (1865), LR by Adjutant General, RG 94, NA; Eaton, *Report,* 19; Rawick, ed., *American Slave* 17: 179; Swint, ed., *Dear Ones,* 52; *FDHE,* ser. 1, 2: 40 Yellin, ed., *Jacobs Family Papers* 2: 469 (quoted).

64. Cecelski, *Fire of Freedom,* 73–80; *US Statutes,* 12: 129, 144, 379; *FDHE,* ser. 2, 1: 136.

65. Cimprich, *Slavery's End,* 50; *New York National Antislavery Standard,* July 2, 1864; *FDHE,* ser. 1, 2: 475; Rawick, *American Slave* 7: OK-358 (quoted); Yeatman, *Report,* 7; H. Porter, report, March 24, 1865, 11, consolidated file V-87 (1865), LR by Adjutant General, RG 94, NA; *OR,* ser. 3, 3: 1140–41.

66. Sears, ed., *Camp Nelson,* 114; *New York Tribune,* November 4, 1863; Joseph B. Kinsman to Benjamin F. Butler, December 12, 1863, Joseph B. Kinsman, charges and testimony, January 20, 1864, LR by Department of Negro Affairs, Ft. Monroe, VA, field office, RG 105, NA; W. Perkins to Simeon S. Jocelyn, January 19, 1863, Samuel G. Wright to Simeon S. Jocelyn, January 20, 1863, Kentucky file, AMAA; Ripley, *Slaves and Freedmen,* 109. See *US Statutes,* 12: 11, for Congress' approval of the practice in February, 1864.

67. Pearson, ed., *Letters,* 174, 188, 240; *OR,* ser. 3, 4: 1028; Rose, *Rehearsal,* 267–68; Allen, *Yankee,* 71; *New York Tribune,* August 24, 1863; H. S. Beals to Benjamin F. Butler, December 10,

1863, and John H. Holman to Joseph B. Kinsman, December 25, 1863, LR by Department of Negro Affairs, Ft. Monroe, VA, field office, RG 105, NA; Higginson, *Army Life,* 48.

68. E. C. Brott to unknown, October 14, 1863, vol. 167/196: 106, LS by US Forces at Gallatin, Tennessee, RG 393, NA; D. C. Houston to Orville Leonard, March 30, 1863, Leonard Papers; *OR,* ser. 1, 31 (pt. 3): 367; Cimprich, *Slavery's End,* 86.

69. Glatthaar, *Forged in Battle,* 76–77; Leonard, *Slaves, Slaveholders,* 53–54.

70. Glatthaar, *Forged in Battle,* 40–42, 79, 109–20; *New York Anglo-African,* July 16, 1864; Higginson, *Army Life,* 259; Singleton, *Recollections,* 95; Thomas Trauernicht to Lorenzo Thomas, August 12, 1864, LR by 13th US Colored Infantry, RG 94, NA; Ramold, *Slaves, Sailors, Citizens,* 154; Marrs, *Life,* 25.

71. Glatthaar, *Forged in Battle,* 79, 101, 110–13; *Nashville Union,* March 10, 1864 (quoted); Higginson, *Army Life,* 59, 260.

72. Glatthaar, *Forged in Battle,* 104–5; Engs and Brooks, ed., *Their Patriotic Duty,* 141 (quoted); Higginson, *Army Life,* 49.

73. Glatthaar, *Forged in Battle,* 182; Clampitt, *Occupied Vicksburg,* 149–52; Carruthers journal, 1: 118 (January, 1865); *Philadelphia Christian Recorder,* May 7, 1864 (Hatton quote); two Black soldiers quoted in Ash, *Firebrand of Liberty,* 41; Engs and Brooks, ed., *Their Patriotic Duty,* 141, 185–86; Hawks, *Woman Doctor's Civil War,* 41.

74. Jordan, *Black Confederates and Afro-Yankees,* 163; *Philadelphia Christian Recorder,* July 9, 1864, February 4, April 15, 22, 1865; Trudeau, ed., *Voices of the 55th,* 129; Cimprich, *Fort Pillow,* 105–6.

75. Lucas, *From Slavery,* 167; True, "Life aboard a Gunboat," 38; *ORN,* 20: 396.

76. H. Porter, report, March 24, 1865, p. 34, consolidated file V-87 (1865), LR by Adjutant General, RG 94, NA; Glatthaar, *Forged in Battle,* 89.

77. Carruthers journal, 1: 107 (June 1864), 115–116 (December, 1864); Rochester Ladies Antislavery Society, *Fourteenth Annual Report,* 16; Bowley, *Honor in Command,* 824; Addeman, *Reminiscences,* 28; Edward R. Pierce to Simeon S. Jocelyn, August 7, 1863, Mississippi file, AMAA; Clara Duncan to George Whipple, February 22, 1865, Virginia file, AMAA; Rein, *Alabamians in Blue,* 136; Corbin, *Autobiography,* 37–38.

78. Glatthaar, *Forged in Battle,* 116, 169–75; Hawks, *Woman Doctor's Civil War,* 40; Orlando Brown to Joseph B. Kinsman, June 22, 1864, LR by Department of Negro Affairs, Ft. Monroe, VA, field office, RG 105, NA; Stephen Burbridge to J. B. Dickson, February 8, 1864, LS by Organization of USCT, Department of Kentucky, RG 393, NA.

79. Rawick, ed., *American Slave* 19: 179–80 (quoted); Reidy, *Illusions,* 149; Longacre, *Regiment of Slaves,* 30; *Philadelphia Christian Recorder,* March 4, 1865; Glymph, "This Species of Property," 66; Crane, "Demise of Slavery on the Border," 601; Williams, *I Freed Myself,* 155–56.

80. Dougherty, *Port Royal,* 58, 61.

7. Church and Community

1. Wilbur journal, May 22, 1864; Fountain, *Slavery,* 97–105; J. M. Mace to George Whipple, December 5, 1864, District of Columbia file, G. Greely to Simeon S. Jocelyn, June 3, 1863, James P. Stone to AMA, July 1, 1863, George N. Greene to Simeon S. Jocelyn, July 2, 15, 1863, Danforth B. Nichols to George Whipple, January 2, 1865, and Robert Harris to George Whipple, April 29,

1865, Virginia file, AMAA; Timothy Lyman to George Whipple, November 3, 1864, North Carolina file, AMAA; Redkey, ed., *Grand Army of Black Men,* 168–70; Engs, *Freedom's First,* 78; *New York Anglo-African,* August 1, 1863.

2. Blum, *Reforging,* 61–62; Indiana Yearly Meeting, *Report,* 25; H. S. Beals to Simeon S. Jocelyn, May 9, 1863, Joel Baker to George Whipple, February 28, 1865, G. Greeley to George Whipple, February 19, 1864, William S. Bell to Simeon S. Jocelyn, July 20, August 8, 1863, William S. Bell to Michael E. Strieby, March 24, 1865, Virginia file, AMAA.

3. William S. King to Simeon S. Jocelyn, August 4, 1863, Annie P. Wilkins to Michael E. Strieby, February 8, 1864, E. Eliza Lewis to George Whipple, December 28, 1864, and J. N. Mars to George Whipple, August 29, October 5, 1864, Virginia file, AMAA.

4. J. N. Mars to George Whipple, October 5, 1864, Virginia file, AMAA; Harriet Townsend to Simeon S. Jocelyn, February 24, 1864, Missouri file, AMAA; Samuel G. Wright to C. B. Boynton, February 10, 1863, Kentucky file, AMAA; Laura M. Towne testimony, n.d., South Carolina file, 63–64, AFIC; freedman quoted in Horst, *Education,* 125.

5. Mrs. Coleman to J. M. Mace, November report, 1864, District of Columbia file, Rhoda W. Smith to Simeon S. Jocelyn, July 8, 1863, Annie R. Wilkins to George Whipple, May 10, 1864, Virginia file, AMAA; *Friends' Review* 17 (November 7, 1863): 154; *Home Evangelist* 15 (April 1864): 15; Allen, *Yankee,* 79; Wilbur journal, March 12, June 14, November 3, 1863, March 27, 1864.

6. George N. Greene to Simeon S. Jocelyn, July 2, 1863, William H. Woodbury to Simeon S. Jocelyn, September 7, 1863, Charles B. Wilder to AMA, August 19, September 9, 1863, Louise A. Woodbury to Simeon S. Jocelyn, September 10, 1863, and H. C. Beals to George Whipple, February 29, 1864, Virginia file, AMAA; Timothy Lyman to George Whipple, February 1, 1865, North Carolina file, AMAA; Harrold, *Subversives,* 249–50; *New York Anglo-African,* July 9, 1864.

7. Timothy Lyman to George Whipple, August 30, 1864, North Carolina file, Charles B. Wilder to AMA, December 12, 1864, E. Eliza Lewis to George Whipple, December 28, 1864, Virginia file, AMAA; Kinsley, *Diary,* 130; *Friends' Intelligencer* 21 (February 4, 1864): 159.

8. Sobel, *Trabelin' On,* 160; Sears, ed., *Camp Nelson,* 132; Samuel G. Wright to Whipple, June 25, 1864, Mississippi file, AMAA; Lynch, *A Few Things,* 34.

9. *American Missionary* 7 (November 1863): 255; Charles P. Day to William E. Whiting, May 23, 1863, Virginia file, AMAA; Ella Roper to AMA, August 5, 1864, North Carolina file, AMAA; Charles Strong to Simeon S. Jocelyn, April 11, 1864, Louisiana file, AMAA; Butler, *Sketch,* 5; *Home Evangelist* 16 (May 1865): 19.

10. Walker, *Rock,* 64–69, 76–79, 84–87; Harper, *End of Days,* 31–32; Boakyewa-Ansah, "Crafted," 330; Lynch, *A Few Things,* 34–40; Foner and Walker, ed., *Proceedings of the Black National and State Conventions,* 1: 79; Sobel, *Trabelin' On,* 290–91, 296–98, 303, 312–13.

11. James F. Sisson to George Whipple, March 7, 1864, and J. N. Mars to George Whipple, May 27, July 1, 1864, Virginia file, AMAA; William A. Batchelor to Simeon S. Jocelyn, July 1, 1863, District of Columbia file, AMAA; Hurton Reedy to AMA, March 28, 1865, Louisiana file, AMAA; Allen, *Yankee,* 115–16.

12. Marcia Cotton to George Whipple, May 19, September 1, October 7, November 1, 1864, February 21, 1865, Virginia file, AMAA.

13. DeBoer, *His Truth Is Marching On,* 8; Cabral, "Letters," 121; W. T. Richardson to Simeon S. Jocelyn, August 7, 1863, Anna Carter to Simeon S. Jocelyn, December 12, 1863, and Samuel C.

Hale to George Whipple, July 20, 1864, South Carolina file, AMAA; Annie R. Wilkins, report, January 31, 1864 (quoted), William D. Harris to George Whipple, June 30, 1864, Nellie E. Parmenter to Michael E. Strieby, February 1, 1865, Charles P. Day to George Whipple, December 26, 1864, and Mary D. Williams to Simeon S. Jocelyn, July 4, 1864, Virginia file, AMAA; Lydia Montagne to Michael E. Strieby, June 20, 1864, Missouri file, AMAA; I.A. McMasters to George Whipple, May 2, 1864, Frank H. Green to George Whipple, February 16, 1864, Louisiana file, AMAA; D. T. Allen to George Whipple, May 1, 1864, Arkansas file, AMAA; Susan A. Hosmus to father, September 11, 1863, North Carolina file, AMAA; Botume, *First Days,* 101–2; *Freedman's Friend* 1 (June 1864): 12.

14. Howard et al., "Domestic History,"(typescript), 174: Browning, *Shifting Loyalties,* 89; Warren, ed., *Extracts from Reports,* ser. 1: 40; Lorenzo Thomas, S.O. 15, March 28, 1864, Mississippi Freedmen's Department Orders, RG 105, NA; Eberhart, *History,* 248; Edwin S. Williams to Simeon S. Jocelyn, April 26, 1863, South Carolina file, AMAA; Mary M. Reed to George Whipple, December 30, 1864, Virginia file, AMAA; W. W. Wheeler to George Whipple, December 2, 1864, Maryland file, AMAA; Towne testimony, n.d., 70–71, South Carolina file, 49, AFIC; Allen Journal, September 28, 1864; Hunter, *Bound in Wedlock,* 153.

15. Cimprich, *Slavery's End,* 75; Eberhart reminiscences, 39; Ripley, *Slaves and Freedmen,* 156; Bercaw, *Gendered Freedoms,* 45; Swint, ed., *Dear Ones,* 100.

16. Eberhart, *History,* 248; Hunter, *Bound in Wedlock,* 130; Williams, *Help Me,* 186–87; Swint, ed., *Dear Ones,* 34, 123–24; Botume, *First Days,* 155–56, 159, 160–61, 163.

17. Lee testimony, n.d., South Carolina file, 51–52, AFIC; Williams, *Help Me,* 186–87; Ames, *New England Woman's Diary,* 15–16; Mary M. Reed to George Whipple, December 30, 1864, Virginia file, AMAA; Edwin S. Williams to Simeon S. Jocelyn, April 26, 1863, South Carolina file, AMAA; Nordhoff, *Freedmen,* 23–24; Swint, ed, *Dear Ones,* 121.

18. *FDHE,* ser. 1, 2: 292; Friends' Association of Philadelphia, *Report,* 13; Ripley, *Slaves and Freedmen,* 153–55; Johnston, *Surviving Freedom,* 139; *Philadelphia Christian Recorder,* May 27, 1865; Bercaw, *Gendered Freedoms,* 36, 42–43, 46; Click, *Time Full,* 91, 101.

19. Botume, *First Days,* 105, 146, 151–54; Henry Rountree to Abram M. Taylor, May 7, 1863, Taylor Family Papers; Ann Schofield to Sarah Cope, April 3, 1864, LR by Women's Aid Committee, FFAR; Elizabeth James to George Whipple, August 13, 1864, North Carolina file, AMAA; Howard et al., "Domestic History"(typescript), 176.

20. Lovey A. Eberhart to C. H. Fowler, February 1, 1864, Mississippi file, AMAA; George N. Carruthers journal, 1: 119 (January 1865); Kickler, "Black Children," 33; Click, *Time Full,* 91, 102; *FDHE,* ser. 2, 1: 667, 712, 719; *National Freedmen* 1 (April 1865): 84.

21. *FDHE,* ser. 1, 2: 184, 3: 824, 846, ser. 2: 212, 709, ser. 3, 1: 845–46; Warren, ed., *Extracts from Reports,* ser. 1: 8, ser. 2: 22; Frankel, *Freedom's Women,* 30, 46; Clampitt, *Occupied Vicksburg,* 125.

22. *Friends' Review* 18 (February 4, 1865): 363; Ella Roper to AMA, August 5, 1864, North Carolina file, AMAA; *Freedman's Friend* 1 (July 1864): 8; Orlando Brown endorsement, October 27, 1864, on J. B. Kinsman to Brown, October 25, 1864, LR by Department of Negro Affairs, Ft. Monroe, VA, field office, RG 105, NA; Swint, ed., *Dear Ones,* 60; Cimprich, *Slavery's End,* 75.

23. James F. Sisson to AMA, July 16, 1863, Virginia file, AMAA; *FDHE,* ser. 1, 2: 331; Emerson, *Gibbons,* 2: 74; Yellin, *Harriet Jacobs,* 161, 165–66, 168; Yellin, ed., *Jacobs Family Papers* 2: 406, 461 (Wilbur quotes); Rochester Ladies Antislavery Society, *Thirteenth Annual Report,* 20.

24. Emerson, *Gibbons*, 74; Conway, *Final Report*, 14; Hawks, *Woman Doctor's Civil War*, 99, 126; Kilham, "Sketches," 210; Eaton, *Grant, Lincoln, and the Freedmen*, 202; Indiana Yearly Meeting, *Report*, 43; Warren, ed., *Extracts from Reports*, ser. 2, 47; Henry Rountree to Abram M. Taylor, October 8, 1863, Taylor Family Papers; *Friends' Review* 17 (December 1864): 211, (February 4, 1865): 363; Rochester Ladies Antislavery Society, *Fourteenth Annual Report*, 17.

25. *New York Principia*, August 20, 1863; Colman, *Reminiscences*, 62; Indiana Yearly Meeting, *Report*, 17; *Freedman's Advocate* 2 (February, 1865): 5; *Freedmen's Bulletin* 1 (September, 1864): 24, (November, 1864 supplement): 38.

26. Robinson, *Yankee*, 110; Rachel G.C. Patten to Simeon S. Jocelyn, July 28, 1863, Rachel G.C. Patten to William E. Whiting, April 29, 1864, January 4, 1865, James F. Sisson to AMA, July 23, 1863, Mary J. Doxey to William E. Whiting, November 14, 1863, Orlando Brown to Rachel G. C. Patten, February 20, 1864, Virginia file, AMAA; "Memphis Colored Orphan Asylum" (broadside, 1864), Taylor Family Papers; *National Freedman* 1 (April 1865): 79; *Freedmen's Bulletin* 1 (July 1864): 24, (November 1864 supplement): 48; Rochester Ladies Antislavery Society, *Twelfth Annual Report*, 14.

27. W. O. King to Simeon S. Jocelyn, April 2, 1864, William H. Woodbury to AMA, September 1, 1863, Rachel G. C. Patten to AMA, April 6, 1864, Virginia file, AMAA; *Friends' Review* 17 (March 19, 1864): 324, 461; Indiana Yearly Meeting, *Minutes*, 42; Indiana Yearly Meeting, *Report*, 48–49; *Freedmen's Advocate* 1 (May 1864): 19.

28. *National Freedman* 1 (April 1865): 79, (July 1865): 179; *Freedman's Advocate* 2 (February 1865): 5; "Freedmen's Schools," 1863–79 account book, Howland Family Papers; J. B. Kinsman to Benjamin F. Butler, July 14, 1864, LR by Department of Negro Affairs, Ft. Monroe, VA field office, RG 105, NA; Indiana Yearly Meeting, *Report*, 48–49; Emerson, *Gibbons*, 2: 74; *Pennsylvania Freedmen's Bulletin* 1 (August 1865): 51.

29. Henry Rountree to Abram M. Taylor, April 8, 1863, Taylor Family Papers; *Freedman's Advocate* 1 (May 1864): 18; Friends' Association for the Aid and Elevation of Freedmen. *Extracts from Letters*, 4; Botume, *First Days*, 121; *Freedmen's Record* 1 (March 1865): 39; Edward R. Pierce to Simeon S. Jocelyn, August 7, 1863, Mississippi file, AMAA; Annie R. Wilkins to George Whipple, May 10, 1864, and Mary M. Reed to George Whipple, December 30, 1864, Virginia file, AMAA; F. L. Williams to Simeon S. Jocelyn, April 28, 1863, South Carolina file, AMAA; Wilbur journal, May 20, June 2, October 10, 17, 29, 1863.

30. Greene, *Regulations* (poster).

31. *FDHE*, ser. 1, 2: 292; Rachel G. C. Patten to George Whipple, October 25, 1864, Virginia file, AMAA; Tacy Hadley reminiscences, 2–3; Wilbur journal, April 4, 1865.

32. Gerteis, *From Contraband to Freedman*, 193–94; Yellin, ed., *Jacobs Family Papers*, 2: 451; Wilbur journal, June 9, 1864; *American Missionary* 7 (September 1863): 207; Browning, *Shifting Loyalties*, 93–94.

33. Wilbur journal, June 16, October 30, 1863, January 9, 1864; Allen, *Yankee*, 168; Grimke, *Journals*, 495; Towne, *Letters and Diary*, 115–16; Freedmen and Soldiers' Relief Association, *Second Annual Report*, 6; Forbes, *African American Women*, 52–53, 106–8; *OR*, ser. 1, 45 (pt.1): 698; *New York Tribune*, November, 2, 1863; *New York Anglo-African*, September 3, 1864, quoted in Yellin, *Harriet Jacobs*, 182.

34. Clark, *Defining Moments*, 6, 9, 20, 31–35; E. H. Alden to George Whipple, June 11, 1864, Louisiana file, AMAA; Danforth B. Nichols to George Whipple, July 10, 1863, District of

Columbia file, AMAA; *Boston Liberator,* January 15, June 11, 1864; *New York Tribune,* April 4, 1865; Trumbull, *War Memories,* 402–3; *Freedmen's Record* 1 (February 1865): 21; *Freedman's Advocate* 2 (January 1865): 3; *New York National Antislavery Standard,* August 13, 20, 1864.

35. Danforth B. Nichols to George Whipple, July 10, 1863, Virginia file, AMAA; William McClue to Simeon S. Jocelyn, August 22, 1863, South Carolina file, AMAA; *New York Anglo-African,* August 1, 1863; *First Anniversary of the Proclamation of Freedom in South Carolina,* passim (Beaufort, SC: Free South Printing, 1864); Allen, *Yankee,* 176–77; *Freedman's Advocate* 2 (February 1865): 6; *Boston Liberator,* February 3, 1865.

36. Clark, *Defining Moments,* 38–39; *New York Tribune,* April 4, 1865; *New York National Antislavery Standard,* January 21, 1865; *New York Anglo-African,* January 28, 1865.

37. Berlin, *Slaves without Masters,* 284, 390; Reidy, *Illusions,* 43, 46–47, 333; Escott, *Worst Passions,* 169–71; *New York Anglo-African,* August 1, December 5, 26, 1863, July 16, 1864, March 25, April 22, 29, May 13, 1865; Cecelski, *Fire of Freedom,* 103–14.

38. Everett, "Demand," 45–48; *New York Tribune,* February 19, 1864; *Boston Liberator,* January 15, July 30, 1864; *New York Anglo-African,* July 9, 1864, April 8, 15, 1865.

39. Cecelski, *Fire of Freedom,* 115–21; *New York Tribune,* February 27, 1864; Harris, *With Charity for All,* 182; Everett, "Demand," 51–52.

40. Cimprich, *Slavery's End,* 112–113; Allen, *Yankee,* 15; William H. Woodbury to AMA, March 26, 1865, and Samuel G. Wright to George Whipple, March 28, 1865, Mississippi File, AMAA; *New York Anglo-African,* July 2, 1864; Friends' Association for the Aid and Elevation of Freedmen, *Extracts from Letters,* 3–4.

41. Rose, *Rehearsal,* 316–17; Knox, *Startling Revelations,* 5; Cimprich, *Slavery's End,* 110–13; *Nashville Times and True Union,* October 25, November 14, 1864.

42. National Convention of Colored Men, *Proceedings,* 5–6, 17, 25–29, 34, 42.

43. Cimprich, *Slavery's End,* 110, 112; Wilbur journal, January 2, 3, February 25, March 4, 1865. For Blacks' mock elections in Alexandria and Beaufort, South Carolina, see Yellin, ed., *Jacobs Family Papers,* 2: 588; *Boston Liberator,* December 9, 1864.

44. Cecelski, *Fire of Freedom,* 158; Cimprich, *Slavery's End,* 110, 115; Ripley, *Slaves and Freedmen,* 164, 179; Williams, *I Freed Myself,* 210; *New York Anglo-African,* January 17, 28, 1865.

45. *Boston Liberator,* November 14, 1862; New England Educational Commission, *Extracts,* ser. 4: 5; *Philadelphia Christian Recorder,* April 22, 1865; Tetzlaff, "Mitchelville," 83; Gerteis, *From Contraband to Freedman,* 179; Reidy, *Illusions,* 179.

46. *American Missionary* 8 (February 1864): 39; *National Freedman* 1 (June 1865): 152; Blassingame, *Testimony,* 377–78, 384; W. T. Eaton to George Whipple, May 26, 1865, Georgia file, AMAA.

47. Sheridan, "From Slavery in Missouri," 46–47; *New York Anglo-African,* July 2, 1864, and January 28, April 8, 1865; *FDHE,* ser. 1, 2: 359.

48. E. Eliza Lucas to George Whipple, June 28, 1864 (Portsmouth freedman quote), Virginia file, AMAA; *New York Tribune,* November 9, 1863 (Rivers quote); Parsons, *Memoir,* 139–41; Jacob West to J. Burnham Kinsman, July 26, 1864, LR by Department of Negro Affairs, Ft. Monroe, VA, field office, RG 105, NA; Winkle, *Lincoln's Citadel,* 396–400; Truth, *Narrative,* 184; *New York Anglo-African,* April 8, 1865; Wilbur journal, April 22, 1864.

49. *New York National Antislavery Standard,* January 30, 1864; Cimprich, *Slavery's End,* 45; Romeo, *Gender and the Jubilee,* 69–74, 78, 80, 87–94; White, "Martial Law," 567-60.

50. *New York Principia,* February 25, 1864.

8. Education

1. George Condee to Simeon S. Jocelyn, July 3, 1863, February 5, 1864, H. R. Revels to Simeon S. Jocelyn, February 24, 1864, and George Condee to George Whipple, April 8, June 1 (quoted), 9, July 15, 1864, Missouri file, AMAA.

2. J. L. Richardson to Simeon S. Jocelyn, July 4, 1863, George Condee to George Whipple, April 4, June 9, 1864, Lydia A. Hess to Simeon S. Jocelyn, March 28, 1864, George C. Booth to AMA, October 20, 1864, and M. M. Clark to George Whipple, February 2, 1865, Missouri file, AMAA; N. Noyes to George Whipple, January 16, 1865, Maryland file, AMAA; *New York National Antislavery Standard,* October 1, 1864; *American Missionary* 8 (April 1864): 145.

3. *American Missionary* 8 (April 1864): 101; Warren, ed., *Final Report,* 9; Sears, ed., *Camp Nelson,* 101, 120; *New York Anglo-African,* December 19, 1863; A. G. Marsh to George Whipple, February 18, 1864, and Thomas James to George Whipple, January 24, 1865, Kentucky file, AMAA; Fuke, "Baltimore Association," 373, 377–78.

4. Horst, *Education,* 183, 199; *"Evening School for Freedmen in Washington and George-town"* (flyer, 1864), District of Columbia file, AMAA; Ellen W. Dickinson to George Whipple, May 2, 1864, J. R. Brown to George Whipple, August 13, 1864, J. W. Fox to George Whipple, September 26, 1864, and J. F. Norris to George Whipple, December 28, 1864, Kansas file, AMAA.

5. William S. Bell to AMA, January report, 1864, Charlotte MacDonald to George Whipple, February 27, 1864, and Charlotte MacDonald to William H. Woodbury, May 2, 1864, Virginia file, AMAA; Lucy Chase testimony, May 10, 1863, Virginia file, 23, AFIC.

6. George Condee to George Whipple, August 15, 1864, Missouri file, AMAA; J. R. Blake to George Whipple, April 30, 1864, Virginia file, AMAA; L. L. Hammonds to Michael E. Strieby, August 23, November 29, 1864, Michael E. Strieby to George Whipple, December 3, 1864, N. Noyes to Michael E. Strieby, December 12, 1864, and N. Noyes to George Whipple, January 4, 1865, Maryland file, AMAA.

7. Charles P. Day to George Whipple, April 27, 1863, Charles P. Day to William E. Whiting, March 26, December 31, 1864, and William S. Bell to George Whipple, November 14, 1864, Virginia file, AMAA; George N. Greene to William E. Whiting, North Carolina file, AMAA; *Pennsylvania Freedmen's Bulletin* 1 (March, 1865): 31.

8. Orlando Brown to J. B. Kinsman, June 20, 1864, LR by Department of Negro Affairs, Ft. Monroe, VA, field office, RG 105, NA; *Freedmen's Journal* 1 (January 1865): 9; Board of Education for Freedmen, *Report,* 5–7; Ripley, *Slaves and Freedmen,* 128–31, 136; Edwin M. Wheelock to John McNair, May 13, 1864, Edwin M. Wheelock to Mr. Aldrich, May 17, 1864, LS by Louisiana Board of Education for Freedmen, RG 105, NA; Cimprich, *Slavery's End,* 77; David Todd to George Whipple, February 25, 1864, Arkansas file, AMAA.

9. Morris, *Reading, 'Riting, and Reconstruction,* 23–26; Ripley, *Slaves and Freedmen,* 131, 135–40, 142; Messner, "Black Education," 48–49, 55–56; B. F. Burnham to Michael E. Strieby, September 12, 1864, Louisiana file, AMAA; Kinsley, *Diary,* 175; Edwin M. Wheelock to Stephen A. Hurlbut, February 7, 1865, LS by Louisiana Board of Education for Freedmen, RG 105, NA; *Freedmen's Bulletin* 1 (May 1864): 103.

10. Ripley, *Slaves and Freedmen,* 131; J. H. Ford, reports, May 23, July 22, August 19, 1864, Inspections for the Louisiana Board of Education for Freedmen, RG 105, NA; Board of Education

for Freedmen, *Report,* 15; L. M. Binge to AMA, June 27, 1864, Daniel W. Knowles to George Whipple, September 30, 1864, Louisiana file, AMAA.

11. Cimprich, *Slavery's End,* 77–78; Eaton, *Report,* 86; Eaton, Circular 4, October 20, 1864, Orders of the Mississippi Freedmen's Department, RG 105, NA; J. M. Palmer endorsement, January 20, 1864, on John P. Hunting to Palmer, January 15, 1864, LR by Department of Negro Affairs, Ft. Monroe, VA, field office, RG 105, NA; Allen journal, October 31, 1864; *Freedmen's Bulletin* 1 (May 1865): 97. During the war Allen worked for Black school systems in three locations, each at a different time.

12. Allen journal, October 4, 1864, November 23, 30, January 4, 1865; Cimprich, *Slavery's End,* 78; J. P. Bardwell to Michael E. Strieby, January 5, 1865, Mississippi file, AMAA; Warren, ed., *Final Report,* 14.

13. New England Yearly Meeting, *Report to the Executive Committee,* 6; George F. Shepley, G.O. 30, September 21, 1864, William L. Coan to George Whipple, March 29, 1864, H. L. True to William H. Woodbury, March 29, 1864, Ellen L. Benton to Whipple, October 11, 1864, William S. Bell to George Whipple, October 31, 1864, and Sallie L. Daffin to George Whipple, February 2, 1865, Virginia file, AMAA; *Freedmen's Journal* 1 (January 1865): 9; H. Porter, report, March 24, 1865, pp. 16, 27 (quoted), 31, consolidated file V-87 (1865), LR by the Adjutant General, RG 94, NA.

14. Williams, *Self-Taught,* 87–90; *Friends' Intelligencer* 21 (February 25, 1865): 815; W. T. Richardson, January 2, 1865, and Donald Brown to Samuel Hunt, January 20, 1865, Georgia file, AMAA; *Freedmen's Record* 1 (June 1865): 92.

15. *Freedman's Record* 1 (April 1865): 61, 73, (July 1865): 112; T. W. Cardozo to Michael E. Strieby, April 29, 1865, H. H. Hunter to Michael E. Strieby, May 6, 1865, South Carolina file, AMAA; *National Freedman* 1 (June 1865): 150.

16. L. S. Hascall to Michael E. Strieby, April 8, 1865, Virginia file, AMAA; Swint, ed., *Dear Ones,* 154–55; *American Missionary* 9 (July 1865): 153.

17. *Philadelphia Christian Recorder,* May 6, 1865; Browning, "Bringing Light," 9, 12; *Freedman's Advocate* 1 (March 1864): 9; *Freedmen's Journal* 1 (January 1865): 4; Click, *Time Full,* 85; *American Missionary* 7 (September 1863): 205; Ripley, ed., *Black Abolitionist Papers,* 5: 292 (Mars quote).

18. Samuel G. Wright to George Whipple, October 12, 1864, Mississippi file AMAA; William H. Woodbury to George Whipple, February 10, 1864, Virginia file, AMAA; J. W. Magill to AMA, February 3, 1864, Georgia file, AMAA; George Condee to George Whipple, June 1, 1864, Missouri file, AMAA; W. T. Richardson to George Whipple, January 24, 1865, South Carolina file, AMAA; John G. Fee to Michael E. Strieby, May 30, 1865, Kentucky file, AMAA; N. Noyes to Michael E. Strieby, May 30, 1865, Maryland file, AMAA; *New York Anglo-African,* April 8, 1865.

19. William H. Woodbury to Simeon S. Jocelyn, November 7, 1863, February 10, 1864, Virginia file, AMAA: Horace James to George Whipple, September 13, 1863, North Carolina file, AMAA; George F. Needham to George Whipple, October 14, 1864, William J. Wilson to George Whipple, December 7, 1864, District of Columbia file, AMAA; Harrold, *Subversives,* 234; Jones, *Soldiers of Light,* 69; Richardson, *Christian Reconstruction,* 23–24; Wilson quoted in DeBoer, *His Truth,* 92; Perkins, "Black Female," 128–29.

20. Susan Drummond to Miss Dodge, December 21, 1863, J. N. Mars to George Whipple, November 14, 1864, James E. Edwards to AMA, February 28, 1865, William H. Woodbury to George Whipple, February 10, 1864, Virginia file, AMAA; J. W. Fox to Simeon S. Jocelyn, February 8, 1864, Kansas file, AMAA; J. L. Richardson to Simeon S. Jocelyn, April 30, 1863,

Missouri file, AMAA; J. P. Bardwell to Michael E. Strieby, January 5, 1865, Mississippi file, AMAA; Allen, *Yankee,* 41; Allen journal, December 20, 1864 (Black teacher quote); Swint, ed., *Dear Ones,* 144; Blassingame, *Testimony,* 742; New York Yearly Meeting, *Report,* 8; Click, *Time Full,* 85.

21. Samuel A. Walker to George Whipple, March 28, 1864 (quoted), Virginia file, AMAA; Edmonia G. Highgate to Michael E. Strieby, March 10, 31, April 13, 1865, and N. Noyes to George Whipple, April 17, 1865, Maryland file, AMAA. Also see Lynch, *A Few Things,* 32–33, on discrimination in transportation.

22. Yellin, ed., *Jacobs Family Papers,* 2: 534–36, 553 (quoted); Yellin, *Harriet Jacobs,* 161, 177–78; McGranahan, ed., *Historical Sketch,* 2–3; William S. Bell to George Whipple, May 9, 1865, Virginia file, AMAA.

23. Browning, *Shifting Loyalties,* 110; Cimprich, *Slavery's End,* 79; *Freedman's Record* 1 (April 1865): 61, (July 1865): 110; *American Missionary* 19 (May 1865): 104; *New York Tribune,* March 18, 1865; McKivigan, *Forgotten Firebrand,* 105–7; *Pennsylvania Freedmen's Bulletin* 1 (March 1865): 29; J. L. Richardson to Simeon S. Jocelyn, March 23, 1864, Missouri file, AMAA; J. W. Duncan to George Whipple, April 1, 1864, and E. W. Douglas to George Whipple, January 14, 1865, Virginia file, AMAA; Susan A. Hosmus to father, September 11, 1863, North Carolina file, AMAA; *New York National Antislavery Standard,* August 20, 1864 (quoted).

24. Cimprich, *Slavery's End,* 77; Allen, *Yankee,* 193, 197; Reidy, *Illusions,* 200.

25. Forten, "Life," 592; E. Congden to Sarah Cope, July 9, 1864, LR by Women's Aid Committee, FFAR; Joseph Warren, *Extracts from Reports,* ser. 1: 43; D. W. Knowles to George Whipple, June 24, 1864, Louisiana file, AMAA; J. H. Ford report, June 6, 1864, Inspections for the Louisiana Board of Education for Freedmen, RG 105, NA; Powers, *Hospital Pencilings,* 61; Clifford, *Those Good Gertrudes,* 32; *Pennsylvania Freedmen's Bulletin* 1 (April 1865): 30.

26. Misses Smith, Burnap, and Gill, January report, 1864, North Carolina file, AMAA; Charles P. Day to Simeon S. Jocelyn, October 13, 1863, William H. Woodbury to Simeon S. Jocelyn, October 29, 1863, William H. Woodbury to George Whipple, December 9, 1863, and Annie R. Wilkins to George Whipple, May 18, 1864, Virginia file, AMAA; H. J. Heilman to George Whipple, March 4, 1864, Arkansas file, AMAA; William J. Wilson to George Whipple, November 15, 1864, William S. Tilden to Mr. Hunt, May 13, 1865, District of Columbia file, AMAA; E. Congdon to Sara Cope, July 9, 1864, LR by Women's Aid Committee, FFAR; Moore, *In Christ's Stead,* 328–29.

27. Williams, *Self-Taught,* 151; William T. Briggs to George Whipple, June 21, 1864, North Carolina file, AMAA; Charles B. Wilder to AMA, June 14, 1864, Virginia file, AMAA; John Eaton, Circular, April 12, 1864, Mississippi Freedmen's Department orders, RG 105, NA; *American Missionary* 7 (July 1863): 160, (September 1863): 211, 8 (December 1864): 285; Maria Mann to Aunt Mary, May 18, 1863, Mann Papers; *Freedmen's Record* 1 (February 1865): 29; *New York Anglo-African,* September 5, 1863.

28. Harrold, *Subversives,* 250; *Pennsylvania Freedmen's Bulletin* 1 (March 1865): 32; *Freedmen's Journal* 1 (January 1865): 7–8; William J. Wilson to Michael E. Strieby, April 12, 1865, and William S. Tilden to Mr. Hunt, May 14, 1865, District of Columbia file, AMAA; A. W. Eastman to George Whipple, September 29, 1864, and Joel Baker to George Whipple, January 31, April 1, 1865, Virginia file, AMAA; J. H. Ford, report, February 6, 1865, Inspections for Louisiana Board of Education for Freedmen, RG 105, NA; Friends' Association for the Aid and Elevation of the Freedmen, *Report,* 21.

29. Henry Rountree to Abram M. Taylor, June 2, 1863, Taylor Family Papers; Butler, *Sketch,* 2; Horace James to friends, May 25, 1863, James Papers; Burton, *Penn Center,* 25; Towne, *Letters and Diary,* 148; William H. Woodbury to Simeon S. Jocelyn, October 29, 1863, Virginia file, AMAA.

30. Anna A. Carter to Simeon S. Jocelyn, June 13, 1864 (quoted), South Carolina file, AMAA; Elizabeth James, April report, 1865, North Carolina file, William L. Coan to AMA, October 10, 1863, Charles P. Day to William E. Whiting, December 5, 1863 and January 28, 1864, Harriet Taylor to William H. Woodbury, December 10, 1863, Annie R. Wilkins to George Whipple, May 10, 1864, Mary M. Reed, June report, 1864, Charles B. Wilder to AMA, June 14, 1864, H. C. Percy to George Whipple, November 2, 1864, March 31, 1865, H. E. Flagg to George Whipple, December 31, 1864, Sarah A. MacDonald to George Whipple, May 1, 1865, Virginia file, AMAA; Friends' Association for the Aid and Elevation of the Freedmen, *Report,* 15, 21; Laura M. Towne testimony, n.d., South Carolina file, 60, AFIC; New England Educational Commission for Freedmen, *Extracts,* ser. 4: 11; *Pennsylvania Freedmen's Bulletin,* 1 (March 1865): 24, (April 1865): 30; Friends' Association for the Aid and Elevation of Freedmen, *Extracts from Letters,* 3–4; *Freedmen's Bulletin* 1 (May 1865): 99.

31. Lydia Thompson to George Whipple, June 28, 1864, Mississippi file, AMAA; Elizabeth James, April report, 1865, North Carolina file, AMAA; George Condee to George Whipple, November 30, 1863, Missouri file, AMAA; *Friends' Review* 17 (November 7, 1863): 154; Moore, *In Christ's Stead,* 30–31; Trumbull, *War Memories,* 401; *Freedman's Advocate* 1 (July/August 1864): 25; J. H. Ford, report, May 23, 1864, Inspections for Louisiana Board of Education for Freedmen, RG 105, NA; Davis, *History of Black Catholics,* 104.

32. Frank H. Green to George Whipple, August 12, 1864, Louisiana file, AMAA; Butchart, *Schooling,* 125–26; Brosnan, "Representations of Race and Racism," 729–31; *Freedman's Advocate* 1 (July/August 1864): 25; American Tract Society, *The Freedman's Primer or First Reader* (Boston: privately printed, 1864), esp. 40; American Tract Society, *The Freedman's Second Reader* (Boston: George C. Rand & Avery, 1865), esp. 35–37; Morris, *Reading, 'Riting, and Reconstruction,* 189–91.

33. Charles P. Day to William E. Whiting, December 25, 1863, Virginia file, AMAA; *American Missionary* 7 (April 1863): 89 (quoted); *Freedmen's Bulletin* 1 (January 1865): 61; Botume, *First Days,* 110; James Hawks to Esther Hawks, August 14, 1862, Hawks Papers; *Freedman's Friend* 1 (May 1865): 54.

34. *Freedman,* 1 (esp. August, 1864); Butchart, *Schools,* 139–43, 151.

35. Susan Drummond to Simeon S. Jocelyn, January 1, 1864, W. O. King to AMA, June 1, 1864, Virginia file, Anna A. Carter to Simeon S. Jocelyn, June 13, 1864, South Carolina file, Sarah M. Pearson, May report, 1864, North Carolina file, AMAA; Jones, *Soldiers of Light,* 115; *Freedman's Friend* 1 (May 1865): 55; New England Education Commission, *Extracts,* ser. 4: 8; Association of Friends for the Aid and Elevation of Freedmen, *Report,* 21; Towne, *Letters and Diary,* 163; *Pennsylvania Freedmen's Bulletin* 1 (January 1865): 6; *Freedmen's Record* 1 (July 1865): 111.

36. Warren, ed., *Extracts from Reports,* ser. 1: 19; *Friends' Review* 17 (January 2, 1864): 282; *Friends' Review* 18 (April 1, 1865): 490; *Friends' Review* 18 (May 13, 1865): 587; Horst, *Education,* 65; *New York Tribune,* August 21, 1863, and May 14, 1864; Greene, *Regulations* (poster); Indiana Yearly Meeting, *Minutes,* 43–44; *Freedman's Advocate* 1 (April 1864): 13 (June 1864 supplement): 2.

37. Daniel Breed to Anna M. C. Barnes, December 29, 1863, Rochester Ladies Antislavery Society Papers; *Evening Schools for Freedmen in Washington and Georgetown* (flyer), District of Columbia file, AMAA.

38. *Friends' Intelligencer* 20 (January 9, 1864): 694; Ann Schofield to Sarah Cope, April 3, 1864, LR by Women's Aid Committee, FFAR; Charlotte S. MacDonald to George Whipple, February 28, 1865, Virginia file, AMAA.

39. *American Missionary* 8 (December 1864): 293; J. H. Ford, report, October 1, 1864, Inspections for Louisiana Board of Education for Freedmen, RG 105, NA; *Freedman's Advocate* 1 (March 1864): 10; (quoted), (May 1864): 18; *National Freedman* 1 (June 1865): 169; Allen, *Yankee,* 197; *Freedmen's Record* 1 (July 1865): 112; Northwestern Freedmen's Aid Commission, *Second Annual Report,* 14.

40. Clifford, *Those Good Gertrudes,* 215–217; Charles P. Day to Simeon S. Jocelyn, May 8, 1863, J. W. Coan to Simeon S. Jocelyn, May 18, 1863, William D. Harris to George Whipple, July report, 1864, Virginia file, AMAA; William T. Briggs to George Whipple, July 9, 1864, North Carolina file, AMAA; Frank H. Green to George Whipple, September 23, 1864, Louisiana file, AMAA; Allen journal, January 3–4, 1865.

41. Glatthaar, *Forged in Battle,* 223–27; Williams, *Self-Taught,* 37–52; Allen journal, November 6, 1864; Hawks, *Woman Doctor's Civil War,* 37, 42; Walker, "Corinth," 15; R. H. Manley to George Whipple, February 13, July report, 1864, Virginia file, AMAA; W. T. Richardson to Simeon S. Jocelyn, January 5, 1864, Jonathan J. Wright to Michael E. Strieby, May 5, 1865, P. Gustave Barnswell to Michael E. Strieby, May 11, 1865, South Carolina file, AMAA; T. A. McMasters to George Whipple, May 2, 1864, Louisiana file, AMAA.

42. Samuel G. Wright to George Whipple, January 3, 1865, Mississippi file, AMAA; W. B. Wooster to Simeon S. Jocelyn, February 17, 1865, R. H. Manley, July report, 1864, Virginia file, AMAA; Sears, ed., *Camp Nelson,* xlv–xlvi; *Freedman's Advocate* 1 (June 1864): 21, (June 1864 supplement): 2; Williams, *Self-Taught,* 51; Cimprich, *Slavery's End,* 89; Swint, ed., *Dear Ones,* 119 (quoted).

43. *Freedmen's Journal* 1 (January 1864): 4; Sarah Pearson and Elizabeth James, March reports, 1865, North Carolina file, AMAA; S. L. Drummond to George Whipple, April 27, 1864, Nannie I. Partridge to George Whipple, January 3, 1865, Virginia file, AMAA; George Sisson, March report, 1864, Nelson Scoval, April report, 1864, South Carolina file, AMAA; Ann Schofield to Sarah Cope, April 3, 1864, LR by Women's Aid Committee, FFAR; Botume, *First Days,* 94–95; *Freedmen's Bulletin* 1 (November 1864 supplement): 50; Williams, *Self-Taught,* 163.

44. Greene, *Regulations* (poster); Swint, ed., *Dear Ones,* 147; Joel Baker to George Whipple, May 31, 1865, Virginia file, AMAA; William McClue to Simeon S. Jocelyn, July 14, 1863, South Carolina file, AMAA; New York Yearly Meeting, *Report,* 5 (quoted).

45. Cecelski, *Waterman's Song,* 171; Cyrus Jordan to George Whipple, March 11, 1864, Emily Stewart to George Whipple, February 2, 1865, Virginia file, AMAA; Click, *Time Full,* 94; Women's Aid Committee Minutebook #1, E-12, FFAR; Browning, *Shifting Loyalties,* 110; *Freedman's Advocate* 1 (April 1864): 14; *Pennsylvania Freedmen's Bulletin* 1 (February 1865): 7; New England Freedmen's Aid Society, *Extracts,* ser. 5: 15.

46. New England Freedmen's Aid Society, *Extracts,* ser. 5: 17; H. E. Flagg to George Whipple, December 31, 1864, William Davis to George Whipple, February 27, 1865, William L. Coan to George Whipple, March 29, 1864, Virginia file, AMAA; W. Hamilton to Simeon S. Jocelyn, January 25, 1864, North Carolina file, AMAA; Alma Baker to George Whipple, January 20, 1865, Missouri file, AMAA; J. H. Ford report, July 22, 1864, Inspections for Louisiana Board of Education for Freedmen, RG 105, NA; Allen, *Yankee,* 88; Browning, *Shifting Loyalties,* 110; Wilbur journal, December 14, 1864; Friends' Association of Philadelphia, *Second Report,* 24.

47. Williams, *Self-Taught,* 163–64; Clara Duncan to George Whipple, February 22, 1865, Virginia file, AMAA; Rhoda W. Smith et al., January report, 1864, W. Hamilton to Simeon S. Jocelyn, January 25, 1864, North Carolina file, AMAA; Allen, *Yankee,* 56; E. Congdon to Sara Cope, July 9, 1864, LR by Women's Aid Committee, FFAR.

48. *Pennsylvania Freedmen's Bulletin* 1 (April 1865): 32; Isabella McKetchie to George Whipple, December 2, 1864, Charles P. Day to George Whipple, January 31, 1865, Sarah M. Gill to George Whipple, May 31, 1865, Virginia file, AMAA; *Freedmen's Record* 1 (February 1865): 20.

49. *New York Principia,* June 25, July 23, 1863; William J. Wilson to George Whipple, August 27, 1864, District of Columbia file, AMAA; Lydia Montague to Michael E. Strieby, June 20, 28, 1864, George Condee to Simeon S. Jocelyn, June 30, 1863, Lydia A. Hess to Simeon S. Jocelyn, March 28, 1864, J. L. Richardson to Simeon S. Jocelyn, July 4, 1863, Missouri file, AMAA; W. W. Wheeler to George Whipple, June 22, 1864, West Virginia file, AMAA: William L. Coan to William E. Whiting, October 21, 1863, Josephine E. Strong to Michael E. Strieby, Virginia file, AMAA; Cimprich, *Slavery's End,* 76; *Pennsylvania Freedmen's Bulletin* 1 (April 1865): 35; *Freedmen's Bulletin* 1 (September 1864): 21; Board of Education for Freedmen, Department of the Gulf, *Report,* 10.

50. Browning, "Vision," 88; Warren, *Extracts from Documents,* 6; Robert Harris to George Whipple, December 29, 1864, Virginia file, AMAA; Edwin M. Wheelock to William Fiske, January 18, 1865, C. H. Newton to Edwin M. Wheelock, January 20, 1865, LS by Louisiana Board of Education for Freedmen, RG 105, NA; Ash, *Middle Tennessee,* 134.

51. *Pennsylvania Freedmen's Bulletin* 1 (April 1865): 28, 35, (August 1865): 46; W. W. Wheeler to George Whipple, June 22, 1864, West Virginia file, Lydia A. Hess to Simeon S. Jocelyn, March 28, 1864, Missouri file, AMAA; George N. Greene to Simeon S. Jocelyn, May 15, June 24, 1863, William D. Harris to Willian H. Woodbury, April 1, 1864, William H. Woodbury to AMA, November 30, 1863, William L. Coan to Simeon S. Jocelyn, May 9, 1863, (quoted) Virginia file, AMAA; *Freedman's Advocate* 1 (May 1865): 9; Job Hadley reminiscences, 10.

52. Freedwoman quoted in Greenwood, *First Fruits,* 75; *Freedmen's Record* 1 (February 1865): 29, (July 1865): 114, (June 1865): 97 (freedman's quote); Charles Wilder to William E. Whiting, July 23, 1864, H. M. Reed to George Whipple, May 31, 1865, Susan Drummond to AMA, May 9, 1863, Harriet Taylor to Simeon S. Jocelyn, February 24, 1864 (boy's quote), Sarah A. Vinton to George Whipple, June 21, 1864, Virginia file, AMAA; Butler *Sketch,* 2.

9. Freedpeople and Reformers at the War's End

1. Hodes, *Mourning Lincoln,* 65–66, 143; two Washington freedpersons quoted in Yellin, *Harriet Jacobs,* 187; Laura Towne to S., April 23, 1865, Towne letters, Penn School Papers; *Freedmen's Record* 1 (June 1865): 98; Chester, *Black Civil War Correspondent,* 329; T. E. Ruggles to Charles P. Ware, May 5, 1865, Ware Papers; Pearson, ed., *Letters,* 311.

2. Botume, *First Days,* 191–93; *American Missionary* 9 (July 1865): 157 (Roper quote); H. C. Percy to George Whipple, May 7, 1865, Virginia file, AMAA.

3. *FDHE,* ser. 3, 1: 83; W. T. Richardson to George Whipple, May 25, 1865, South Carolina file, AMAA; Rochester Ladies Antislavery Society, *Fourteenth Annual Report,* 15; *Philadelphia Christian Recorder,* May 6, 1865; Wise et al., *Rebellion,* 376; Wilbur journal, May 31, 1865; Williams, *Help Me,* 152–53, 221.

4. Foner, *Reconstruction,* 21; Ellen Wheeler to Miss Smith, May 29, 1865, Scott Family Papers; Wilbur journal, May 29, 31, 1865; Rochester Ladies Antislavery Society, *Fourteenth Annual Report,* 15–17.

5. *FDHE,* ser. 1, 2: 260, ser. 2, 1: 721; Click, *Time Full,* 139–40; *National Freedman* 1 (April 1865): 84; Charles P. Day to George Whipple, February 25, 1865, H. S. Beals to George Whipple, April 29, 1865, Virginia file, AMAA; Towne, *Letters and Diary,* 154–57; Ellen Wheeler to Miss Smith, May 29, 1865, Scott Family Papers.

6. Ellen Wheeler to Miss Smith, May 29, 1865, Scott Family Papers; *FDHE,* ser. 3, 1: 36, 198, 313–14, 332–33; *OR,* ser. 1, 47 (pt. 3): 331; James, *Annual Report,* 59–60; Foner, *Reconstruction,* 164–67.

7. Cimbala, *Under the Guardianship,* 167–70; Manning, *Troubled Refuge,* 265; Ochiai, *Harvesting Freedom,* 143–44; *FDHE,* ser. 3, 1: 199; Click, *Time Full,* 160–161.

8. *National Freedman* 1 (June 1865): 166, (July 1865): 190; daily record book, 7, 15, New England Freedmen's Aid Society Papers; G. N. Greene to Simeon S. Jocelyn, July 2, 1863, E. P. Worthington to George Whipple, May 1, 1865, Virginia file, AMAA; Litwack, *Been in the Storm,* 465–68; Warren, ed., *Final Report,* 14; *Philadelphia Christian Recorder,* May 6, 1865.

9. H. C. True to George Whipple, April 4, 1865, North Carolina file, AMAA; *Freedmen's Bulletin* 1 (July 1865): 134; McPherson, *Struggle,* 172; Manning, *Troubled Refuge,* 265–66.

10. Allen, *Yankee,* 195–96.

11. Inadequate records prevent an exact headcount of Black refugees behind Federal lines, including those who died there. Low estimates are based on reformers' actual counts or estimates in particular locations, all made at different times during the war. High estimates primarily count all living in occupied areas as of the 1860 census. The estimate in *FDHE,* ser. 1, 2: 76–79 is a plausible minimum, but also see Gerteis, *From Contraband to Freedman,* 193–94; Blight, ed., *A Slave No More,* 160; Ash, *Black Experience,* 74–75. The New England Freedmen's Aid Society estimate in *Freedmen's Journal* 1 (January 1865): 15, of two million, around half of all slaves, seems excessively high.

12. Ash, *Black Experience,* 5; Fuke, *Imperfect Equality,* 120; Harrison, *Washington,* 25; Wise et al., *Rebellion,* 376; Edward S. Philbrick to Charles P. Ware, September 24, 1863, Ware Papers.

13. Eliza Lewis to George Whipple, April 1, 1865, Charles P. Day to George Whipple, April 29, 1865, Augustus M. Weeks to George Whipple, May 3, 1865, Robert Harris to George Whipple, April 1, 1865, Virginia file, AMAA; H. E. Gaylord to George Whipple, May 1, 1865, Mississippi file, AMAA; *Pennsylvania Freedmen's Bulletin* 1 (May 1865): 28, 36; William F. Allen to Ned, May 21, 1865, Allen Papers.

14. Foner, *Reconstruction,* 119; Chester, *Black Correspondent,* 330, 333; H. C. Percy to George Whipple, May 31, 1865, Virginia file, AMAA; Swint ed., *Dear Ones,* 159 (quoted).

15. Manning, *Troubled Refuge,* 247–48; Harris, *With Charity for All,* 29; Cimprich, *Slavery's End,* 103.

16. Gerteis, *From Contraband to Freedman,* 188–91; Foner, *Reconstruction,* 153–58; Kolchin, *American Slavery,* 212; *Nashville Press and Times,* October 18, 1865; Cimprich, *Slavery's End,* 50; Cimbala, *Under the Guardianship,* 84; *FDHE,* ser. 1, 2: 476, 531; Rochester Ladies Antislavery Society, *Fourteenth Annual Report,* 13.

17. McElya, *Politics of Mourning,* 122–24, 133–35; Blum, *Reforging,* 59; Colman, *Reminiscences,* 61; Holt et al., *Special Mission,* 7; Osthaus, *Freedmen, Philanthropy, and Fraud,* 3–5, 16,

32; Cimprich, *Slavery's End,* 127; Taylor, *Embattled Freedom,* 235–37; *Freedmen's Bulletin* 1 (June 1865): 122; Minutes, May 10, 1865, New England Freedmen's Aid Society Papers.

18. Manning, *Troubled Refuge,* 272; Rose, *Rehearsal,* 357; Weicksel, "Fitted up," 169; Click, *Time Full,* 177–90; Ross, "Freed Soil, Freed Labor," 223; Gerteis, *From Contraband to Freedman,* 47–48; Taylor, *Embattled Freedom,* 216–30, 237–38.

19. Manning, *Troubled Refuge,* 253; Sears, ed., *Camp Nelson,* 174, 207; Warren, ed., *Final Report,* 11; *Freedmen's Record* 1 (May 1865): 73; Oakes, *Freedom,* 440, 479–80; Littlefield, *Africans and Seminoles,* 193.

20. Berlin, *Slaves without Masters,* 55, 96–97, 286, 305, 317.

21. Manning, *Troubled Refuge,* 222, 225–26.

22. Glymph, "Black Women and Children," 124–26; Eberhardt, *Reminiscences,* 33; Pearson, ed., *Letters,* 1; Kolchin, *American Slavery,* 230.

23. Blum, *Reforging,* 71–75; Ferebee, *Brief History,* 9–10; Breitborde, "Discourse," 428.

24. Wilbur journal, February 22, 1864 (quote); Chang, "Angels of Peace," 31.

Bibliography

Manuscript Collections

Abraham Lincoln Presidential Library, Springfield, IL
    Eberhart Papers
American Antiquarian Society, Worcester, MA
    Horace James Papers.
Amistad Research Center, Tulane University, New Orleans, LA
    American Missionary Association Archives.
Duke University Library Special Collections, Durham, NC
    Edward Gray Stetson Papers.
Earlham College Library Friends Collection, Richmond, IN
    Job Hadley Reminiscences. Typescript, n.d.
    Tacy Burgess Hadley Reminiscences. Typescript, n.d.
Haverford College Library Special Collections, Haverford, PA
    Taylor Family Papers.
    Julia Wilbur Papers.
Howard University Library Special Collections, Washington, DC
    Charles P. Ware Papers.
Library of Congress, Washington, DC
    George N. Carruthers Journals.
    Esther H. Hawks Papers.
    Low-Mills Family Papers.
    Mary Mann Papers.
    D. B. Nichols Papers.
    Benjamin Franklin Whitten Papers
Massachusetts Historical Society, Boston, MA
    William H. Eastman Letters.

Bibliography

Ebenezer Hunt Correspondence.
Orville W. Leonard Military Papers.
New England Freedmen's Aid Society Papers.
National Archives, Washington, DC
    Microcopy 619: American Freedmen's Inquiry Commission Records.
    RG 92: Quartermaster General's Office Records.
    RG 94: Adjutant General's Office Records.
    RG 105: Records of the Bureau of Refugees, Freedmen, and Abandoned Lands.
    RG 393: Records of the United States Army Continental Commands, 1821–1920.
Southern Historical Collection, University of North Carolina, Chapel Hill, NC
    Thomas D. Howard et al., "Charles Howard Family Domestic History" (typescript, 1910).
    Penn School Papers.
    Scott Family Papers.
State Historical Society of Wisconsin, Madison, WI
    William F. Allen Papers.
Swarthmore College Friends Historical Library, Swarthmore, PA
    Friends' Freedmen's Association Records.
    Abby Hopper Gibbons Papers.
    Howland Family Papers.
    Anna Wharton Papers.
University of Michigan Library Special Collections, Ann Arbor, MI
    Phillip Bacon Papers, James Schoff Civil War Collection
    Eaton-Shirley Papers
    Rochester Ladies Antislavery Society Papers.
Western Reserve Historical Society, Cleveland, OH
    John Butler Papers.
    Isaac G. Thorne Papers.

Newspapers and Periodicals

American Missionary, 1861–1865
Boston Advertiser, 1861–1865
Boston Liberator, 1861–1865
Cleveland Herald, 1861–1865
Douglass' Monthly, 1861–1863
Freedman, 1864–1865
Freedman's Advocate, 1864
Freedman's Friend, 1864–1865
Freedmen's Bulletin, 1864–1865
Freedmen's Journal, 1865
Freedmen's Record, 1865
Friend, 1861–1865
Friends' Intelligencer, 1861–1865
Friends' Review, 1861–1865

Home Evangelist, 1863–65

Home Mission Record, 1862

Home Missionary, 1862–1865

Nashville Banner, March 9, 1888

Nashville Press and Times, 1865

Nashville Times and True Union, 1864

Nashville Union, 1864

National Freedman, 1865

New York Anglo-African, 1861–1865

New York Herald, 1861–1865

New York National Antislavery Standard, 1861–1865

New York Principia, 1861–1865

New York Times, 1861–1865

New York Tribune, 1861–1865

Pennsylvania Freedmen's Bulletin, 1865

Philadelphia Christian Recorder, 1861–1865

Philadelphia Press, November 3, 1862

Washington National Intelligencer, 1861–1865

Published Primary Sources

Addeman, J. M. *Reminiscence of Two Years with the Colored Troops.* Providence, RI: N. Bangs Williams & Co., 1890. No. 7 in ser. 2 of Rhode Island Soldiers and Sailors Historical Society, *Personal Narratives.*

Allen, William Francis. *A Yankee Scholar in Coastal South Carolina.* Edited by James Robert Hester. Columbia: University of South Carolina Press, 2015.

American Freedmen's Union Commission. *The Results of Emancipation in the United States of America.* New York: privately printed, n.d.

American Tract Society. *The Freedmen's Primer or First Reader.* Boston: privately printed, 1864.

———. *The Freedmen's Second Reader.* Boston: George C. Rand & Avery, 1865.

Ames, Mary. *From a New England Woman's Diary in Dixie in 1865.* Springfield, MA: Plimpton Press, 1906.

Anders, Olney. *Civil War Letters.* Edited by Fred A. Shannon. Urbana: University of Illinois Press, 1947.

Anderson, Robert. *From Slavery to Affluence.* Hemingford, NE: Hemingford Ledger, 1927.

Barnard Freedmen's Aid Society of Dorchester. *First Annual Report of the Executive Committee.* Dorchester, MA: privately printed, 1865.

Beecham, Robert. *As if It Were Glory.* Edited by Michael E. Stevens. Madison, WI: Madison House, 1998.

Berlin, Ira, Barbara J. Fields, Thavolia Glymph, Joseph P. Reidy, and Leslie S. Rowland, eds. *Destruction of Slavery.* Ser. 1, vol. 1 of *Freedom: A Documentary History of Emancipation, 1861–1867.* New York: Cambridge University Press, 1985.

Berlin, Ira, Barbara J. Fields, Steven F. Miller, Joseph P. Reidy, and Leslie S. Rowland, eds. *Free at Last: A Documentary History of Slavery, Freedom, and the Civil War.* New York: New Press, 1993.

Berlin, Ira, Thavolia Glymph, Steven F. Miller, Joseph P. Reidy, Leslie S. Rowland, and Julie Saville, eds. *Wartime Genesis of Free Labor: Lower South.* Ser. 1, vol. 3 of *Freedom: A Documentary History of Emancipation, 1861-1867.* New York: Cambridge University Press, 1990.

Berlin, Ira, Steven F. Miller, Joseph P. Reidy, and Leslie S. Rowland, eds. *Wartime Genesis of Free Labor: Upper South.* Ser. 1, vol. 2 of *Freedom: A Documentary History of Emancipation, 1861-1867.* New York: Cambridge University Press, 1993.

Berlin, Ira, Joseph P. Reidy, and Leslie S. Rowland, eds. *Black Military Experience.* Ser. 2 of *Freedom: A Documentary History of Emancipation, 1861-1867.* New York: Cambridge University Press, 1982.

Blassingame, John W., ed. *Slave Testimony: Two Centuries of Letters, Speeches, Interviews, and Autobiographies.* Baton Rouge: Louisiana State University Press, 1977.

Blight, David W., ed. *A Slave No More: Two Men Who Escaped to Freedom.* New York: Harcourt, 2007.

Board of Education for Freedmen, Department of the Gulf. *Report for the Year 1864.* New Orleans: Office of the True Delta, 1865.

Botume, Elizabeth H. *First Days amongst the Contrabands.* Boston: Lee and Shepherd Publishers, 1893.

Bowley, Freeman S. *Honor in Command.* Edited by Keith Wilson. Gainesville: University Press of Florida, 2006.

Boyer, Samuel Pellman. *Naval Surgeon Blockading the South, 1862-1866: The Diary.* Edited by Elinor Barnes and James A. Barnes. Bloomington: Indiana University Press, 1963.

Bruce, Henry Clay. *The New Man, Twenty-nine Years a Slave, Twenty-nine Years a Free Man: Recollections.* York, PA: P. Anstadt & Sons, 1895.

Bucklin, Sophronia E. *In Hospital and Camp: A Woman's Record of Thrilling Incidents among the Wounded in the Late War.* Philadelphia: J. E. Potter and Company, 1869.

Burton, E. P. *Diary.* Des Moines, IA: Historical Records Survey, 1939.

Buss, Harriet M. *My Work among the Freedmen: Civil War and Reconstruction Letters.* Edited by Jonathan W. White and Lydia J. Davis. Charlottesville: University of Virginia Press, 2021.

Butler, Benjamin F., et al. *Private and Official Correspondence.* 5 vols. Norwood, MA: Plimpton Press, 1917.

Butler, Josiah, *A Sketch of My Work among the Freedmen.* n.p.: privately printed, n.d.

Chester, Thomas Morris. *Black Civil War Correspondent: His Dispatches from the Virginia Front.* Edited by R. J. M. Blackett. Baton Rouge: Louisiana State University Press, 1989.

Coffin, Levi. *Reminiscences.* New York: Arno Press, 1968.

Colman, Lucy. *Reminiscences.* Buffalo, NY: H. L. Green, 1891.

Colyer, Vincent. *Report of the Services Rendered by the Freed People to the United States Army in North Carolina.* New York: privately printed, 1864.

Committee on Freedmen in Parts of Tennessee and the Mississippi Valley. *Report to Friends Board of Control* [probably for Ohio Yearly Meeting]. Cincinnati: R. W. Carroll & Company, 1865.

Contraband Relief Commission. *Report.* Cincinnati: Gazette Steam Printing, 1863.

Contraband Relief Commission, *To the Public* (flyer, 1863), Cincinnati and Hamilton County Public Library Rare Book Room.

Convention of Freedmen's Commissions. *Minutes.* Cincinnati: Methodist Book Concern, 1864.

Conway, Moncure. *Testimonies Concerning Slavery.* London: Chapman and Hall, 1864.

Conway, Thomas. *Final Report of the Bureau of Free Labor.* New Orleans: New Orleans Times, 1865.

Cope, M. C. *Report of a Visit to Hampton, Norfolk, & Yorktown*. Philadelphia: Ringwalt & Brown, 1863.

Corbin, Henry Clark. *Autobiography*. Edited by Gary L. Knepp. Milford, OH: Cragburn Publishing Company, 2003.

Doster, William E. *Lincoln and Episodes of the Civil War*. New York: G. P. Putnam's Sons, 1915.

Eaton, John. *Grant, Lincoln and the Freedmen: Reminiscences of the Civil War*. New York: Longmans, Green, and Co., 1907.

————. *Report of the General Superintendent of Freedmen, Department of the Tennessee and State of Arkansas for 1864*. Memphis: privately printed, 1865.

Eberhart, Uriah. *History of the Eberharts in Germany and the United States*. Chicago: Donohue & Henneberry, 1891.

Educational Commission for Freedmen. *First Annual Report*. Boston: Prentiss & Deland, 1863. Educational Commission of Boston.

————. *Extracts from Letters from Teachers*. Boston: privately printed, 1863. Ser. 3.

————. *Extracts from Letters Received*. Boston: privately printed, 1862. Ser. 1.

————. *Extracts from Letters Received*. Boston: privately printed, 1862. Ser. 2.

Emancipation League. *Facts Concerning the Freedmen*. Boston: Commercial Printing House, 1863.

Engs, Robert F., and Corey M. Brooks, eds. *Their Patriotic Duty: The Civil War Letters of the Evans Family of Brown County, Ohio*. New York: Fordham University Press, 2007.

Ferebee, London R. *A Brief History of the Slave Life*. Raleigh, NC: Edwards Broughton & Co., 1882.

First Anniversary of the Proclamation of Freedom in South Carolina. Beaufort, SC: Free South Print, 1864.

Foner, Philip S., and George E. Walker, eds. *Proceedings of the Black National and State Conventions, 1865–1900*. 2 vols. Philadelphia: Temple University Press, 1986.

Forten, Charlotte. "Life on the Sea Islands," *Atlantic Monthly* 13 (May–June, 1864): 587–96, 666–76.

Freedmen and Soldiers' Relief Association. *Second Annual Report*. Washington: Chronicle Printing, 1864.

French, A. M. *Slavery in South Carolina and the Ex-Slaves*. New York: Winchell M. French, 1862.

Friends' Association for the Aid and Elevation of the Freedmen. *Extracts from Letters*. Philadelphia: privately printed, 1865.

————. *Report*. Philadelphia: Merrihew & Son, 1865.

Friends' Association of Philadelphia and Its Vicinity. *Report*. Philadelphia: C. Sherman, Sons, & Co., 1864.

————. *Second Report*. Philadelphia: Ringwalt & Brown, 1865.

————. *Statistics of the Operations of the Executive Board*. Philadelphia: Inquirer Printing Office, 1864.

Fry, Alice L., ed. *Following the Fifth Kansas Cavalry: Letters*. n.p.: privately published, 1998.

Greene, Elias M. *"Regulations for the Government of Freedmen's Village, Greene Heights, Arlington, Va."* (poster, 1863), Boston Public Library Special Collections.

Grimke, Charlotte Forten. *Journals*. Edited by Brenda Stevenson. New York: Oxford University Press, 1988.

Hancock, Cornelia. *South after Gettysburg*. Edited by Henrietta Stratton Jaquette. Philadelphia: University of Pennsylvania Press, 1937.

Haviland, Laura S. *A Woman's Life Work*. Grand Rapids, MI: S. B. Shaw, 1881.

Hawks, Esther Hill. *A Woman Doctor's Civil War.* Edited by Gerald Schwartz. Columbia: University of South Carolina Press, 1984.

Higginson, Thomas Wentworth. *Army Life in a Black Regiment.* New York: W. W. Norton, 1984.

———. *Complete Civil War Journal and Selected Letters.* Edited by Christopher Looby. Chicago: University of Chicago Press, 2000.

Indiana Freedmen's Aid Commission. *Report of the Board of Managers to the First Annual Meeting.* Indianapolis: Elias Barnes Book and Job Printer, 1864.

Indiana Yearly Meeting of Friends. *Report of the Executive Committee for the Relief of Colored Freedmen.* Richmond, IN: Holloway and Davis, Printers, 1864.

———. *Minutes, 1865.* Cincinnati: E. Morgan & Co., 1865.

James, Horace. *Annual Report of the Superintendent of Negro Affairs in North Carolina, 1864, with an Appendix Containing the History and Management of the Freedmen in This Department up to June 1st, 1865.* Boston: W. F. Brown & Co., 1865.

James, Thomas. *Wonderful, Eventful Life.* 3rd ed. Rochester, NY: Post-Express Printing, 1887.

Kilham, Elizabeth. "Sketches in Color." *Putnam's Magazine* 15 (February 1870): 205–10.

King, James W. *Conspicuous Gallantry.* Edited by Eric R. Faust. Kent, OH: Kent State Press, 2015.

Kinsley, Rufus. *Diary of a Christian Soldier.* Edited by David C. Rankin. New York: Cambridge University Press, 2004.

Kinsman, J. Burnham. *Report of the General Sup't of Negro Affairs.* Ft. Monroe, VA: privately printed, 1864.

Knox, Thomas P. *Startling Revelations from the Department of South Carolina.* Boston: William M. Kendall, Printer, 1864.

Livermore, Mary A. *My Story of the War: A Woman's Narrative of Four Years Personal Experience.* Hartford, CT: A. D. Worthington and Company, 1889.

Lockwood, Lewis C. *Mary S. Peake: The Colored Teacher at Fortress Monroe.* Boston: American Tract Society, n.d.

Lynch, James. *A Few Things about the Educational Work among the Freedmen of South Carolina and Georgia.* 2nd ed. Baltimore: William K. Boyle, 1865.

Lyon, William P., and Adelia C. Lyon. *Reminiscences of the Civil War.* San Jose, CA: William P. Lyon, Jr., 1907.

Mann, N. M. "*Condition of the Negroes Who Came into Vicksburg with Sherman's Army*" (flyer 1864), Massachusetts Historical Society, Boston, MA.

Marrs, Elijah P. *Life and History.* Louisville: Bradley & Gilbert Company, 1885.

Mazzagetti, Dominick, ed. *"True Jersey Blues": The Civil War Letters of Lucien A. Voorhees and William Mackenzie Thompson.* Madison, NJ: Fairleigh Dickinson University Press, 2011.

McGranahan, R. W., ed. *Historical Sketch of the Freedmen's Missions of the United Presbyterian Church, 1862–1902.* Knoxville, TN: Knoxville College Printing, 1904.

McKaye, James. *The Mastership and Its Fruits: The Emancipated Slave Face to Face with His Old Master.* New York: William C. Bryant & Co., 1864.

McShane, Alice, ed. "Reading, Writing, and War: A Vermonter's Experience in the Port Royal Experiment, 1863–1871." *Vermont History* 67, no. 3/4 (1999): 101–14.

Miller, Stephen F., Susan E. O'Donovan, John C. Rodrigue, and Leslie S. Rowland, eds. *Land and Labor, 1865.* Ser. 3, vol. 1 of *Freedom: A Documentary History of Emancipation, 1861–1867.* Chapel Hill: University of North Carolina Press, 2008.

Moore, Francis T. *The Story of My Campaign*. Edited by Thomas Bahde. DeKalb: Northern Illinois University Press, 2011.

Moore, Joanna P. *In Christ's Stead: Autobiographical Sketches*. Chicago: Women's Baptist Home Mission Society, 1902.

Nanzig, Thomas P., ed. *The Badax Tigers: From Shiloh to the Surrender with the 18th Wisconsin Volunteers*. Lanham, MD: Rowman and Littlefield Publishers, 2002.

National Convention of Colored Men. *Proceedings*. Boston: J. S. Rockford and Geo. L. Ruffin, 1864.

National Freedmen's Relief Association of the District of Columbia. *First Annual Report*. Washington: M'Gill & Witherow, Printers, 1863.

New England Educational Commission for Freedmen. *Extracts from Letters of Teachers and Superintendents*. Boston: David Clapp, Printer, 1864. Ser. 4.

New England Freedmen's Aid Society. *Extracts from Letters of Teachers and Superintendents*. Boston: John Wilson and Son, 1864. Ser. 5.

———. *Second Annual Report*. Boston: privately printed, 1864.

New England Yearly Meeting of Friends. *Report to the Executive Committee upon the Conditions and Needs of the Freed People of Color in Washington and Virginia*. New Bedford, MA: E. Anthony & Sons, Printers, 1864.

———. *Second Report of the Executive Committee in Behalf of the Freed People of Color*. New Bedford, MA: E. Anthony & Sons, Printers, 1865.

New York Yearly Meeting of Friends. *Report of a Committee of Representatives upon the Condition and Wants of the Colored Refugees*. New York: privately printed, 1862.

———. *Second Report of a Committee of Representatives upon the Condition and Wants of the Colored Refugees*. n.p.: privately printed, 1863.

———. *Third Report of a Committee of Representatives upon the Condition and Wants of the Colored Refugees*. n.p.: privately printed, 1864.

Nordhoff, Charles. *The Freedmen of South Carolina*. n.p.: privately printed, 1863.

Northwestern Freedmen's Aid Commission. *Minutes of the First Annual Meeting*. Chicago: James Barnet, Printer, 1864.

———. *Second Annual Report of the Board of Managers*. Chicago: James Barnet, Printer, 1865.

Parsons, Emily Elizabeth. *Memoir*. Edited by Theophilus Parsons. Boston: Little, Brown and Co., 1880.

Pearson, Elizabeth Ware, ed. *Letters from Port Royal Written at the Time of the Civil War*. Boston: W. B. Clarke Company, 1906.

[Pennsylvania Freedmen's Relief Association.] *Report of the Proceedings of a Meeting Held at Concert Hall*. Philadelphia: Merrihew & Thompson, Printers, 1863.

Pierce, Edward. "The Contrabands at Fortress Monroe." *Atlantic Monthly* 8 (November 1861): 626–40.

———. "The Freedmen at Port Royal." *Atlantic Monthly* 12 (September 1863): 291–315.

Port Royal Relief Committee [of Philadelphia]. *First Annual Report*. Philadelphia: Merrihew & Thompson, Printers, 1863.

Powers, Elvira J. *Hospital Pencilings*. Boston: Edward L. Mitchell, 1866.

Rawick, George P. *The American Slave: A Composite Autobiography*. 41 vols. in 3 ser. Westport, CT: Greenwood Press, 1972–79.

Redkey, Edwin S., ed. *A Grand Army of Black Men: Letters from African American Soldiers, 1861–1865.* New York: Cambridge University Press, 1992.

Richards, Channing. "Dealing with Slavery" in Military Order of the Loyal Legion of the United States, Ohio Commandery, *Sketches of War History.* Cincinnati: Robert Clarke Co., 1896. Vol. 4: 315–26.

Ripley, C. Peter, ed. *Black Abolitionist Papers.* 5 vols. Chapel Hill: University of North Carolina Press, 1985–1992.

Robinson, Calvin L. *A Yankee in a Confederate Town.* Edited by Anne Robinson Clancy. Sarasota, FL: Pineapple Press, Inc., 2002.

Rochester Ladies Antislavery Society. *Twelfth Annual Report.* Rochester, NY: Press of A. Strong, 1863.

———. *Thirteenth Annual Report.* Rochester, NY: Democrat Steam Printing House, 1864.

———. *Fourteenth Annual Report.* Rochester, NY: William S. Falls, 1865.

Rogers, J. B. *War Pictures: Experiences and Observations of a Chaplain in the U.S. Army in the War of the Southern Rebellion.* Chicago: Church & Goodman, 1863.

Salemson, Daniel J., ed. "The Civil War Writings of Elkanah Beard." *Southern Friend* 20, no. 1 (1998): 21–75.

Sears, Richard D., ed. *Camp Nelson, Kentucky: A Civil War History.* Lexington: University Press of Kentucky, 2002.

Sherwood, Henry Noble, ed. "Journal of Miss Susan Walker." *Quarterly Publication of the Historical and Philosophical Society of Ohio* 7, no. 1 (1912): 11–48.

Singleton, William Henry. *Recollections of My Slavery Days.* Edited by Catherine Mellon Charon and David S. Cecelski. Raleigh: North Carolina Division of Archives and History, 1999.

Sterling, Dorothy, ed. *We are Your Sisters: Black Women in the Nineteenth Century.* New York: W. W. Norton & Company, 1984.

Superintendents of Freedmen for the State of Arkansas and District of West Tennessee. *Reports.* Memphis: Freedmen's Press, 1865.

Swint, Henry L., ed. *Dear Ones at Home: Letters from Contraband Camps.* Nashville: Vanderbilt University Press, 1966.

Thompson, Mitchel Andrew. *Dear Eliza: Letters.* Ames, IA: Carter Press, 1976.

Tourgee, Albion W. *The Story of a Thousand.* Buffalo, NY: S. McGerald & Son, 1896.

Towne, Laura. *Letters and Diary.* Edited by Rupert S. Holland. New York: Negro Universities Press, 1969.

———. *Pioneer Work on the Sea Islands.* Hampton, VA: privately printed, 1901.

Trudeau, Noah A., ed. *Voices of the 55th: Letters from the 55th Massachusetts Volunteers, 1861–1865.* Dayton, OH: 1996.

Trumbull, H. Clay. *War Memories of an Army Chaplain.* New York: Charles Scribner's Sons, 1898.

Truth, Sojourner, *Narrative.* Battle Creek, MI: privately printed, 1878.

US Congress. *Africans in Fort Monroe Military District.* 37 Cong., 2 Sess., House Exec. Doc. 85 (serial 1135).

———. *Colored Refugees in Kentucky, Tennessee, and Alabama.* 38 Cong., 2 Sess., Senate Exec Doc. 28 (serial 1209).

———. *Statutes at Large, Treaties, and Proclamations of the United States of America.* Vol. 12. Edited by George P. Sanger. Boston: Little, Brown and Company, 1863.

US Department of the Interior. Census Office. *Eighth Census of the United States, 1860.* 4 vols. Washington: GPO, 1864.

US Navy Department. *Official Records of the Union and Confederate Navies in the War of the Rebellion.* 31 vols. Washington: GPO, 1894–1927.

US War Department. *The War of the Rebellion: A Compilation of the Official Records of the Union and Confederate Armies.* 131 vols. Washington: GPO, 1880–1901.

Warren, Joseph, ed. *Extracts from Documents in the Office of the General Superintendent of Refugees and Freedmen.* Memphis: Freedmen Press. 1865.

———. *Extracts from Reports of Superintendents of Freedmen.* 2 series. Vicksburg: Freedmen Press, 1864.

———. *Final Report of Freedmen Schools in the Department Lately under the Supervision of Col. John Eaton, Jr., 1864–65.* Vicksburg: Freedmen Press, 1865.

Western Freedmen's Aid Commission, *Report.* Cincinnati: privately published, 1864.

———. *Second Annual Report.* Cincinnati: Methodist Book Concern, 1865.

Western Yearly Meeting of Friends. *Minutes.* n.p.: privately printed, 1865.

Wistar, Isaac Jones. *Autobiography.* New York: Harper & Brothers, 1937.

Women's Association of Philadelphia. *Second Annual Report.* Philadelphia: Merrihew & Thompson, Printers, 1864.

———. *Third Annual Report.* Philadelphia: Merrihew & Thompson, Printers, 1865.

Yeatman, James E. *A Report on the Condition of the Freedmen of the Mississippi.* St. Louis: Western Sanitary Commission, 1864.

Yellin, Jean Fagin, ed. *Harriet Jacobs Family Papers.* 2 vols. Chapel Hill: University of North Carolina Press, 2008.

Secondary Sources

Asch, Chris Myers, and George Derek Musgrove. *Chocolate City: A History of Race and Democracy in the Nation's Capital.* Chapel Hill: University of North Carolina Press, 2017.

Ash, Stephen V. *The Black Experience in the Civil War South.* Dulles, VA: Potomac Books, 2013.

———. *Firebrand of Liberty: The Story of Two Black Regiments That Changed the Course of the Civil War.* New York: W. W. Norton & Company, 2008.

———. *Middle Tennessee Society Transformed, 1860–1870: War and Peace in the Upper South.* Baton Rouge: Louisiana State University Press, 1988.

———. *When the Yankees Came: Conflict and Chaos in the Occupied South, 1861–1865.* Chapel Hill: University of North Carolina Press, 1995.

Barnickel, Linda. *Milliken's Bend: A Civil War Battle in History and Memory.* Baton Rouge: Louisiana State University Press, 2013.

Belz, Herman. *A New Birth of Freedom: The Republican Party and Freedmen's Rights, 1861–1865.* Westport, CT: Greenwood Press, 1976.

Bercaw, Nancy. *Gendered Freedoms: Race, Rights, and the Politics of Household in the Delta.* Gainesville: University Press of Florida, 2003.

Berlin, Ira. *Slaves without Masters: The Free Negro in the Antebellum South.* New York: Random House, 1974.

Besterbreurtje, Lindsay. "Beyond the Plantation: Freedmen, Social Experimentation, and

African American Community Development in Freedmen's Village, 1863–1900." *Virginia Magazine of History and Biography* 126, no. 3 (2018): 334–65.

Blum, Edward J. *Reforging the White Republic: Race, Religion, and American Nationalism, 1865–1898.* Baton Rouge: Louisiana State University Press, 2005.

Boakyewa-Ansah, Abena. "Crafted 'By Their Own Hands:' The African American Religious Experience in Union-Occupied North Carolina, 1862–1865." *North Carolina Historical Review* 94, no. 3 (2017): 299–332.

Bradford, Sarah. *Scenes in the Life of Harriet Tubman.* Auburn, NY: W. J. Moses, 1869.

Brasher, Glenn David. *The Peninsula Campaign & the Necessity of Emancipation: African Americans & the Fight for Freedom.* Chapel Hill: University of North Carolina Press, 2012.

Breault, Judith Colucci. *The World of Emily Howland: Odyssey of a Humanitarian.* Milbrae, CA: Les Femmes, 1976.

Breitborde, Mary-Lou. "Discourse, Education, and Women's Public Culture in the Port Royal Experiment: Interpreting the Life and Work of Laura Towne." *American Educational History Journal* 38, no. 2 (2011): 427–46.

Brent, Joseph E. *Occupied Corinth: The Contraband Camp and the First Alabama Regiment of African Descent, 1862–1864.* Washington: GPO, 1995.

Bremner, Robert. *The Public Good: Philanthropy and Welfare in the Civil War Era.* New York: Knopf, 1980.

Brosnan, AnneMarie. "Representations of Race and Racism in the Textbooks Used in Southern Black Schools during the American Civil War and Reconstruction Era, 1861–1876." *Paedagogia Historica* 52, no. 6 (2016): 718–33.

Brown, William Wells. *The Negro in the American Rebellion.* Edited by John David Smith. Athens: Ohio University Press, 2003.

Browning, Judkin. "'Bringing Light to Our Land . . . She Was Dark as Night': Northerners, Freedpeople, and Education during Military Occupation in North Carolina, 1862–1865." *American Nineteenth Century History* 9, no. 1 (2008): 1–17.

———. *Shifting Loyalties: The Union Occupation of Eastern North Carolina.* Chapel Hill: University of North Carolina Press, 2011.

———. "Visions of Freedom and Civilization Opening before Them: African Americans Search for Autonomy during Military Occupation in North Carolina." In *North Carolinians in the Era of the Civil War and Reconstruction,* edited by Paul D. Escott, 69–100. Chapel Hill: University of North Carolina Press, 2008.

Bryant II, James K. *The 36th Infantry United States Colored Troops in the Civil War.* Jefferson, NC: McFarland & Company, 2012.

Buker, George E. *Blockaders, Refugees, & Contrabands: Civil War on Florida's Gulf Coast 1861–1865.* Tuscaloosa: University of Alabama Press, 1993.

Burton, Orville Vernon. *Penn Center: A History Preserved.* Athens: University of Georgia Press, 2014.

Butchart, Ronald E. *Northern Schools, Southern Blacks, and Reconstruction: Freedmen's Education, 1862–1875.* Westport, CT: Greenwood Press, 1980.

———. *Schooling the Freedpeople: Teaching, Learning, and the Struggle for Black Freedom, 1861–1876.* Chapel Hill: University of North Carolina Press, 2010.

Cabral, Linda Britton. "Letters from Four Antebellum Black Women Educators to the American Missionary Association, 1863–1870." D.Ed. diss., University of Massachusetts Boston, 2006.

Cecelski, David S. *The Fire of Freedom: Abraham Galloway & the Slaves' Civil War.* Chapel Hill: University of North Carolina Press, 2012.

———. *The Waterman's Song: Slavery and Freedom in Maritime North Carolina.* Chapel Hill: University of North Carolina Press, 2001.

Chambers-Schiller, Lee Virginia. *Liberty, a Better Husband: Single Women in America, the Generations of 1780–1840.* New Haven, CT: Yale University Press, 1984.

Chang, Perry. "'Angels of Peace in a Smitten Land': The Northern Teachers' Crusade in the Reconstruction South Reconsidered," *Southern Historian* 16 (April 1995): 26–45.

Churchill, Robert H. "When the Slave Catchers Came to Town: Cultures of Violence along the Underground Railroad." *Journal of American History* 105, no. 3 (2018): 514–37.

Cimbala, Paul A. *Under the Guardianship of the Nation: The Freedmen's Bureau and the Reconstruction of Georgia, 1865–1870.* Athens: University of Georgia Press, 1996.

Cimprich, John. *Fort Pillow: A Civil War Massacre, and Public Memory.* Baton Rouge: Louisiana State University Press, 2005.

———. *Slavery's End in Tennessee, 1861–1865.* Tuscaloosa: University of Alabama Press, 1985.

Clampitt, Bradley R. *Occupied Vicksburg.* Baton Rouge: Louisiana State University Press, 2016.

Clark, Kathleen Ann. *Defining Moments: African American Commemorations & Political Culture in the South, 1863–1913.* Chapel Hill: University of North Carolina Press, 2005.

Click, Patricia C. *Time Full of Trial: The Roanoke Island Freedmen's Colony, 1862–1867.* Chapel Hill: University of North Carolina Press, 2001.

Clifford, Geraldine J. *Those Good Gertrudes: A Social History of Women Teachers in America.* Baltimore: Johns Hopkins Press, 2014.

Crane Jr., Michael J. "The Demise of Slavery on the Border: Federal Policy and the Union Army in Henderson, Kentucky." *Register of Kentucky Historical Society* 113, no. 4 (2015): 601–40.

Danielson, Joseph W. *War's Desolating Scourge: The Union's Occupation of North Alabama.* Lawrence: University of Kansas Press, 2012.

Davis, Cyprian. *History of Black Catholics in the United States.* New York: Crossroad, 2004.

DeBoer, Clara Merritt. *His Truth Is Marching On: African Americans Who Taught the Freedmen for the American Missionary Association, 1861–1877.* New York: Garland, 1995.

Doddington, David Stefan. *Contesting Slave Masculinity in the American South.* New York: Cambridge University Press, 2018.

Dougherty, Kevin. *The Port Royal Experiment: A Case Study in Development.* Jackson: University Press of Mississippi, 2014.

Downs, Jim. *Sick from Freedom: African American Illness and Suffering during the Civil War and Reconstruction.* New York: Oxford University Press, 2012.

Eiss, Paul K. "A Share in the Land: Freed People and the Government of Labour in Southern Louisiana, 1862–65." *Slavery and Abolition* 19, no. 1 (1998): 46–89.

Emerson, Sarah Hopper. *Life of Abby Hopper Gibbons.* 2 vols. New York: G. P. Putnam's Sons, 1897.

Engs, Robert Francis. *Freedom's First Generation: Black Hampton, Virginia, 1861–1890.* Philadelphia: University of Pennsylvania Press, 1979.

Epps, Kristen. *Slavery on the Periphery: The Kansas-Missouri Border in the Antebellum and Civil War Eras.* Athens: University of Georgia Press, 2016.

Escott, Paul D. *Rethinking the Civil War Era: Directions for Research.* Lexington: University Press of Kentucky, 2018.

———. *Slavery Remembered: A Record of Twentieth Century Slave Narratives.* Chapel Hill: University of North Carolina Press, 1979.

———. *The Worst Passions of Human Nature.* Charlottesville: University of Virginia Press, 2020.

Everett, Donald E. "Demand of the New Orleans Free Colored Population for Political Equality, 1862–1865." *Louisiana Historical Quarterly* 38, No. 2 (1955): 43–64.

Faulkner, Carol. *Women's Radical Reconstruction: The Freedmen's Aid Movement.* Philadelphia: University of Pennsylvania Press, 2004.

Finley, Randy. "In War's Wake: Health Care and Arkansas Freedmen, 1863–1868." *Arkansas Historical Quarterly* 51, no. 2 (1992): 135–63.

Fliss, William M. "Wisconsin's 'Abolition Regiment': The Twenty-Second Volunteer Infantry in Kentucky, 1862–63." *Wisconsin Magazine of History* 86, no. 2 (2002–03): 2–17.

Foner, Eric. *The Fiery Trial: Abraham Lincoln and American Slavery.* New York: W. W. Norton, 2010.

———. *Reconstruction: America's Unfinished Revolution, 1863–1877.* New York: Harper & Row, 1988.

Forbes, Ella. *African American Women during the Civil War.* New York: Garland, 1998.

Forman, Jacob G. *The Western Sanitary Commission.* St Louis: R. P. Studley, 1864.

Foster, Gaines M. "The Limitations of Federal Health Care for Freedmen, 1862–1868." *Journal of Southern History* 48, no. 3 (1982): 349–72.

Fountain, Daniel A. *Slavery, Civil War, and Salvation: African American Slaves and Christianity, 1830–1870.* Baton Rouge: Louisiana State University Press, 2010.

Frankel, Noralee. *Freedom's Women: Black Women and Families in Civil War Era Mississippi.* Bloomington: Indiana University Press, 1999.

Franklin, John Hope. *The Emancipation Proclamation.* Wheeling, IL: Harlan Davidson, 1995.

Franklin, John Hope and Loren Schweninger. *Runaway Slaves: Rebels on the Plantation.* New York: Oxford University Press, 1999.

Fredrickson, George M. *The Black Image in the White Mind: The Debate on Afro-American Character and Destiny, 1817–1914.* Middletown, CT: Wesleyan University Press, 1987.

Fuke, Richard Paul. "The Baltimore Association for the Moral and Educational Improvement of the Colored People, 1864–1870." *Maryland Historical Magazine* 66, no. 4 (1971): 369–404.

———. *Imperfect Equality: African Americans and the Confines of White Racial Attitudes in Post-Emancipation Maryland.* New York: Fordham University Press, 1999.

Gerteis, Lewis S. *From Contraband to Freedman: Federal Policy toward Southern Blacks, 1861–1865.* Westport, CT: Greenwood Press, 1973.

Ginzberg, Lori D. *Women and the Work of Benevolence: Morality, Politics, and Class in the Nineteenth Century United States.* New Haven: Yale University Press, 1990.

Glatthaar, Joseph T. *Forged in Battle: The Civil War Alliance of Black Soldiers and White Officers.* New York: Free Press, 1990.

Glymph, Thavolia. "Black Women and Children in the Civil War: Archive Notes." In *Beyond Freedom: Disrupting the History of Emancipation,* edited by David W. Blight and Jim Downs, 121–35. Athens: Georgia University Press, 2017.

———. "This Species of Property: Female Slave Contrabands in the Civil War." In *A Woman's War: Southern Women, Civil War, and the Confederate Legacy,* edited by Edward D. C. Campbell and Kym S. Rice, 54–71. Richmond: Museum of the Confederacy, 1996.

———. *The Women's Fight: The Civil War's Battles for Home, Freedom, and Nation.* Chapel Hill: University of North Carolina Press, 2020.

Greenwood, Janette Thomas. *First Fruits of Freedom: The Migration of Former Slaves and Their Search for Equality in Worcester, Massachusetts, 1862–1900.* Chapel Hill: University of North Carolina Press, 2009.

Hahn, Steven. *A Nation under Our Feet: Black Political Struggles in the Rural South from Slavery to the Great Migration.* Cambridge, MA: Harvard University Press, 2003.

Harper, Matthew. *The End of Days: African American Religion and Politics in the Age of Emancipation.* Chapel Hill: University of North Carolina Press, 2016.

Harris, William C. *With Charity for All: Lincoln and the Restoration of the Union.* Lexington: University Press of Kentucky, 1997.

Harrison, Robert. *Washington during Civil War and Reconstruction: Race and Radicalism.* New York: Cambridge University Press, 2011.

Harrold, Stanley. *Subversives: Antislavery Community in Washington, D.C., 1828–1865.* Baton Rouge: Louisiana State University Press, 2003.

Hermann, Janet Sharp. *The Pursuit of a Dream.* New York: Random House, 1981.

Hilliard, Kathleen M. *Masters, Slaves, and Exchange: Power's Purchase in the Old South.* New York: Cambridge University Press, 2014.

Hodes, Martha. *Mourning Lincoln.* New Haven: Yale University Press, 2015.

Holt, Thomas, Cassandra Smith Parker, and Rosalyn Terborg-Penn. *A Special Mission: The Story of Freedmen's Hospital, 1862–1962.* Washington: Howard University Press, 1975.

Horst, Samuel L. *Education for Manhood: The Education of Blacks in Virginia during the Civil War.* Lanham, MD: University Press of America, 1987.

Hunter, Tera W. *Bound in Wedlock: Slave and Free Black Marriage in the Nineteenth Century.* Cambridge, MA: Harvard University Press, 2017.

James, Felix. "The Establishment of Freedmen's Village in Arlington, Virginia." *Negro History Bulletin* 33, no. 4 (1970): 90–93.

Jimerson, Randall C. *Private Civil War: Popular Thought during the Sectional Conflict.* Baton Rouge: Louisiana State University Press, 1988.

Johnston, Allan. *Surviving Freedom: The Black Community of Washington, D.C., 1860–1880.* New York: Garland Press, 1993.

Jones, Jacqueline. *Saving Savannah: The City and the Civil War.* New York: Alfred A. Knopf, 2008.

———. *Soldiers of Light and Love: Northern Teachers and Georgia Blacks, 1865–1873.* Chapel Hill: University of North Carolina Press, 1980.

Jordan, Ervin L. *Black Confederates and Afro-Yankees in Civil War Virginia.* Charlottesville: University Press of Virginia, 1995.

Kachun, Mitch. *Festivals of Freedom, Memory, and Meaning in African American Emancipation Celebrations.* Amherst: University of Massachusetts Press, 2003.

Katz, Michael B. *In the Shadow of the Poorhouse: A Social History of Welfare in America.* New York: Basic Books, 1986.

Kaye, Anthony E. *Joining Places: Slave Neighborhoods in the Old South.* Chapel Hill: University of North Carolina Press, 2007.

Kickler, Troy Lee. "Black Children and Northern Missionaries, Freedmen's Bureau Agents, and Southern Whites in Reconstruction Tennessee, 1865–1869." Ph.D. diss., University of Tennessee, 2005.

Kisacky, Jeanne. *Rise of the Modern Hospital: An Architectural History of Health and Healing, 1870–1940.* Pittsburgh: University of Pittsburgh Press, 2017.

Kolchin, Peter. *American Slavery, 1619–1877.* New York: Hill & Wang, 2003.

Krauthamer, Barbara. *Black Slaves, Indian Masters: Slavery, Emancipation, and Citizenship in the Native American South.* Chapel Hill: University of North Carolina Press, 2013.

Larson, Kate Clifford. *Bound for the Promised Land: Harriet Tubman, Portrait of an American Hero.* New York: Random House, 2004.

Leonard, Elizabeth D. *Slaves, Slaveholders, and a Kentucky Community's Struggle towards Freedom.* Lexington: University Press of Kentucky, 2019.

Levine, Bruce. *The Fall of the House of Dixie: The Civil War and the Social Revolution That Transformed the South.* New York: Random House, 2013.

Lineberry, Cate. *Be Free or Die: The Amazing Story of Robert Smalls' Escape from Slavery to Union Hero.* New York: St. Martin's Press, 2017.

Littlefield Jr., Daniel F. *Africans and Seminoles: From Removal to Emancipation.* Westport, CT: Greenwood Press, 1977.

———. *The Cherokee Freedmen: From Emancipation to American Citizenship.* Westport, CT: Greenwood Press, 1978.

Litwack, Leon F. *Been in the Storm So Long: The Aftermath of Slavery.* New York: Knopf, 1979.

Long, Gretchen. *Doctoring Freedom: The Politics of African American Medical Care in Slavery and Emancipation.* Chapel Hill: University of North Carolina Press, 2012.

Longacre, Edward G. *A Regiment of Slaves: The Fourth United States Colored Infantry.* Mechanicsburg, PA: Stackpole Books, 2003.

Lovett, Bobby L. "African Americans, Civil War, and Aftermath in Arkansas." *Arkansas Historical Quarterly* 54, no. 3 (1995): 304–58.

Lucas, Marion B. *From Slavery to Segregation.* Vol. 1 of *A History of Blacks in Kentucky.* Frankfort: Kentucky Historical Society, 1992.

Mabee, Carleton, and Susan Mabee Newhouse. *Sojourner Truth: Slave, Prophet, Legend.* New York: New York University Press, 1995.

Magdol, Edward. *A Right to the Land: Essays on the Freedmen's Community.* Westport, CT: Greenwood Press, 1977.

Mann, Robert G. "The 'Contact of Living Souls': Shepherd Gilbert's Civics Education in Reconstruction South Carolina." *New England Historical Quarterly* 88, no. 2 (2015): 286–315.

Manning, Chandra. *Troubled Refuge: Struggling for Freedom in the Civil War.* New York: Vintage Books, 2016.

———. *What This Cruel War Was Over: Soldiers, Slavery, and the Civil War.* New York: Knopf, 2007.

Masur, Kate. *An Example for All the Land: Emancipation and the Struggle over Equality in Washington, D.C.* Chapel Hill: University of North Carolina Press, 2010.

———. "'A Rare Phenomenon of Philological Vegetation': The Word 'Contraband' and the Meanings of Emancipation in the United States." *Journal of American History* 93, no. 4 (2007): 1050–84.

McCurry, Stephanie. *Women's War: Fighting and Surviving the American Civil War.* Cambridge, MA: Harvard University Press, 2019.

McElya, Micki. *The Politics of Mourning: Death and Honor in Arlington National Cemetery.* Cambridge, MA: Harvard University Press, 2016.

McKivigan, John R. *Forgotten Firebrand: James Redpath and the Making of Nineteenth Century America*. Ithaca, NY: Cornell University Press, 2008.

McPherson, James M. *The Struggle for Equality: Abolitionists and the Negro in the Civil War and Reconstruction*. Princeton, NJ: Princeton University Press, 1964.

Messner, William F. "Black Education in Louisiana, 1863–1865." *Civil War History* 22, no. 1 (1976): 41–59.

Miller, Randall M., and John David Smith, eds. *Dictionary of Afro-American Slavery*. Westport, CT: Greenwood Press, 1988.

Mohr, Clarence L. *On the Threshold of Freedom: Masters and Slaves in Civil War Georgia*. Athens: University of Georgia Press, 1986.

Morris, Robert C. *Reading, 'Riting, and Reconstruction: The Education of Freedmen in the South, 1861–1870*. (Chicago: University of Chicago Press, 1976).

Nelson, Megan Kate. *Ruin Nation: Destruction and the American Civil War*. Athens: University of Georgia Press, 2012.

Nicholson, Elizabeth. "A Contraband Camp." *Indiana Historical Bulletin* 1, no. 11/12 (1924): 131–40.

Oakes, James. *Freedom National: The Destruction of Slavery in the United States*. New York: W. W. Norton Company, 2013.

Ochiai, Akiko. *Harvesting Freedom: African American Agrarianism in Civil War Era South Carolina*. Westport, CT: Praeger, 2004.

Osthaus, Carl R. *Freedmen, Philanthropy, and Fraud: A History of the Freedman's Savings Bank*. Urbana: University of Illinois Press, 1976.

Pease, William H. "Three Years among the Freedmen: William C. Gannett and the Port Royal Experiment." *Journal of Negro History* 42, no. 2 (1957): 98–117.

Penningroth, Dylan C. *The Claims of Kinfolk: African American Property and Community in the Nineteenth Century South*. Chapel Hill: University of North Carolina Press, 2003.

Perkins, Linda M. "The Black Female American Missionary Association Teacher in the South, 1861–1870." In *Black Americans in North Carolina and the South*, edited by Jeffrey J. Crow and Flora J. Hatley, 122–36. Chapel Hill: University of North Carolina Press, 1984.

Rable, George C. *God's Almost Chosen Peoples: A Religious History of the American Civil War*. Chapel Hill: University of North Carolina Press, 2010.

Ramold, Stephen J. *Slaves, Sailors, Citizens: African Americans in the Union Navy*. DeKalb: Northern Illinois University Press, 2002.

Reidy, Joseph P. *Illusions of Emancipation: The Pursuit of Freedom and Equality in the Twilight of Slavery*. Chapel Hill: University of North Carolina Press, 2019.

Rein, Christopher M. *Alabamians in Blue: Freedmen, Unionists, and the Civil War in the Cotton State*. Baton Rouge: Louisiana State University Press, 2019.

Richardson, Joe M. *Christian Reconstruction: The American Missionary Association and Southern Blacks, 1861–1890*. Athens: University of Georgia Press, 1986.

Ripley, C. Peter. *Slaves and Freedmen in Civil War Louisiana*. Baton Rouge: Louisiana State University Press, 1976.

Rodrigue, John C. *Reconstruction in the Cane Fields: From Slavery to Free Labor in Louisiana's Sugar Parishes, 1862–1880*. Baton Rouge: Louisiana State University Press, 2001.

Roediger, David R. *Seizing Freedom: Slave Emancipation and Liberty for All*. New York: Verso, 2014.

Romeo, Sharon. *Gender and the Jubilee: Black Freedom and the Reconstruction of Citizenship in Civil War Missouri*. Athens: University of Georgia Press, 2016.

Rose, Willie Lee. *Rehearsal for Reconstruction: The Port Royal Experiment.* Indianapolis: Bobbs-Merrill, 1964.

Ross, Steven Joseph. "Freed Soil, Freed Labor, Freed Men: John Eaton and the Davis Bend Experiment." *Journal of Southern History* 44, no. 2 (1978): 213–32.

Saville, Julie. *The Work of Reconstruction: From Slave to Wage Labor in South Carolina, 1860–1870.* New York: Cambridge University Press, 1996.

Schafer, Daniel L. *Thunder on the River: The Civil War in Northeast Florida.* Gainesville: University Press of Florida, 2010.

Schultz, Jane E. *Women at the Front: Hospital Workers in Civil War America.* Chapel Hill: University of North Carolina Press, 2004.

Schwalm, Leslie A. *A Hard Fight for We: Women's Transition from Slavery to Freedom in South Carolina.* Urbana: University of Illinois Press, 1997.

———. "Between Slavery and Freedom: African American Women and Occupation in the Slave South." In *Occupied Women: Gender, Military Occupation, and the American Civil War,* edited by Leann Whites and Alicia P. Long, 137–54. Baton Rouge: Louisiana State University Press, 2009.

———. *Emancipation's Diaspora: Race and Reconstruction in the Upper Midwest.* Chapel Hill: University of North Carolina Press, 2009.

———. "Surviving Wartime Emancipation: African Americans and the Cost of Civil War." *Journal of Law, Medicine, and Ethics* 39, no. 1 (2011): 21–28.

Selleck, Linda B. *Gentle Invaders: Quaker Women Educators and Racial Issues during the Civil War and Reconstruction.* Richmond, IN: Friends United Press, 1995.

Sheridan, Richard B. "From Slavery in Missouri to Freedom in Kansas: The Influx of Black Fugitives and Contrabands into Kansas, 1854–1865." *Kansas History* 12, no. 1 (1989): 28–47.

Small, Sandra E. "The Yankee Schoolmarm in Freedmen's Schools: An Analysis of Attitudes," *Journal of Southern History* 45, no. 3 (1978): 381–402.

Smith, David G. *On the Edge of Freedom: The Fugitive Slave Issue in South Central Pennsylvania, 1820–1870.* New York: Fordham University Press, 2013.

Smith, Timothy B. *Corinth 1862: Siege, Battle, Occupation.* Lawrence: University Press of Kansas, 2012.

Sobel, Mechal. *Trabelin' On: The Slave Journey to an Afro-Baptist Faith.* Westport, CT: Greenwood Press, 1979.

Span, Christopher M. *From Cotton Field to Schoolhouse: African American Education in Mississippi, 1862–1875.* Chapel Hill: University of North Carolina, 2009.

Spurgeon, Ian Michael. *Soldiers in the Army of Freedom: The First Kansas Colored, the Civil War's First African American Combat Unit.* Norman: University of Oklahoma Press, 2014.

Stanley, Amy Drew. "Slave Emancipation and the Revolutionizing of Human Rights." In *The World the Civil War Made,* edited by Gregory P. Downs and Kate Masur, 269–303. Chapel Hill: University of North Carolina Press, 2015.

Stealey, John E. *West Virginia's Civil War Era Constitution: Loyal Revolution, Confederate Counter-Revolution, and the Convention of 1872.* Kent, OH: Kent State University Press, 2013.

Stephens, Gail. *Shadow of Shiloh: Major General Lew Wallace in the Civil War.* Indianapolis: Indiana Historical Society Press, 2010.

Taylor, Amy Murrell. *Embattled Freedom: Journeys through the Civil War's Slave Refugee Camps.* Chapel Hill: University of North Carolina Press, 2018.

Teed, Paul E. *Joseph and Harriet Hawley's Civil War: Partnership, Ambition, and Sacrifice.* Lanham, MD: Lexington Books, 2019.

Terry, Fiona. *Condemned to Repeat? The Paradox of Humanitarian Action.* Ithaca, NY: Cornell University Press, 2002.

Teters, Kristopher A. *Practical Liberators: Union Officers in the Western Theater during the Civil War.* Chapel Hill: University of North Carolina Press, 2018.

Tetzlaff, Monica. "Mitchelville: An Early Experiment in Self-Governance." In *The Forgotten History: A Photographic Essay on Civil War Hilton Head Island,* edited by Charles C. McCracken and Faith M. McCracken, 81–90. Hilton Head Island: Time Again Publications, 1993.

Tomblin, Barbara Brooks. *Bluejackets and Contrabands: African Americans and the Union Navy.* Lexington: University of Kentucky Press, 2009.

Trefousse, Hans L. *Ben Butler: The South Called Him Beast!* New York: Octagon Books, 1974.

True, Roland Stafford. "Life aboard a Gunboat: A First Person Account." *Civil War Times Illustrated* 9, no. 10 (1971): 36–43.

Walker, Cam. "Corinth: The Story of a Contraband Camp." *Civil War History* 20, no. 1 (1974): 5–22.

Walker, Clarence E. *A Rock in a Weary Land: The African Methodist Episcopal Church during the Civil War and Reconstruction.* Baton Rouge: Louisiana State University Press, 1982.

Weicksel, Sarah Jones. "Fitted up for Freedom: The Material Culture of Refugee Relief." In *War Matters: Material Culture in the Civil War Era,* edited by Joan E. Cashin, 151–75. Chapel Hill: University of North Carolina Press, 2018.

Whitacre, Paula Tarnapol. *A Civil Life in an Uncivil Time: Julia Wilbur's Struggle for Purpose.* Lincoln: University of Nebraska Press, 2017.

White, Jonathan W. "Martial Law and the Expansion of Civil Liberties during the Civil War." In *Ex Parte Milligan Reconsidered: Race and Civil Liberties from the Lincoln Administration to the War on Terror,* edited by Stewart L. Winger and Jonathan W. White, 52–62. Lawrence: University of Kansas Press, 2020.

Wiley, Bell Irvin. *The Life of Billy Yank: The Common Soldier of the Union.* Indianapolis: Bobbs-Merrill Company, 1952.

Williams, David. *I Freed Myself: African American Self-Emancipation in the Civil War Era.* New York: Cambridge University Press, 2014.

Williams, Heather Andrea. *Help Me to Find My People: The African American Search for Family Lost in Slavery.* Chapel Hill: University of North Carolina Press, 2012.

——. *Self-Taught: African American Education in Slavery and Freedom.* Chapel Hill: University of North Carolina Press, 2005.

Williams, William H. *Slavery and Freedom in Delaware, 1639–1865.* Wilmington, DE: SR Books, 1996.

Winkle, Kenneth J. *Lincoln's Citadel: The Civil War in Washington, D.C.* New York: W. W. Norton & Company, 2013.

Wise, Stephen R., Lawrence S. Rowland, and Gerhard Spieler. *Rebellion, Reconstruction, and Redemption,* Vol. 2 of *History of Beaufort County, South Carolina.* Columbia: University of South Carolina Press, 2015.

Woods, Michael E. "Mountaineers Becoming Free: Emancipation and Statehood in West Virginia." *West Virginia History* 9 (new series), no. 2 (2015): 37–72.

Yellin, Jean Fagan. *Harriet Jacobs: A Life.* New York: Basic Civitas Books, 2004.

Index

Index